Praise for *Secrets and*

'*Secrets and Spies* is a cry from the heart. Every page took me further and deeper into an experience I'd not had before, not even after four years in Russia, listening to the horror stories of people who, though their souls had taken a beating, had survived Stalinism—the darkest of the dark years. Mara Moustafine uses extraordinary descriptive power to bring back to life a family she has never met. She has transformed Stalin's victims into people you can almost touch and speak with, so detailed is her portrayal of their lives. The research is impeccable. The story compelling. Each page is a passionate tribute to a family defiant till death against a machine so insidious that its leader was mourned when he died. *Secrets and Spies* is a protest, an expression of indignation at the inhumanity of one of the twentieth century's worst evils. It is a tribute to Moustafine and the past she has turned into a present.'

Monica Attard, former ABC correspondent to Russia
and author of *Russia: Which Way Paradise?*,
Doubleday, 1997

Secrets AND Spies

THE HARBIN FILES

Mara Moustafine (signature)

Mara Moustafine

VINTAGE

A Vintage Book
Published by
Random House Australia Pty Ltd
20 Alfred Street, Milsons Point, NSW 2061
http://www.randomhouse.com.au

Sydney   New York   Toronto
London   Auckland   Johannesburg

Copyright © Mara Moustafine 2002

All rights reserved. No part of this publication may be reproduced, stored
in a retrieval system or transmitted in any form or by any means, electronic,
mechanical, photocopying, recording or otherwise, without the prior permission
of the publisher.

National Library of Australia
Cataloguing-in-Publication data:

ISBN: 1 74051 091 7

Moustafine, Mara. 2. Consultants – Australia – Biography. 3. Russians – China
– Harbin. 4. Political persecution – Soviet Union. I. Title

920.72

Cover photograph of Manya Onikul, courtesy of Mara Moustafine
Cover design by Justine O'Donnell for jmedia design
Typeset by Midland Typesetters, Maryborough, Victoria
Printed and bound by Griffin Press, Netley, South Australia

10 9 8 7 6 5 4 3 2 1

Mara Moustafine was born in Harbin, China, into a family with Jewish, Russian and Tatar roots and came to Sydney as a child in 1959. Bilingual in Russian and English, Mara completed a Masters in International Relations at the Australian National University. She has worked as a diplomat, intelligence analyst, journalist and a senior business executive in Australia and Asia. This is her first book.

CONTENTS

'History keeps her secrets longer than most of us'
—John le Carré, *The Secret Pilgrim*

'If you spit on the past, it will land on the future'
—A Russian saying

'A human being is stronger than stone'
—Chesna Abramovna Onikul

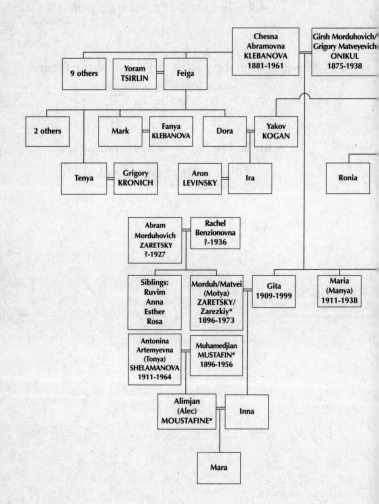

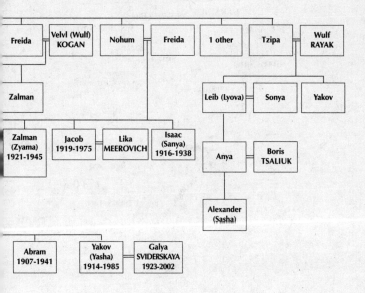

Onikul Family

* as transliterated by Australian immigration authorities.

(   ) indicates commonly used name.

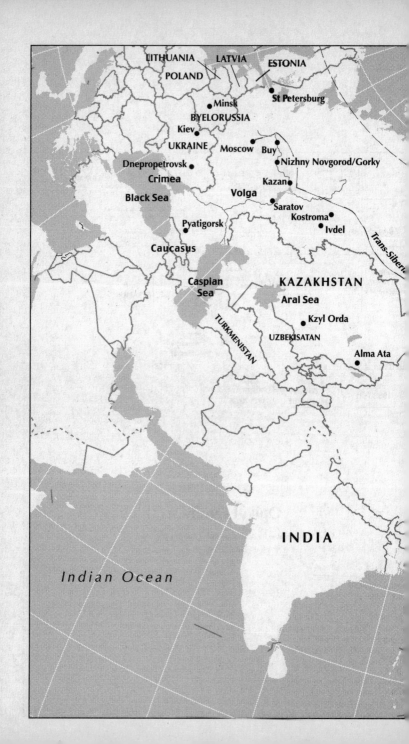

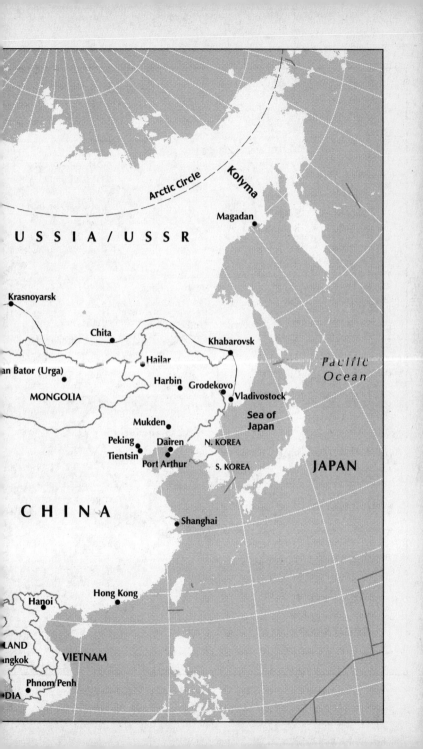

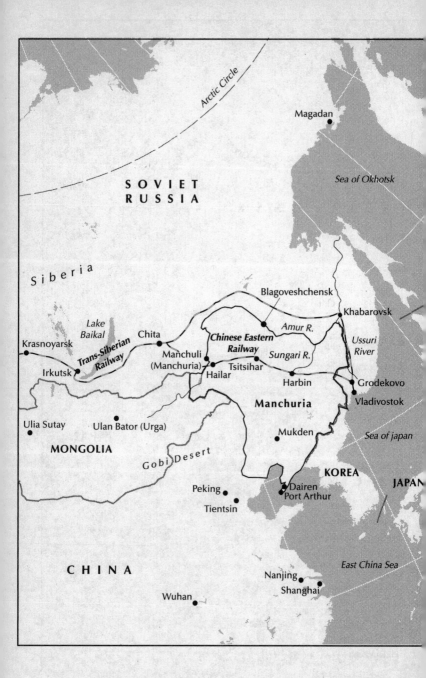

GLOSSARY

Article 58
: key article of the Criminal Code that dealt with counterrevolutionary activity

ASIO
: Australian Secret Intelligence Organisation

BREM
: Bureau of Russian Émigré Affairs in Manchukuo

CER
: Chinese Eastern Railway

Cheka
: All-Russian Extraordinary Commission for Combating Counter-Revolution and sabotage (Soviet security service 1917–22)

chekist
: Member of the Soviet or Russian security service (derives from Cheka, above)

CIA
: Central Intelligence Agency (USA)

Comintern	Communist International
DOB	Public Security Bureau in China (Russian acronym) after 1949
FSB	Federal Security Service (security service of the Russian Federation 1991–)
GAZ	Gorky Avtozavod (auto works)
glasnost	openness
GPU	State Political Directorate (Soviet security service 1922–23)
GUGB	Chief Directorate of State Security (Soviet security service within NKVD 1934–43)
Gulag	Chief Directorate of Corrective Labour Camps of the NKVD
Harbintsy	people of Harbin
HIAS	Hebrew Immigrant Aid Society
HPI	Harbin Polytechnical Institute
INO	Foreign Intelligence Department of Cheka/ GPU/OGPU/GUGB/NKVD 1920–41
ITL	corrective labour camp
Kempeitai	Japanese Gendarmerie (military police)
KGB	Committee of State Security (Soviet security service 1954-91)

kolkhoz	Soviet collective farm
Komsomol	Communist Youth League (for 14–28 year olds)
kulak	prosperous peasant
Manchukuo	The Japanese puppet state proclaimed in March 1932 under former Chinese Emperor Pu Yi following the Japanese occupation of Manchuria. Ended with Japanese capitulation in August 1945.
Memorial	Russian human rights movement
MGB	Soviet Ministry of State Security 1946–54
MVD	Soviet Ministry of Internal Affairs 1946–91
NKVD	People's Commissariat for Internal Affairs, which from 1934–41 included the political and civilian police and other agencies; acronym also used to refer to the NKVD Chief (Commissar)
OGPU	Unified State Political Directorate (Soviet security service 1923–34)
ONA	Office of National Assessments (Aust)
Otmol	Youth department of railway union in Manchuria modelled on the Komsomol
perestroika	restructuring

Pioneers	Soviet youth group (for children up to 14 years old)
pogranichniki	NKVD border guards
RFP	Russian Fascist Party
shtetl	village (Yiddish)
Smersh	Death to Spies! Soviet military counter-intelligence, 1943–46
spravka	certificate
SSC	Society of Soviet Citizens, established in 1945 to administer the affairs of Soviets in China
SSM	Union of Soviet Youth, organisation established in 1945 for Soviets in China on the Komsomol model
troika	three-person judicial board revived during the purges to expedite processing of political cases
UGB	Directorate of State Security of the NKVD
VMN	capital punishment
zek	Soviet prison slang for prisoner

KEY HISTORICAL DATES

1896	China and Russia sign agreement for construction of Chinese Eastern Railway (CER) across Manchuria
1898	start of construction of CER and Harbin
1904–05	Russo–Japanese War
Oct 1917	Bolshevik Revolution in Russia
1918–20	Russian Civil War
1920	China withdraws recognition from Tsarist representatives and ends Russian extraterritoriality in Manchuria
Oct 1922	collapse of the Far Eastern republic marks the end of the Russian Civil War
1924	China recognises Soviet government and agrees to joint administration of the CER

1928–31	Stalin's collectivisation campaign
Nov–Dec 1929	Sino–Soviet conflict over CER
1931	Mukden incident used as pretext for Japanese occupation of Manchuria
Feb 1932	Japanese occupy Harbin
Mar 1932	establishment of Japanese puppet state of Manchukuo
Dec 1932	Japanese occupy Hailar
Dec 1934	murder of Leningrad Communist party chief Kirov, which precipitates the purges
Mar 1935	Soviets sell CER to Japan
Aug 1936	First Moscow show trial (Zinoviev and Kamenev)
Nov 1936	new Soviet constitution proclaimed
Jan 1937	second Moscow show trial
June 1937– Nov 1938	the Great Terror
June 1937	arrest for treason and execution of Marshal Tukhachevsky and ten senior Red Army officers
July 1937	mass NKVD operation ordered against kulaks, criminals and anti-Soviet elements, then against suspect nationalities
Sept 1937	mass NKVD operation ordered against *Harbintsy*
Nov 1938	crackdown on NKVD excesses

Nov 1938	NKVD chief Yezhov resigns; replaced by Beria
June 1941	Germany invades USSR
Dec 1941	Japan bombs Pearl Harbor; start of Pacific War
Feb 1945	Yalta Conference, where US President Roosevelt, British Prime Minister Churchill and Soviet leader Stalin redraw the post-World War II borders and agree on spheres of influence
May 1945	Germany's unconditional surrender marks the end of the USSR's War against Nazism
Aug 1945	Soviet Red Army enters Manchuria
Aug 1945	Japan's unconditional surrender
1948	new wave of terror begins in the USSR
Oct 1949	Mao Zedong proclaims People's Republic of China after Communist forces defeat Chiang Kai-shek's Nationalists
Jan 1953	alleged Kremlin doctor's plot exposed
Mar 1953	Stalin dies. Khrushchev becomes Soviet Communist Party leader
July–Dec 1953	arrest and execution of NKVD chief Beria
Apr 1954	'Virgin lands' program launched for Soviet citizens in China
Feb 1956	Khrushchev's secret speech at the 20th CPSU Congress exposes Stalin's crimes
1966	Chinese Cultural Revolution

KEY HISTORICAL FIGURES

BAKSHEEV, General Alexei   Cossack leader who briefly headed BREM in 1937; tried by a Soviet Military Tribunal as a Japanese collaborator and executed in 1946

BERIA, Lavrenty   Chief of NKVD and successor services 1938–53; executed for conspiracy in 1953

BREZHNEV, Leonid   Soviet Communist Party leader (1964–82)

CHANG HSUE-LIANG   (aka 'the Young Marshal'), son of Chang Tso-lin, who succeeded him as Governor of Manchuria in 1928; ousted by the Japanese in 1931

CHANG TSO-LIN   warlord governor of Manchuria 1918–28, when he was murdered by the Japanese

CHIANG KAI-SHEK   leader of the Chinese Nationalists (Kuomintang); defeated by Mao Zedong's Communists in 1949

DZERZHINSKY, Feliks   ('Iron Feliks'), Chief of Cheka/ GPU/OGPU

1920–26 GORBACHEV, Mikhail the last Soviet Communist Party leader and President of the USSR 1985–91

KAGANOVICH, Lazar Commissar for Transportation 1935–38, later Heavy Industry

KHRUSHCHEV, Nikita Soviet Communist Party leader 1953–64

KRYUCHKOV, Vladimir the last KGB chief of the USSR 1988–91

LAVRUSHIN, Ivan Gorky regional NKVD chief 1937–38; executed in 1940 as an 'enemy of the people'

LYUSHKOV, Genrikh NKVD chief of the Far East region 1937–38 who, fearing a purge, defected to Japan

MAO ZEDONG leader of Chinese Communist revolutionary forces; proclaimed People's Republic in October 1949

MATKOVSKY, Mikhail Deputy of the Russian Fascist Party and Head of BREM's administrative department; a suspected Soviet agent

NAGOLEN, Colonel Head of Asano unit of the Russian Detachment in the Kwantung Army; a suspected Soviet agent

NEMTSOV, Boris Governor of Nizhny Novgorod (1991–96) and Deputy Prime Minister of the Russian Federation (1997–98); now parliamentary leader of the Union of Rightist Forces

ORDZHONIKIDZE, Sergo Commissar for Heavy Industry 1932–37; died mysteriously at height of the purges

PU YI   the last emperor of China (Hsuan T'ung) who was enthroned as Emperor of the Japanese puppet state of Manchukuo in 1933

PUTIN, Vladimir   former KGB officer, now President of the Russian Federation 2000–

RODZAEVSKY, Konstantin   leader of the Russian Fascist party in Harbin; tried by a Soviet Military Tribunal as a Japanese collaborator and executed in 1946

SEMYONOV, Ataman Grigory   Japanese-backed Cossack warlord during Civil War, leader of militant White émigrés in Manchuria; tried by Soviet Military Tribunal as a Japanese collaborator and hanged in 1946

STALIN, Josef   Soviet Communist Party leader 1922–53

TUKHACHEVSKY, Marshal Mikhail   Deputy Defence Commissar, arrested and executed for alleged treason and conspiracy in June 1937; rehabilitated 1958

UNGERN-STERNBERG, Baron Roman   anti-Bolshevik warlord during the Civil War, cohort of Ataman Semyonov

VYSHINSKY, Andrei   Procurator (attorney general) of the USSR 1935–39 and chief Public Prosecutor of the Moscow show trials

YEZHOV, Nikolai   NKVD chief 1936–38; executed as a spy in 1940

*To my family across continents and generations
and to their courage*

CURIOSITY

I DIDN'T KNOW much about her when, in my early twenties, I stole her photograph from my grandmother's drawer. But I sensed she was important to me somehow. I carefully slid the picture into the tiny Chinese leather album with cut-out frames I had found among my family's treasures from Harbin.

Manya was my grandmother Gita's younger sister. Her photograph was a perfect fit for the small rectangular space next to the picture Gita had inscribed to my grandfather four months before their marriage in 1927.

At seventeen, Gita was a classic beauty. Her dark, knowing eyes stared directly out of the photo with a quiet certainty. But her simple, sombre dress with white lace collar—perhaps her school uniform—gave away her wholesome innocence. I adored my grandmother, but could never imagine living her life, defined as it was by marriage and family.

Manya was quite different. Photographed in her early twenties, she looked more worldly-wise and modern. Dressed in an open-necked trench coat, with dark shoulder-length hair, Manya had a certain 1930s glamour. Gazing mysteriously into the distance, she looked like she was going places. Though I had never known her, Manya struck me as someone I could relate to.

Why didn't I ask my grandmother for the photo? I knew there was nothing she would ever deny me. But instinct told me there would be less pain caused this way. Besides, I did not know how to explain why I was filling the little album with photographs of myself and my family. Some had been taken in Sydney, but most were from Harbin, the city in north China where several generations of my family had lived and where I was born. At that stage, my fascination with the lost world of Russian Harbin was still ill-defined. And my vague yearning to connect to family across continents and generations was something I had not articulated, even to myself.

Russian Jews have a tradition of naming a child after a dead relative. I am named after Manya, whose full name in Russian was Maria. They called me Marianna as this name derives from the same Hebrew root as Maria—shortened in my case to the Russian 'Mara'. Why not 'Manya'? In 1950s Harbin, my family thought it too reminiscent of the *shtetls* (Jewish villages) of Byelorussia, which my great-grandparents had left behind—together with poverty and pogroms—at the turn of the twentieth century.

All I knew about Manya when I was growing up was that she had been a dentist and had died in Stalin's purges along with her father, Girsh, and brother, Abram. She was twenty-six years old. 'What was she like? Why did they kill her?' I remember asking. The most I ever got in reply was, 'She wasn't as beautiful as your grandmother, but she was very clever. As for her death—you know she died in the purges. Stalin didn't need a reason.'

From my grandmother's stories, I knew that in the mid-1930s, Manya, her parents Girsh and Chesna Onikul, and two brothers Abram and Yasha, left Hailar, a small town in the Manchurian steppes north-west of Harbin, to escape the Japanese occupation and build a new life in the Soviet Union. Gita, who was already married, stayed in Harbin with my grandfather, Motya Zaretsky, and my mother, Inna.

The Onikuls went to Gorky, the city I knew as the place of exile in the 1980s of the Nobel Prize-winning human rights activist Andrei Sakharov. Formerly Nizhny Novgorod, the city was renamed in Soviet times after the proletarian writer Maxim Gorky, who was born there. How appropriate that in Russian *gorky* means 'bitter'. In hindsight, it seems bizarre that, after twenty-five years in Manchuria, the Onikuls chose to go there on the eve of the Great Terror. But life in Manchuria under Japanese occupation in the 1930s was full of menace for many Russians, particularly those who, like the Onikuls, had Soviet identity papers.

In the late 1930s, a wall of silence descended between the Onikuls, caught in the Stalinist terror followed by the war, and my grandparents, the Zaretskys, living under the Japanese puppet regime in 'Manchukuo'. Only in the mid-1950s, after the death of Stalin, did news reach Harbin that two of the Onikuls—Gita's mother, Chesna, and her younger brother, Yasha—had survived the purges. By some miracle, in the late 1950s, each separately visited Harbin from Riga, the capital of Latvia where they were then living. Chesna brought the news that her husband, Girsh, and two other children, Manya and Abram, had perished. I was too young then to understand what was going on.

In 1959, a couple of years after these visits, my family left Harbin for Australia. By that time, the once thriving Russian community had become an anachronistic enclave of some one thousand people. The Chinese Revolution was in full swing and we were not wanted.

⎯⎯⎯•⎯⎯⎯

Growing up Russian in Sydney in the 1960s, one couldn't escape reminders of the Cold War world. The spy drama that gripped Australia after the defection of two Soviet agents, the Petrovs, in 1954 was still fresh in people's minds. I would often be put on the spot when asked where I came from.

'China,' I would answer.

'That's funny, you don't look Chinese.'

'No, I'm Russian.'

'Are you a Communist?', the next question might be, or 'Are you White Russian or Red Russian?' These were not the sort of questions most Australian children my age had to field.

'No, I'm Russian from China. I've never even been over there.'

'Yes, but what about your parents?'

'They haven't either.'

The ideological divide between Soviet and émigré Russians was accentuated at Russian school, which I attended on Saturdays for ten years. Organised by Russian *Harbintsy* (people of Harbin) to ensure their children preserved their heritage, we were taught language, literature and history, as well as singing and ballet. The standard of teaching was generally very high and enabled most of us to take Russian as an extra subject for matriculation. But it had its idiosyncrasies.

Although the text books we used were printed in the Soviet Union, they were censored before they were handed out to us. This meant that all references to the Soviet Union, Communist Party, the Pioneers (a youth group most Soviet children attended), the *kolkhoz* (collective farm) and other Soviet concepts were glued over with paper. So were Soviet symbols in illustrations, such as the Soviet crest with hammer and sickle and even the red stars on top of the Kremlin towers.

Predictably, our study of Russian history, taught by a woman whom we nicknamed 'Catherine the Great' because of her pompadour hairstyle and elaborate dresses, ended with the fall of the House of Romanov in 1917. 'What happened after that?' I remember asking, mischievously. In fact, I knew full-well having already studied the Bolshevik Revolution at high school. The teacher looked disapproving, as if I had asked her where babies came from, and suggested that I go home and ask my mother.

Still, I knew that 'over there', behind the infamous 'iron curtain', I had relatives whom I would probably never see again. My great-grandmother, Chesna, and my paternal grandmother, Tonya, had died in the Soviet Union in the early 1960s. But Gita's brother Yasha still lived in Riga with his wife Galya. He was some sort of doctor, working for the Soviet airline Aeroflot. He corresponded regularly with my grandmother and sometimes sent me books and Latvian souvenirs.

Curiously, the return address on anything Yasha sent us was always in his wife Galya's surname. My mother explained that Yasha was afraid that contact with foreigners might impinge negatively on his career. I would write him a few lines in my grandmother's letters. Once in the mid-1970s, I mentioned that I had visited Israel, among some other Mediterranean countries. My mother crossed it out. 'But the Soviet Union has diplomatic relations with Israel,' I protested. 'It might still be dangerous for them. You just never know,' she replied.

Such exchanges frequently reminded me how much I took for granted, living in a democratic country where law and logic governed and a premium was placed on a humane and civil society. Letters from our relative, Ira Kogan in Kazakhstan, underlined my family's good fortune to have made it to Australia at all. Still in Harbin in the early 1960s, she and her family had not been able to get Australian entry visas. It could so easily have been our story too.

⬥

Perhaps it was my family's history of journeys across borders and political systems which in some part drove me to study politics and international relations at university in the 1970s. I read a lot of Soviet history but my focus was on contemporary Soviet politics and the dynamics of the bipolar world. By the late 1970s, I was working on my Masters degree in international relations at the Australian National University (ANU) in Canberra, with a doctoral scholarship in the offing. It occurred to me then that the stories of Harbin Russians like my family were an invaluable historical source on extraordinary events in Russia and China, and should be recorded. But I was too busy with issues of high policy—US-Soviet détente, the Middle East conflict and Eurocommunism. Set on the path to an academic career, I left the Harbin project on the back-burner, thinking there would always be time for it later.

But halfway through my Masters, I began to question my career direction. Having spent five years in academe, I became impatient to get out into the real world—or at least, the world of diplomacy. To my chagrin, I discovered that the Department of Foreign Affairs was not recruiting new entrants that year. I happened to mention my disappointment to the director of the Australian Institute of International Affairs, a distinguished, retired ambassador whose office was in my department at university. Several months later, his secretary summoned me from an end-of-year picnic near the lake in the university grounds for an urgent meeting.

'Right now?' I asked in dismay. I was dressed in tight, red jeans and a black T-shirt—the colours of anarchy.

'If possible, yes.' I straightened myself up as best I could and went immediately to the distinguished gentleman's office.

'It's about your future, my dear,' he said, reminding me of our earlier conversation. 'Have you ever considered intelligence?'

I was stunned. Only one intelligence agency sprang to mind—ASIO, the domestic security service—not really the place for a committed left-leaning liberal.

'Do I look like the sort of person who would work for ASIO?' I asked.

'Do I look like the sort of person who would recruit for them?' he responded.

'No', I said, thinking 'yes'.

In fact, the organisation the ambassador had in mind was the Office of National Assessments (ONA), a new intelligence assessment organisation set up to provide the government with strategic analysis on international matters. Sensing my hesitation, he described it as a 'quasi-academic think tank'. He told me he had been asked to keep an eye out for potential candidates. If I was interested, he would pass on my curriculum vitae.

Though I devoured the novels of Graham Greene and John le Carré, I had never contemplated a career in intelligence. Not in my wildest dreams. But what did I have to lose? It was a new and prestigious organisation that reported directly to the prime minister. It was bound to be interesting.

After several interviews and rigorous security checking, I was granted a Top Secret security clearance and went to work as a strategic analyst. Who would have believed it? A migrant with such a confusing background; Australia really was the land of opportunity! During my induction, I was warned about hostile intelligence services and made to understand that travel to the Soviet Union, China or other Eastern bloc countries was practically out of the question. It was not something I was contemplating in any case.

This was the start of my twelve-year career with the Australian government. After four years in intelligence, I moved to diplomacy, with policy assignments in Canberra, a term as ministerial adviser and a senior posting to the embassy in Bangkok. It was here that I became involved in the Australian peace initiative for Cambodia in the early 1990s. Cambodia and its people captured my heart and my imagination. By 1992, I had moved to the private sector and was heading up the Cambodian operations of Australia's national telecommunications company, Telstra, in Phnom Penh, just as the reconstruction of the war-ravaged country was getting underway.

In July 1992, I managed to escape Cambodia briefly for a long-planned holiday in Moscow with my friends, Olga and Bradley Wynne, where Olga was in the final year of her posting at the Australian embassy.

I had in fact been to Moscow once before in late 1987, during a brief stint as a foreign affairs journalist. At that time, President Mikhail Gorbachev was still trying to reform the Soviet Union within the parameters of a Communist system and his new buzz words, *perestroika* (restructuring) and *glasnost* (openness), were on everybody's lips.

By the early 1990s, everything had been turned on its head. Though he survived a coup by Communist Party hardliners, Gorbachev was no longer leader. Boris Yeltsin, Gorbachev's radical reform rival who had rallied opposition against the coup, was now the first elected president of the Russian Federation. The red Communist flag with hammer and sickle had been replaced by the old Russian white, blue and red minus the Tsarist double-headed eagle. The final curtain had descended on the Soviet Union.

CHAPTER 1

RIGA TREASURES

As the Moscow express train pulls into Riga station, I immediately recognise the woman standing on the platform in the smart beige coat as Galya, the wife of my grandmother's brother, Yasha. True to my grandmother Gita's description, she is attractive, light-haired and in her seventies. Besides, who else would be dressed in their best on a weekday morning, holding a bunch of red carnations?

'Oh Marochka, Marochka! Finally I get to meet Gita's granddaughter! You know Yasha absolutely adored you! What a pity he did not live to see you now!' Galya gushes with excitement and chastises me for coming to Riga for only two days. I am overwhelmed by the torrent of affection from someone I don't really know and stifled by all the superlatives. I only ever met Yasha once and Galya has never met Gita. Can one absorb family ties by osmosis?

It was my grandmother's suggestion that I come to Riga to see Galya, whom no-one in our family has ever met. Gita also asked me to visit the cemetery where Yasha and my great-grandmother Chesna are buried.

Galya has arranged for a friend to take us there in his car—Yasha's old car, in fact. On the way, the two of them talk about their fears of living as ethnic Russians in the new Latvian republic since the collapse of the Soviet Union. They are understandably worried about the impact of their loss of citizenship on their pensions.

I soon realise that politically, Galya and I will never see eye to eye. She remembers with fondness the Brezhnev years, when Yasha held a senior post in Aeroflot's health administration in Riga. There were holidays at resorts in the Crimea and they wanted for nothing. Galya rues the passing of the Soviet regime. 'At least there was order and the USSR was a world power to be reckoned with— unlike now . . .' she says. It is a common refrain from elderly people in Russia. I struggle to bite my tongue, but cannot resist pointing out that it was the economic stagnation and corruption of the Brezhnev years that precipitated the Soviet Union's collapse. This only leads to more bickering.

Yasha and Chesna are buried together at the Jewish cemetery on the outskirts of Riga. The graves are laid out between alleys of tall, leafy trees. In traditional Russian style, most of the gravestones have small, oval photographs of the deceased with their names and dates written underneath. Standing before the Onikul grave shaded by an enormous beech tree, the stress of my encounter with Galya begins to dissipate, and I start to feel calm. For the sake of family, I resolve to steer clear of politics and other contentious subjects for the duration of my visit.

———•••••———

Back at Galya's apartment, I am drawn to the Chinese artefacts in the living room—a fat, pale green jade Buddha; a gold tea set; a painting of the Bund waterfront in Shanghai. A silver Mongolian tea bowl and a couple of Chinese scrolls are identical to those in my parents' house in Sydney. Yasha or Chesna must have brought them back from China.

It occurs to me then that Galya might be able to fill me in on some family history. I tell her that apart from vague recollections of meeting Yasha and Chesna in Harbin as a very young child, I know little about my grandmother's family or what happened to them. I ask her to tell me what she knows.

'I only met Yasha in 1946 after the war ended and later I met his mother. By that time the others were long dead . . .'

'What happened to them?' I ask.

'All I know is that they were arrested during the purges. They were innocent of course, and rehabilitated after Stalin died. Somewhere your great-grandmother kept the certificates of "rehabilitation", which cleared their names.'

'Do you have them here? Oh please, please find them . . .'

'I think they're probably in the box with her photographs. I'll look for them later. I thought you wanted to go out to see the old town,' Galya says.

'Photos!' I shriek in delight. 'Oh please, please can you get them now. I can see the old town tomorrow.'

From the top of the cupboard in her bedroom, Galya brings a box of old photographs and documents which once belonged to Yasha and Chesna. My attention is immediately captured by two Chinese photograph albums. From their contents, it is clear that one belonged to Yasha's sister Manya and the other one to Chesna. Manya's is small, clothbound in beige with a floral motif and full of her photos from Hailar and Harbin. Chesna's is larger, dark green with embossed flying cranes. Inside are photographs of her children and relatives over the years, including many of myself as a child, mounted in no particular order. There are also loose photographs going back to Minsk and Moghilev, towns in Byelorussia from which the family had originally come. What a miracle that all these photos survived the years and so many upheavals.

Poring over these old photographs as well as a pile of Galya's own, we pack more than fifty years into two days. I gain some real insight into the Onikul family. Over the years, my grandmother told me stories about her father, Girsh, whom she adored. He always came across as quite a character. Now I see him in family photographs. Yasha and Chesna are relatively familiar figures. I met both of them as a child when they visited Harbin, and know them through the letters and photographs they used to send us from Riga.

Galya's stories fill out the picture. She tells me how she met Yasha while he was visiting friends in the Ukraine after the war, about their romance and their life together. She shows me photographs of the two of them in places where they lived and worked—Latvia, Estonia, Lithuania, Uzbekistan—he as a medical administrator, she as a pharmacist. I thumb through Yasha's personal papers and impressive work references. My grandmother had so hoped that one day he would visit us in Australia. What a pity he died before this was possible.

The biggest gap in my knowledge of the Onikuls is about Manya and Abram, whose lives were cut off so senselessly at an early age. Having never known them, Galya can cast no light. But the papers and photographs of their lives in China and the Soviet Union do. Among them are Manya's academic records for her final year in high school in Hailar and her graduation from dentistry school in Harbin. In the albums, I see Manya photographed with school friends in Hailar; nursing my mother as a tiny child outside Harbin's famous Hotel Moderne; in her dentist surgery in Gorky; with a group, visiting resorts on the Black Sea.

I ask Galya the identity of a handsome, dark-haired young man whose face appears regularly among Chesna's photos. It turns out to be my grandmother's older brother, Abram. I vaguely recall Gita showing me his photo in Sydney. Now I see what she meant by her constant reference to how handsome he was. Many of his photographs are inscribed with place names on the back—Abram with friends in Hailar; standing in a field in the Mongolian capital of Ulan Bator; in Vladivostok reading a book; dressed in some sort of military uniform. He was clearly a young man who travelled. Galya remembers Yasha telling her that Abram lived somewhere in the Far East, not in Gorky. I am tantalised by these beautiful images frozen in time. What is their story?

At the end of my stay, Galya suggests that I take Chesna's photographs and papers. 'They're your family,' she says, 'I didn't even know them. Of what possible use are they to me?'

Among the papers I find five small, official certificates, each headed *Spravka*—one for each member of the family. These are the certificates of 'rehabilitation' Galya had mentioned.

Typed on the letterhead of the Military Collegium of the USSR Supreme Court on 22 October 1956, with the Soviet crest printed in dark blue and signed by a 'colonel of the judiciary', Manya's reads:

Spravka

The charges against Onikul, Maria Grigorievna, have been reviewed by the Military Collegium of the USSR Supreme Court on 6 October 1956.

The sentence of the USSR NKVD of 7 January 1938 relating to Onikul M.G. is revoked and the case is dropped in the absence of criminal evidence.

Onikul M.G. is posthumously rehabilitated.

Girsh's *spravka* is identical and issued on the same day. Abram's, dated in February 1957, differs in the second paragraph. It reads:

The sentence of the Military Tribunal of the forces of the USSR NKVD of the Khabarovsk district of 4 October 1939 and the determination of the Military Collegium of the USSR Supreme Court of 17 November 1939 relating to Onikul Abram Grigorievich is revoked ... and the case is dropped in the absence of criminal evidence.

All I know about Khabarovsk is that it is a city in the Russian Far East, not far from Vladivostok. The information on the *spravka* seems consistent with what Galya told me. But why is there no mention of his rehabilitation?

Yasha and Chesna's *spravkas*, both dated 28 April 1956, come from a different judicial authority—the Military Tribunal of the Moscow Military District. Its crest is a white hammer and sickle inside a red star. Both have been sentenced by a 'Special Board of the USSR NKVD'—Yasha on 10 January 1938, Chesna on 20 October 1938. Yasha's *spravka* describes him as 'born in 1914, working as an English language interpreter at the automobile works in the city of Gorky prior to his arrest on 3 October 1937'. Chesna's says she was born in 1881.

In themselves, the *spravkas* give away little. But compared to what I knew before, they are full of information. Apart from the fact of their rehabilitation, I now know when each of the Onikuls was sentenced and by which authority. I know where Yasha worked in Gorky and that Abram was arrested in Khabarovsk. But I still have no idea what the Onikuls had been charged with or why.

What I do not yet fully appreciate is that these *spravkas* may be my tickets to information about the people whose names they bear. In a system that still runs on *spravkas*—officious bits of paper with crests, signatures and stamps—I now have something which gives me an entrée with Russian officials. At the very least, they might get me a foot through the door. It is my friends Olga and Bradley Wynne who point this out when I return to Moscow with my Riga treasures.

⋅—•◦•—⋅

Olga and Bradley have now spent almost three years in Moscow, where Olga is the head of migration at the Australian embassy. They are eye-witnesses to the dramatic end of the Soviet empire and the evolution of the new Russia. Olga is my best friend. She too was born in Harbin of Russian parents and grew up in Sydney. Bradley has taken time out from his job as a journalist to study Russian and write.

The Wynnes are a striking couple. With curly hair, beard and strong features, Bradley's face is reminiscent of the great Russian writer Aleksandr Pushkin. Olga, a dreamy, grey-eyed Slav, resembles a princess from a Pushkin fairy tale. But looks can be deceptive as Olga is far from dreamy. With the lifting of previous Soviet restrictions on migration, she has had to initiate processes to cope with the flood of applicants for Australia. For her achievements, she has just been awarded an Australian government medal.

When I show my friends the treasures I have brought

back from Riga, Olga—like me—is captivated by the old photographs. Bradley immediately zeros in on the *spravkas*. He tells me the 'new KGB' is opening up its archives and starting to release information about Stalin's purges.

'You could approach them and see what information they will give you about what happened to your family,' he suggests.

'What? Go to the Lubyanka?' I shudder. The building complex in the centre of Moscow has housed Soviet state security in all its incarnations since the 1917 Bolshevik Revolution, as well as its infamous central prison. First it was the Cheka, then the GPU, OGPU, NKVD, MVD and finally the KGB. Now, since the collapse of communism in 1991, it is called the FSB (Federal Security Service). Has anything else changed, I wonder? There is one way to find out.

Over dinner at *U Pirosmani*, one of the new Georgian restaurants that have sprung up around Moscow, we talk about the KGB and some of the extraordinary events the Wynnes have witnessed over the past three years. Back in 1990, the KGB had tried to present a new face, in line with Gorbachev's *glasnost* and *perestroika*. A press office was opened and a pretty, young woman in a bullet-proof vest was declared 'Miss KGB'. In line with Gorbachev's alcohol ban, she drank orange juice instead of vodka, adored James Bond and could deal a mean karate kick— all in the name of public relations.

The reality became clear to all when in August 1991, KGB chief Kryuchkov appeared on Soviet television to announce the anti-Gorbachev coup. It was not surprising that as the coup collapsed, bringing with it Soviet Communism and its institutions, the first target of the jubilant crowds was the statue of Feliks Dzerzhinsky, founder of the Soviet secret service. With the help of a crane brought from a construction site at the US embassy, the towering figure of 'Iron Feliks' was pulled down from his pedestal at the front of the old Lubyanka, marking the end of the repressive Soviet era.

Olga tells me of a quieter but no less significant ceremony that took place at the other end of Lubyanka Square almost a year earlier. She had been among the crowd that had gathered in the small park opposite the KGB on 30 October 1990 to witness the unveiling of a monument to the victims of totalitarianism. The huge boulder had been brought all the way from Solovki, the first Soviet forced labour camp established on an island just south of the Arctic Circle back in the days of Lenin and Dzerzhinsky.

Who would have believed that the Moscow authorities would approve the erection of a monument to the millions who had perished at the hands of the KGB and its predecessors directly in front of the bastion of Soviet repression?

Bradley explains that it was the work of Memorial, a movement committed to exposing the real history of Stalin's terror and commemorating its victims. The monument is the culmination of a three-year public campaign. 'When Gorbachev told the Communist Party Congress in 1987 that it was time to fill in the "blank spots" of Soviet history, Memorial took him at his word.'

⊷∙∙∙∎∙∙∙⊶

Several days later, Bradley joins me on my Lubyanka mission, as much to satisfy his own curiosity as to make sure I stay out of trouble. We have tried to call the FSB to find out where we should go but the lines are permanently busy. I am beginning to learn that this is typical of Moscow's clogged public phone system. 'Let's just go to the Lubyanka and knock on the door,' I say with false bravado.

Armed with the Onikul *spravkas*, we catch the metro to Lubyanka Square. Neither of us really believes there will be any concrete outcome. We are prepared for the usual bureaucratic run-around—filling in forms, getting proof of identity, being told 'no, no, no'. But what the hell! I have sounded out the Australian ambassador with whom I once worked in Canberra. If my direct approach proves to be unproductive, he is ready to make a formal request on my behalf for information about my family.

After a brief discussion at the FSB reception counter, we are directed first to one building around the corner, then to another down the road in Kuznetsky Most. The receptionist telephones ahead to say we are coming.

Number 22 is a graceful old mansion, apparently the home of a merchant in Tsarist times. A guard points the way to the reception room. Inside, a metal bust of Feliks Dzerzhinsky still oversees proceedings. I desperately want to photograph him, but Bradley reads my mind. 'Don't even think about it,' he warns. 'Just get what you came for.' His eyes flick knowingly to the two-way mirror on the side wall.

A young man appears from behind the screen. Dressed in blue jeans and a pale blue open-necked polo shirt, he is in his thirties. I guess that his closely cropped blond hair is a hangover from military service.

'Good afternoon. I am Vladimir Nikolayevich . . .' He speaks English with a Russian–American accent. I am so taken aback by his informal appearance that I miss his surname. I introduce myself in Russian, as does Bradley, and I start to explain what I am after.

'Reception told me you were Australian . . .' he interjects in English. I wonder whether this is for Bradley's benefit or if he is just showing off. 'But you speak Russian too well for it to be a second language. Yet clearly you are not, "one of us", as they say,' he remarks, raising one eyebrow in a question mark.

In Russian, I tell him that I am indeed Australian, but born in China of Russian parents. I start to explain that I am visiting my friend Bradley and his wife who is on posting with the Australian embassy.

'From Harbin?' Vladimir interjects again, this time in Russian.

I nod.

'Interesting,' he says knowingly and waves us into his office. Vladimir is the face of the new KGB.

I explain to Vladimir the story of my grandmother's family who returned to the Soviet Union in the 1930s and got caught in Stalin's purges. I pass him the rehabilitation *spravkas* and ask him what I need to do to investigate their fate. I also ask why there is no mention of 'rehabilitation' on Abram's *spravka*. Predictably, he tells me I must put my request in writing. Bradley and I exchange glances. Just then the phone rings and Vladimir answers it.

'Here comes the bureaucratic run-around . . .' Bradley whispers to me in English.

'Well, we've got this far, may as well keep going,' I whisper back and smile at Vladimir.

'Nobody is engaged in repression now, madam,' Vladimir tells the caller, 'we are only involved in rehabilitation.' Vladimir winks at me irreverently. He has engaging blue eyes. 'Please send your request to the address I just gave you and it will be dealt with.' He puts down the phone and turns back to us.

'Please excuse me for this interruption, but we are economising on telephonists. Now, as I was saying, you will need to draft a letter formally requesting the information about your relatives. Then, we will try to locate any files that may still be in the archives and get them for you. Let's do the letter right now. I take it you write Russian, as well as speak it?'

I nod.

'Of course. Good. Then I will dictate and you will write. It will be quicker that way.' He hands me some blank paper.

'First write the address—*Rehabilitation Group, Directorate for Moscow and the Moscow Region, Ministry of Security of the Russian Federation*. From—your name.

Then keep it simple—*Please advise on the fate of my relatives, the Onikul family, victims of the purges, whose names are listed below*. Leave the rest of the page blank and I will fill in their names from the *spravkas* and the details of your request. I'll ask for all the standard information: when and why they were arrested, what they were charged with, any other information or remaining personal photographs, letters etc. Let me just photocopy the *spravkas* to attach to your request,' he says turning on a small Xerox machine behind him. I have the sense that Vladimir has been through this routine before.

'What about my question about the rehabilitation of Abram Onikul?' I ask.

'That will need to be addressed to a different agency,' he answers. 'Please write down your question and his details. I will complete the rest. Vladimir returns my *spravkas* and quickly looks over the copies.

'It may take some time to track down your family's files. They are certainly not held here in Moscow.'

'But I'll only be in Russia for a couple more weeks. I'm just visiting my friends who are with the Australian embassy here,' I say pointing to Bradley. Perhaps mention of my 'connections' will help speed things up?

'Then you'd better authorise your friends to receive the information on your behalf,' says Vladimir. 'So, please write: *As I will be leaving Moscow soon, I entrust*— put your friend's name—*of the Australian embassy in Moscow to receive any spravkas and materials*. And put the phone numbers. Then *I also authorise him to familiarise himself with the criminal cases*.

I flinch at the matter-of-fact way the word 'criminal' rolls off his tongue.

'Sign and date. That's all. As soon as we get something, we'll be in touch.'

Bradley and I walk out into the late Moscow afternoon, shell-shocked. Lubyanka Square is almost deserted. Bradley points out the plinth which once held the statue of Dzerzhinsky. 'After Feliks was removed, people chipped away at it for days. They probably figured that if the Germans could sell chunks of the Berlin Wall, why not a piece of Dzerzhinsky's plinth?' We cross to the small park with the memorial boulder from Solovki. The inscription reads simply:

> *In memory of the millions of victims of*
> *the totalitarian regime*

I take a photograph. This may be the only gravestone Manya, Girsh and Abram have.

Hungry and in need of a sanity check, we walk past the ugly grey monoliths of Stalinist realism along Tverskaya, the main street of central Moscow, straight to McDonald's on Pushkin Square. It is four o'clock and the rush hour has not yet started. But soon the queue will stretch around the corner, thanks to the artificially low rouble prices. The popularity of this icon of American cultural imperialism which opened a year and a half ago infuriates communist and Russian ideologues alike, Bradley tells me. But in the absence of Russian fast food of any quality, even to an Australian yuppie sworn off the brand, a 'Big Mak' tastes good.

'Well, that's certainly not your old KGB,' I remark, recalling the treatment I received in the Soviet Union as a visiting journalist in 1987. Bradley is more sober in his appraisal: 'The new look is good, but let's see what they actually deliver.'

———•◦•———

On my last night in Moscow, I visit my grandmother's relatives, whom she told me about just before my trip. Lyova Rayak is the son of Gita's father's older sister, who stayed in Byelorussia while Girsh and his brothers went to Manchuria. In the late 1920s, the Rayaks moved to Moscow. As with Galya, no-one from my family in Sydney has ever met them. 'Why haven't you told me about these relatives before?' I remember asking Gita. 'There was no point,' she replied. 'You couldn't go to Moscow and it was dangerous for them to have contact with foreigners like us.'

Arriving for dinner at the apartment where Lyova's daughter Anya lives with her family, I do not know what to expect. I am met with warmth, traditional Russian family hospitality and, unexpectedly, another of Gita's relatives—a grandson of her mother Chesna's sister Feiga. Now both sides of Gita's family are represented.

Over the course of the evening—and many toasts— we unravel our complex family ties, and try to work out how we are all related. We conclude it doesn't really matter. Family is family.

At eighty-five, Uncle Lyova is the quintessential Russian Jewish grandfather—short, stubborn and hard-of-hearing, but with a quick wit and an encyclopaedic memory. 'Anything you want to know, just ask me,' he says proudly.

'He'll tell you what he should and what he shouldn't,' laughs his daughter, Anya. And he does.

Uncle Lyova gives me a crash-course on the Onikul family's history, going back to the days in Byelorussia. He knows in which year everyone was born and in which *shtetl*. He remembers when my great-grandparents—his uncle Girsh and aunt Chesna—returned from China in the mid-1930s to live in Gorky with their children, Manya and Yasha. The children found work at the big, new Gorky automobile plant. The Onikuls visited Moscow often. Sometimes they stayed with Lyova's family; at other times with Chesna's sister, Feiga.

This all came to an abrupt end with Stalin's great purge in 1937. 'Like all the Russians who came to the USSR from China, the Onikuls were arrested as spies,' Uncle Lyova says matter-of-factly. 'There was a special article in the Criminal Code which covered espionage but I have forgotten the number.'

'What?' I exclaim. 'I thought they left China to get away from the Japanese?'

'Yes of course,' he sighs. 'But don't look for logic. It was a bandit government here. It was the Terror. At least your great-grandmother Chesna and uncle Yasha survived.'

It emerges from the conversation that, with the exception of Uncle Lyova's twenty-two-year-old grandson Sasha, everybody at Anya's dinner knew both Chesna and Yasha. Anya remembers the exotic gifts Chesna brought back from her visit to Harbin in 1957 —black silk pyjamas and a powder compact for her mother and a little handbag for her. As Yasha and Galya had no children of their own, they doted on Anya as a child. Later Anya and her husband visited the couple in Riga.

'What about Abram?' I ask Uncle Lyova, 'did you know him too?'

'No, he didn't come to Gorky or to Moscow. He went to study in Vladivostok, then was recruited into the NKVD—the secret police,' he says without blinking. 'Then they accused him of being a Japanese spy and shot him. Bandits!'

'What?' My great-uncle a Soviet spy? I cannot believe it.

Upon reflection though, I think *why not?* Abram had been a citizen of the Soviet Union and working for the NKVD was not a crime. I did not think twice about Americans working for the CIA. I myself had worked for an Australian intelligence assessment organisation and knew people in the operational agencies. Was working for the NKVD any different?

'What did Abram do for the NKVD?' I ask Uncle Lyova, naively.

'How would I know? I never got to meet him,' he responds. 'And if I had, I doubt he would have told me.'

I tell the family about the rehabilitation *spravkas* I got from Galya in Riga and the story of my meeting with

Vladimir at the FSB. 'Your great-grandmother Chesna fought hard to have her family vindicated,' Lyova tells me. 'She never gave up, in spite of what she herself had been through.'

'Perhaps the FSB will give me some more information on what happened,' I say hopefully.

'We will live and we will see,' Uncle Lyova quotes an old Russian proverb. He has seen too much history since the 'October Pogrom', as he calls the 1917 revolution, to be easily taken in. 'The comrades may have learned to present themselves in a new style, but I'm not sure how much they've changed underneath.'

Three days later I am back in steamy, monsoonal Phnom Penh. My focus has shifted to the challenges of delivering state-of-the-art international communications services in a country with a devastated infrastructure. There are crises to resolve and contract negotiations to conclude. All too soon, my extraordinary Moscow encounters recede, and seem a world away.

And as predicted, we hear nothing from the FSB.

———————

Several months later, conscious that the Wynnes' posting in Moscow is drawing to a close, I telephone Olga to ask if she has heard anything from the FSB regarding my request for information about the Onikuls. Nothing. We agree that the time has come to give the comrades at the new KGB a nudge.

When Olga telephones the number which Vladimir gave me, she gets the old Soviet fob-off—no-one will take ownership or responsibility.

'Yes, I am Vladimir Nikolayevich. No, I was just the duty officer that day. I did not process any such case. Try the duty officer on 9256917.'

'Yes, case number 03214 was processed on 21 July by Victor Alekseyevich, but he's in hospital right now. Perhaps you can Yevgeny Nikolayevich on 9211697.'

Olga's persistent telephone calls eventually prompt some action.

In December 1992, a couple of letters addressed to Bradley on my behalf arrive at the Australian embassy in Moscow, just as it is winding down for the Christmas–New Year break. By this time, the Wynnes are back in Sydney. The letters are sent on to them in the diplomatic bag and arrive several months later. Olga telephones me in Phnom Penh to tell me the news and faxes me the most relevant pages. But in the midst of security threats and pre-election mayhem in Cambodia, my mind is on other matters. Only months later when I am back in Sydney and collect the originals do I have time to focus on the letters.

The first is from the Ministry of Security in Nizhny Novgorod, the city known in Soviet times as Gorky. In two closely typed pages of inimitably turgid Soviet-style prose, it summarises the fate of the four Onikuls who lived in Gorky—Manya, her parents, and her brother Yasha. Regarding Manya, it says:

Onikul, Maria Grigorievna, born 23 March 1911 in Hailar, worked as a dentist at the Avtozavod [Auto Works] Hospital, residing at apartment 19, no 13 Oktyabrskaya Street, Gorky. She was arrested on 2 October 1937 by the Gorky regional NKVD and was accused of, allegedly, conducting espionage activities in the interest of Japan.

By a ruling of the USSR NKVD and the USSR Procurator of 7 January 1938, Onikul, M.G. was sentenced under Article 58.6 of the Criminal Code ... to capital punishment. The sentence was carried out on 14 January 1938 in Gorky Prison.

By the determination of the Collegium of the USSR Supreme Court of 6 October 1956, the ruling of the USSR NKVD and the USSR Procurator of 7 January 1938 was revoked and the case against her was dropped in the absence of criminal evidence.

A similar rundown about her father follows. Then:

Onikul, M.G. and Onikul, G.M. are buried at the Bugrovsky Cemetery in Nizhny Novgorod. Unfortunately, it is impossible to identify their graves as in those days, these were not registered. However, the Regional Administration of Nizhny Novgorod has decided to erect a memorial at the Bugrovsky Cemetery to the victims of illegal repression.

According to the summary, Yasha was arrested along with Manya and on the same grounds. He was sentenced under the same Article 58.6 to ten years hard labour in the NKVD's Ivdel Lag camp in the foothills of the Ural Mountains near Sverdlovsk. Chesna was arrested later, on 14 June 1938, again for allegedly spying for Japan, sentenced to five years' exile and sent to Alma Ata in Kazakhstan in December 1938. Uncle Lyova was right—they had all been arrested as Japanese spies under the notorious article whose number he could not remember—58.6.

Enclosed with the ministry's letter are two yellow *Cartes Postales*, bearing the stamps of the Japanese puppet state of Manchukuo—'the only personal materials found in the Onikul files'. Sent by my grandmother Gita from Harbin to her mother Chesna in Gorky in December 1937 and May 1938, they were never delivered. Both are full of domestic news and concern about the family in Gorky.

A second lot of documents relates to Abram's case. First comes a copy of a letter from the Military Tribunal of the Far East Military Region in Khabarovsk, forwarding my request about Abram to the Military Collegium of the Supreme Court of the Russian Federation. It still bears the Soviet crest—hammer and sickle surrounded by sheaves of wheat. This is proof that action has been taken. Interestingly, it describes Abram as 'rehabilitated'.

A month or so later comes the *spravka* from the supreme court, again with Soviet crest. Sent to the Australian embassy from the Russian foreign ministry under cover of a diplomatic note verbale, it is brief, but loaded with information:

The case of Onikul, Abram Grigorievich, born in 1907, until his arrest—on 17 October 1937—an interpreter of Chinese at the Operational Point of the 7th department of the UGB [Directorate of State Security] of the Far East Regional Directorate of the NKVD, groundlessly convicted under Articles 58.1(a) and 58.11 of the Criminal Code ... to 10 years imprisonment, was reviewed by the Military Collegium of the USSR Supreme Court on 6 February 1957.

The sentence of the Military Tribunal of the ... NKVD of the USSR of the Khabarovsk Region of 4 October 1939 and the ruling of the Military Collegium of the Supreme Court of the USSR of 17 November 1939 regarding Onikul, Abram Grigorievich were revoked and the case dropped in the absence of criminal evidence.

Onikul, A.G. is posthumously rehabilitated.

So Abram was not shot after all! And he was posthumously rehabilitated. But there is no indication of where he was sent to serve his sentence or how and when he died. Article 58.1(a) is 'treason to the motherland' and 58.11 relates to 'organised anti-Soviet activity' but the *spravka* gives no detail about Abram's alleged crime. The fact that he worked for the NKVD is there in black and white—but only as an interpreter. Coming from a family of linguists, I find this career choice a little more comprehensible.

Thanks to the new KGB, I have filled in some blank spots in the Onikul family's history. I now have an official snapshot of their tragic fate: five lives summed up in four and a half pages, complete with absolution.

But I still don't know what *really* happened. Can I ever find out?

I think back to my meeting with Vladimir at the Lubyanka mansion. I am sure he mentioned files. And I remember authorising my friend Bradley to familiarise himself with 'criminal' matters. The materials I have received are obviously based on something. So there must be more. But what? And where? And how do I get it?

I think of contacting the agencies which sent me information—the Ministry of Security in Nizhny Novgorod for the Gorky Onikuls and perhaps the Military Tribunal of the Far East Military Region in Khabarovsk for Abram. But then I think: what would be the use? There is nothing more they can send me. If there are files, I need to be in Russia to read them and they are probably at opposite ends of the country. And what is likely to be in them? More *spravkas*, full of acronyms and legal references? The Soviets were masters of obfuscation. It's a long way to go to discover that there is nothing more meaningful than I already have.

But despite my misgivings, I remain tantalised by the thought that unresolved family secrets may be buried in dusty files in the depths of a Russian archive.

CHAPTER 2

GORKY TEARS

IS IT CHANCE or coincidence that brings me face to face with the dazzling young governor of Nizhny Novgorod in Sydney in 1994? In retrospect, it proves to be the first of many remarkable meetings and strange coincidences that drive my journey of discovery about my family. At the time, however, it is strictly business.

I have just returned to Sydney after five years in Asia and am now working on telecommunications business opportunities in parts of the former Soviet Union. One afternoon, a colleague invites me to a meeting of the Russia-Australia Business Council. The speaker is Boris Nemtsov, the thirty-five-year-old governor of Nizhny Novgorod.

Nemtsov is articulate, intelligent and attractive. In fluent English, he paints a glowing picture of Nizhny and the reforms his administration is implementing to create a positive investment climate to attract foreign business. A physicist by training, he started his political career as an anti-nuclear activist in the wake of the Chernobyl disaster. What a refreshing change from the tired old Soviet apparatchiks who used to come to Australia on the business attraction circuit! I am dying to speak to him but can't find an excuse to make an approach. Telstra's interests in the former Soviet Union do not extend as far as central Russia.

Suddenly I remember my Gorky relatives. I wait for the swarm of people around Nemtsov to disperse before approaching to congratulate him on his fine presentation.

'Some of my relatives once lived and died tragically in your city,' I say, and tell him briefly about the advice on the fate of the Onikuls which I received from the Nizhny Novgorod Ministry of Security. 'How can I find out more information?'

'Many people died in my town during the purges,' Nemtsov answers. 'If you come and visit, we will see what we can find for you in the archives.' He gives me the name of his adviser and suggests that I contact him before I come.

Two years later, in November 1996, I do just that.

By this time, I am again working in Asia, as regional head of Telstra's operations in Vietnam, Cambodia and Laos. While planning a holiday in Moscow and St Petersburg, it dawns on me that this is my chance to visit Nizhny Novgorod and follow up Nemtsov's suggestion. Nizhny is just an overnight train ride from Moscow. Luckily for me, Nemtsov is still governor. Just three months later,

President Yeltsin will appoint him deputy prime minister of Russia.

In arranging my trip, I discover Harbin links between Sydney and Nizhny. A family friend arranges for me to stay with her old Harbin school friend who emigrated to the Soviet Union in the 1950s and is now living in Nizhny.

Before leaving for Moscow, I contact Nemtsov's adviser and fax him a copy of the letter I received from the Nizhny Ministry of Security in 1992, setting out the information on the Onikuls. When I call him from Moscow, he confirms that their files are now in the government archive in Nizhny Novgorod and gives me names and numbers of people to contact. 'Just call the deputy director when you get to Nizhny and arrange a time.' I am amazed at how easy and accessible it all seems.

In Moscow, I again have dinner with Uncle Lyova and his family and tell them where I'm going. Though four years have passed since our last meeting, the atmosphere is warm and familiar. I show them the summary I received and Lyova's daughter Anya reads it aloud to her father, whose eyesight is failing. For the most part, it confirms information Lyova already knows but adds detail and jogs memories. This time, Uncle Lyova's younger brother, Yakov, has also joined us for dinner. A senior bureaucrat in Soviet times, he is dressed in a suit and proudly wears all his wartime medals. He also knew Yasha and Chesna and met Girsh and Manya in the 1930s.

'What was Manya like?' I ask the brothers.

'She was a dentist,' answers Lyova.

'Yes, I know that,' I persist. 'But what was she like as a person?' I am trying to get a sense of Manya's personality, her likes and dislikes; but these two straight-talking, no-nonsense old men clearly don't share my hunger for descriptive detail.

'She was normal,' Lyova answers. Yakov agrees. The rest of us laugh. 'Yes, but what did she look like? Was she fat or thin? What did she do in her spare time? Was she artistic?' I decide there is no point in asking whether she had a lover.

Eventually Anya succeeds in drawing the old men out. The consensus is that Manya was attractive, 'well built', engaging and clever. She worked hard and went on vacation. I accept that this is the most information I am going to get right now.

The brothers also tell me that my great-grandfather Girsh was a pious Jew who studied the Talmud. Though Chesna's parents were religious, she was not and neither were her children. Still, the brothers tell me, Chesna was not happy when Yasha married Galya, a non-Jew, and that there was always tension between the two women, especially when they all lived together in Riga.

Before I leave, Lyova asks me to write down the dates when his uncle Girsh and cousin Manya died so he can say *kaddish*, the traditional Jewish prayer for the dead, on the anniversaries of their deaths as he does for Chesna and Yasha. Though the rest of his family is secular, Uncle Lyova has faithfully attended the great Moscow Choral Synagogue since he arrived in Moscow in 1929, even through the turbulent Soviet years when religious observance was frowned upon. Now his grandson Sasha, a talented young conductor and musician, is reviving the art of Jewish cantorial singing which gave the synagogue its name. As a parting gift, Sasha gives me a tape of his choir's highly acclaimed music. Three years later, I play one of their songs at a memorial service for my grandmother, Gita, at my house in Sydney.

Before going to Nizhny, I also pay a fleeting visit to Galya in Riga. I want to carefully examine Yasha's personal papers and photographs and ask Galya to take me through Yasha's work history. Last time I was there my attention had been focused on Manya and Chesna's photographs, and I had neglected Yasha's story.

Our first stop, however, is the cemetery where we pay respects to Yasha and my great-grandmother Chesna. On the way home, I ask Galya about Yasha's death. She tells me he died in 1985 from a misdiagnosis. First in Riga, then Moscow, the doctors searched for a blood disease. In fact, his spine was disintegrating from osteomyelitis, but they only discovered this in the autopsy. If they had given him the right treatment straight away, Yasha may have still been alive.

In the short time I have to spend with Galya, I fill her in on what has transpired since she gave me the Onikuls' rehabilitation *spravkas* four years earlier and show her the summary I received from the Nizhny Ministry of

Security. I tell her that I am on my way to Nizhny Novgorod where some NKVD files on the Onikuls have been located in the archives. Galya is agitated by what she hears and shakes her head in disbelief at my persistence.

'What did Yasha tell you about his time in prison camp?' I ask.

I am not prepared for her shocked response.

'He told me nothing! I know the rest of his family had been arrested and later rehabilitated. But he never even mentioned that he was arrested, let alone went to camp.'

I am stunned. How could she not know this crucial fact of her husband's life? Is she ashamed or simply avoiding any more of my questions? I leave Riga not knowing whether or not to believe her professed ignorance.

———◆———

Lying in the dark on the night train from Moscow to Nizhny Novgorod, I wonder what on earth I will find in the archives at the other end of my journey. Although it is only November, the train is so overheated that I am suffocating but the window in my cabin won't open. Nizhny/Gorky, Nizhny/Gorky—I try to fall asleep by turning the new and old names of the town over in my head, but to no avail. I am distracted, nervous, full of anticipation about my visit to the archives.

I finally surrender to my insomnia and switch on the

dim bedside light to re-read the two-page summary of the Onikuls' fate in Gorky. Manya, Yasha, Girsh and Chesna—all four charged with 'conducting espionage activities in the interest of Japan'. Why? I know they were later cleared of all charges. Still, I am perplexed by what they could have done to be suspected of such a crime in the first place.

I recall a conversation I had with my mother before leaving for the station that evening. Full of excitement about the Onikul files that had been found in the archives in Nizhny, I called her in Sydney to say that I was on my way at last. Alone and restless on the train— and full of my own eleventh-hour doubts—her words now ring in my ears: 'You already know what happened to the family. What more do you want to find? Why don't you leave well enough alone?'

Despite the passage of history, my mother is still caught in Cold War stereotypes, but her caution has never deterred me. On the contrary. Now I wonder what indeed I *will* find in Nizhny. Probably, some dusty files full of impenetrable Soviet-speak. I remember forcing myself to read *Pravda* and *Izvestia* in the past. The prospect of more of that, and the rhythmic clackety-clack of the train wheels, eventually lull me to sleep.

Next morning, I am met at the railway station by Alyosha Kalinin, the son of Olga Alekseyevna, the woman with whom I am staying. Alyosha is a striking young man in his thirties and works as a research physicist at the University of Nizhny Novgorod. He is with his friend

Vadim, also an academic, who owns a car and has agreed to take me on a tour of the city.

Driving through the early morning streets of Nizhny to Olga Alekseyevna's apartment, I reflect on the gloomy image this city projected during the Soviet years. Gorky: the bitter city; a closed, grey, military industrial bastion; Andrei Sakharov on hunger strike during his six-year exile; the place where Manya and her father were killed.

Yet Nizhny today is not like that at all. It is the attractive, lively city which Governor Nemtsov described. Many of the nineteenth-century European buildings lining its broad avenues have been elegantly restored, recalling the days of former grandeur when Nizhny hosted Russia's international trade fair for more than a hundred years. Now Russia's third largest city, it has again embraced capitalism with a gusto which leaves some of its citizens reeling.

I explain to my hosts that my mission in Nizhny is to visit the archives and see the secret police files of my relatives, as well as seeing something of the city in which they once lived.

'How on earth did you arrange your archive visit from Australia?' Alyosha asks.

He shakes his head in disbelief when I tell him. By coincidence, it turns out that Boris Nemtsov was Alyosha's university classmate. Circumspect and academic, Alyosha stuck with physics while Boris moved to politics.

Although I am itching to get to the archives, I soon discover that Alyosha and Vadim have already arranged the day off to take me sightseeing. I can hardly ask them to change their plans.

After I have dropped off my luggage and greeted Olga Alekseyevna, I telephone the archive and defer my meeting to the following day. Then I set off with Alyosha and Vadim to see the sights of Nizhny. Closed to foreigners until 1990, my two guides are delighted to show off their beautiful city to a visitor from the Antipodes.

'Let's start our tour, as did Nizhny's history, at the ancient Kremlin,' says Vadim, as he drives towards the river. 'Of course, now only the walls and towers are still standing, but they date back to the sixteenth century . . .'

The itinerary I have in mind is somewhat different. The key places I want to visit are the landmarks of the Onikuls' lives in 1930s Gorky. But we are on our way and it is impolite to decline.

Set on a hill overlooking the confluence of the Volga and Oka Rivers, the view from the Kremlin is indeed breathtaking. As we wander around its towers and climb down the hill towards the river, I think of Manya. I feel sure she would have come here. I imagine her spreading out a picnic with a lover on a sunny afternoon or strolling with him arm in arm along the embankment.

Did Manya have a lover in Gorky? One of my relatives vaguely recalls Chesna telling of a complicated romance with a doctor estranged from his wife. No-one knows for sure, but I feel like I know.

In Manya's album there is one photograph where she is pictured with a man whom I am convinced was her lover. Both are dressed in white medical clothes—Manya, a high-collared tunic, her hair pulled back under a white kerchief; the man in a white coat, unbuttoned over a dark suit and tie. It is an ordinary photo, taken near the desk in her surgery. Yet something jumps out through the sepia. Is it the knowing look in Manya's sultry eyes or the way the two lean towards each other? Maybe it is the way she has crossed her arms in front of her, her left hand showing a ring on the fourth finger? Whatever it is, I know.

Over a quick snack in a cafe bar which a young entrepreneur has established in one of the Kremlin towers, I show my friends Manya's photo and the summary on the Onikuls I received from the Nizhny Ministry of Security back in 1992. Here are the landmarks of their lives in Gorky which I want to visit: the houses where they lived, the famous Gorky Avtozavod (Gorky Automobile Works) where Manya and Yasha worked, Gorky Prison where Manya and her father were executed, and the Bugrovsky Cemetery where they are buried.

Alyosha and Vadim shrug—it is certainly not the traditional tourist itinerary. But in terms of distances and time, it is manageable. We head for the Bugrovsky Cemetery first, just in case it closes early.

'The ministry's letter says I won't be able to find their graves,' I say, scanning it quickly as we approach the black cemetery gates with a single bronze bell hanging above their centre. 'It says graves weren't registered in those days.'

'That's a polite way of saying there weren't any graves,' replies Vadim. 'People were all just shot and thrown into a pit.'

'The letter also says the local administration was planning to erect a memorial to the victims of repression,' I continue. 'That was written in 1992—has it happened yet?'

'Yes, the monument was built a couple of years ago. You might want to buy a wreath or some flowers.'

Outside the gates, I buy a fir wreath. As we enter the cemetery, my heart leaps at the sight of gravestones scattered among the birch trees. The trees give Russian cemeteries a warmth and melancholy that Australian cemeteries lack. We find the memorial in a central square, not far from the entrance. Mounted on a platform, a large sandstone slab bears the simple message: *In eternal memory of the victims of the totalitarian regime*. A couple of wreaths hang on each side of the stone, others lie at its foot. People have twisted plastic flowers through the low iron fence around it. I stand silent for a while, then place my wreath before the monument.

Despite the poignancy of the occasion, I feel strangely disconnected. I have absolutely no sense that Manya and Girsh's tortured spirits are here. I remember the monument outside the Lubyanka and the battle waged by the Memorial movement to put it there. This stone is part of the same process of restoring a nation's memory after years of fear and silence.

I begin to feel a stronger connection with my dead relatives when we get back to town and find number 13 Oktyabrskaya Street—a traditional two-storey house with carved wooden casings around the windows. According to the summary, apartment 19, house 13 is the address at which Manya, Yasha and their father were arrested in October 1937. So this must be where the family lived: right here in this house, with its rustic charm. I am overwhelmed by emotion. It is satisfying to find something still standing that was once part of the Onikuls' lives. What's more, the traditional style of the house resonates with my own love of old houses. I photograph it from every angle. I visualise Chesna opening a window and Girsh strolling outside smoking his pipe, as Manya races out the door, late for some appointment.

Where would apartment 19 have been, I wonder? Inside the door are post boxes marked 1 to 8. It strikes me that the house is not really big enough to house nineteen apartments. Alyosha suggests there may have been a renovation after the war and an adjacent building was knocked down. I look outside again and notice jagged bricks on the side of number 13 that flanks an empty block. Yes! It looks like there was another house the same size there, which was knocked down—probably not so long ago.

I ask a woman in a small shoe repair kiosk at the edge of the block. She shakes her head dismissively at my questions. 'How would I know what was here? What was, is no longer. Now leave me alone.' But an invalid wandering near the yard confirms that there was a house on the block until a few years ago. He does not remember what it looked like. 'Was it also part of number 13?' I ask. 'Who knows? Times change. Numbers change.'

Our next stop is Gorky Prison, which stands right in

the centre of town. The outside facings of the two five-storey red brick buildings have recently been painted a mustard yellow. Through the gap between them looms another large red brick building. Flanking it I can just see the ugly, grey prison blocks. This is the prison where Manya and her father were shot. Yasha and Chesna were probably held there also. It makes me shudder. I photograph the building from the street. Then Alyosha and I walk into the small reception office at the gate to catch a better glimpse of the yard.

'My friend here is a visitor from Australia,' Alyosha explains to the guard at reception. 'Her relatives were held here during the purges and she wants to take a look.' The guard raises her eyebrows. 'Fine, take a look, but don't go beyond this room,' she says and continues with her paperwork.

Chancing fate, I decide to take a quick photo of the yard and move towards the window in the adjoining room. But the guard catches me. 'Look, sir,' she addresses Alyosha, ignoring me, 'I don't care whether your visitor is from Australia or the moon. Taking photographs in this prison is forbidden. Please take her and leave now.' And that is that.

We drive past Gorky Square with its elongated statue of Maxim Gorky. Alyosha points to a massive, grey four-storey building to one side.

'That's the Vorobyovka, headquarters of the secret police.' Alyosha explains that the building is so called because it stands on the corner of the street named after Vorobyov, the first local secret police chief of the Cheka.

'Cheka, NKVD, KGB, now it's the FSB—but it's never been a secret.'

Looking at the concrete monolith, I wonder if any of the Onikuls had ever been inside.

Back in old Nizhny, my mood lightens and I remark on the fine restoration of the grand old buildings.

'It is all part of your friend Boris Nemtsov's effort to attract foreign investment,' Alyosha says with a laugh. 'If only it looked like this in the back streets.'

While Alyosha respects his former classmate's bold reforms, like many Russians he worries about the effect of rapid privatisation on the lives of ordinary people. The 'new Russians' are thriving at their expense, while funding for social programs, education and research has dried up. It is impossible to live on an academic's salary. He and his friend Vadim both work second jobs to support their families.

Our next destination is the Gorky Automobile Works. Fifteen kilometres out of town we come to a satellite city, with a massive industrial plant and a sprawl of monotonous concrete buildings. On one side of the road stands a building which looks like company headquarters. Its emblem is a reindeer dancing above the letters 'GAZ' against a red background. On the other side, a road sign proclaims 'Avtozavod'. This is the Gorky Avtozavod where Yasha and Manya once worked.

As we turn off the main road in that direction, Alyosha explains that, over the years, the GAZ has grown into a 'Russian Detroit', with over 250,000 employees. Avto-zavod is now the name of the district, complete with its own metro stop. I realise immediately that finding the buildings where the Onikuls worked will be impossible. But Vadim stops the car and asks if I want to walk around.

'We could ask someone where the hospital is,' I say tentatively, remembering that Manya had worked as a dentist at the Avtozavod Hospital.

We ask a few people and eventually find our way into the vast hospital area. After wandering around various buildings that all look too modern to have been around in the 1930s, telling people my story, a doctor directs us to an old ochre-coloured building across a courtyard. The sign on its wall reads 'City Therapeutic Hospital No. 37, Avtozavod district'. I guess it is a polyclinic of sorts.

Though dusk is fast approaching and the clinic is closed for the day, a nurse and a couple of cleaners let us wander around the ammonia-scrubbed corridors for a while. Unlike many of the other buildings, this one has a 1930s feel about it. I envisage Manya in her white coat treating patients in a surgery behind one of the closed doors or writing reports by the light of the banker's lamp I noticed in a couple of her photos.

Just as we are about to go back to the car, a well-dressed, middle-aged woman with an authoritative air walks out the door. She turns and asks if we are looking for anything in particular.

'Yes,' I say, 'the Avtozavod dental surgery from 1936.'

She smiles and says, 'It was in this building.' At last! A confirmation that this is where Manya once worked. I feel vindicated that I have not taken Alyosha on a wild goose chase.

Before leaving the Avtozavod district, Vadim drives to Kirov Street to look for the second address in the Ministry of Security's letter—the house where my great-grandmother Chesna was arrested, eight months after the others: 'house number 23, apartment 15'.

Kirov Street is lined with grandiose apartment blocks built in that unmistakeable Stalinist style—combining neo-classic features with communist utilitarianism. But number 23 is nowhere to be found. I remember the words of the old man in Oktyabrskaya Street—times change, numbers change. Perhaps the houses here have been renumbered since the 1930s. It strikes me as odd that Chesna came to live in this area—so far from the old house in Oktyabrskaya Street after the others were arrested. This prompts me to wonder how Yasha and Manya commuted between the GAZ and their home at the opposite end of town.

At the end of our day travelling around Gorky, I return to Olga Alekseyevna's house tired but pleased that the city has revealed some of the places where my family lived and worked in their happier days. It is comforting to keep this image in mind while confronting the institutions of their misfortune.

Early the next morning, I make my way to the state archive on Studencheskaya Street. I have absolutely no idea what I will be shown or the bureaucratic processes

I will be put through. But I am certain there *will* be processes. I have brought my passport as identification, copies of the Onikul *spravkas*, the letter from the Nizhny Ministry of Security and my fax to Governor Nemtsov's office. Alyosha insists on meeting me at the archive on his way to work, just in case there are any hitches. Ultimately, it proves to be just as well.

The deputy director of the archive is a pleasant and businesslike woman. She has a job to do and has no time for small talk. This suits me fine because like her, I am here to do business.

'I know you're keen to look at the material and you don't have much time, but first of all you'll need to complete some formalities. If there's any way I can assist you further, please don't hesitate to ask.' She leaves me with the clerk to do the paperwork.

'Good morning,' I say politely. The clerk does not reciprocate. In Russia, there are still officials who maintain the officiousness of the Soviet order. This clerk is one of them.

'Your identification and *spravkas*, please,' she bristles.

I produce my passport and copies of the letter from the Nizhny Ministry of Security which I had received in 1992.

'That's all very well. But what proof do you have that you are related to these Onikuls? You don't have the same name.' The clerk's tone is victorious. 'Do you have a *spravka*?'

Does this woman seriously believe I can produce one of those little certificates with lots of stamps which will certify that 'Moustafine' is related to 'the deceased Onikuls'?

'How can I have? Most of them were dead long before I was born,' I reply, my eyes brimming with tears. 'The KGB did not seem to have any problem believing me,' I say to Alyosha in a voice loud enough for her to hear. Although he has left me to do most of the talking, I am grateful for his presence.

The emotion of being so close to the files I have waited so long to see and now to be confronted by this old-style Soviet bully gets the better of me. I begin to sob. I am embarrassed by my loss of control, but I decide to use it to my advantage. 'Well, I guess I'll just have to thank Nemtsov's office for trying, but say I didn't have the right *spravka* to satisfy the archive,' I sniff to Alyosha.

'Just a minute,' the clerk says, leaving the room. She does not return. Instead, the deputy director enters the room with a man who turns out to be the chairman of the archive. His name is familiar as he is one of the contacts I got from Nemtsov's office. 'Please calm down, Madam, there is no need to cry,' he says. 'Your files are being brought right now. If you have any questions or need any other help, please don't hesitate to ask.'

While Alyosha goes off to work, I am led to the reading room with desks set up in rows, as in a school room. A couple of people sit studying files. Apart from the hollow rustle of old paper and the odd whisper, there is silence. I sit down at a desk and wait for what feels like hours. In fact, the archivist returns in a few minutes.

Five faded, reddish brown files lie before me, each tied

tightly with discoloured cotton tape. I stare at them. Now what? I never quite believed this moment would arrive.

Opening the first file—Manya's—a chill runs down my spine. The first page is a note, neatly handwritten by the Head of the Department of State Security of the Gorky regional NKVD. Dated 7 October 1937, it says Manya is charged under Article 58.6 with 'espionage activities in the interests of one of the foreign intelligence agencies'. She is being held in custody in Gorky Prison. Next comes an order for her search and arrest, dated 2 October, and a form giving personal particulars. Then pages and pages of handwritten interrogation records— question/answer, question/answer. Names I have never heard of jump out at me, as well as names I recognise.

I feel sick. Apart from the people who cleared these files for release, no-one has looked at them for forty years. Laid out here are people's lives—their secrets. I feel like a voyeur. How different is this from reading other people's mail? I am intruding on the lives of people I have never met. What right do I have to do this?

But the injustice of what I am uncovering is so enormous. Do I have the right to stop? I look through Manya's file to get a sense of what is there.

The first record of interrogation starts with a *pro forma* biographical questionnaire. On the second page, Manya answers *nyet* ('no') seven times. Most of the questions relate to activities during the Russian Revolution and the Civil War. Born in 1911, she was too young for that. The next page gets straight to the point:

Question: When were you recruited as an agent of the Japanese secret service?

Answer: I was never recruited into the Japanese secret service.

Question: You are lying. Our investigations have clearly established that, while living in Hailar, you were recruited into the Japanese secret service and were transferred into the territory of the USSR with the objective of espionage. Do you acknowledge that?

Answer: No, I do not.

Question: Your denial is useless. I insist categorically that you give honest evidence on this question.

Answer: I repeat. I have never been an agent of the Japanese secret service.

The evidence was recorded accurately from my words and read by me.

Below is Manya's signature and the signature of her interrogator. I am stunned. Not just by the significance of what I am reading, but by the detail in which it is recorded. From the correspondence I had received from the Ministry of Security, I already knew that Manya had been arrested as a Japanese spy. But here is the allegation in black and white.

Another record is full of questions about Manya's life in Hailar. Suddenly in the middle of a barely legible page, I see the word 'Shanghai'. Manya tells the interrogator she went there in 1933 and worked for a while as a dentist at the 'Women's Studio' before going to

Vladivostok. Shanghai in the 1930s, with its tantalising mix of East and West, is a city which has long captured my imagination. No-one had ever told me that Manya once lived there. Perhaps they didn't know.

A couple of pages later, my grandfather's name—Zaretsky—jumps out at me. This spooks me as it indicates that the NKVD knew about him too. Manya is asked if she knew him.

Answer: *Yes I know Matvei Abramovich Zaretsky well. He is my brother-in-law. He is a business-man—a cattle trader. When I left for the USSR, he was living in Harbin and still is. He has Soviet citizenship.*

That much I know too. Yet I am totally unprepared for the next question. It staggers me.

Question: *What do you know about his membership of the Fascist Party?*

My grandfather a fascist? That is inconceivable. He was a Jew and held Soviet citizenship while living in Harbin. From what I have heard about the Harbin brand of Russian fascists in the 1930s, they were both anti-Semitic and anti-Soviet. What other fabrications are there in these files? Manya answers that she knows nothing about Zaretsky being a fascist.

Leafing further into Manya's file, the page falls open at a sparsely typed page headed 'Extract from Decree No. 273 of 7 January 1938'. This is her sentence:

HEARD:
Materials on the accused, presented by the NKVD of the Gorky region pursuant to NKVD order No 00593 of 20 September 1937,

DECREED:
ONIKUL, Maria Grigorievna   TO BE SHOT
born 1911, Hailar, CER

signed:
People's Commissar for Internal Affairs USSR
Commissar General of Security   —   YEZHOV

Procurator USSR   —   VYSHINSKY

On the right-hand side is a handwritten note: *Shot 14.01.38, Gorky* and an illegible signature.

I freeze. The statement is so stark and impersonal. It took just three words and one week to end Manya's short life.

Yezhov and Vyshinsky are names I have only ever read in books. Yezhov's name in Russian is synonymous with the Great Terror. Vyshinsky was the sinister prosecutor at the 1930s Moscow show trials. What did these people have to do with our Manya, a twenty-six-year-old dentist from Hailar? Did they have any idea what they were signing?

Tears come to my eyes. I want to scream, to break the dreadful, echoing silence. But one look around the room brings me to my senses. People are sitting quietly, leafing through files, page by page, each undoubtedly wrapped in their own private tragedy. I have been oblivious to new readers entering the hall since I arrived. At the front of the room, the bespectacled duty archivist sits head down, doing her work—like a school mistress presiding over an exam. This is no place for drama. I bow my head and return to the files to take notes.

I am overwhelmed by the pages and pages of interrogations: question/answer, question/answer. I never expected these files to be so detailed or so direct. Then again, I hadn't really imagined what they would be like. I just assumed they would be full of impenetrable Soviet-speak.

Suddenly the enormity of my task dawns on me. I am in Nizhny for only two more days. Before me are five files, most of whose contents are handwritten in Russian, in script which is often hard to decipher and in Soviet bureaucratic language which is not immediately clear to me. How on earth am I going to get through it all?

A novice in the Russian archives, I have not thought through this exercise strategically. Is photocopying allowed? And if so, in what quantity?

I take stock of the files before me. Each has a name and a number. There is one each for Manya, Girsh, Chesna and Yasha. But whose is the fifth? The name written across it is 'Onikul, Isaac Naumovich'. As the family patronymics spin round my head, I realise that this was Manya and Yasha's cousin. I remember my aunt Ronia in Sydney talking about her brother Sanya who had gone to the Soviet Union from Hailar in the 1930s and disappeared. Sanya is short for Isaac, so this must be him! She never told me he had gone to Gorky, so it never occurred to me to ask for his file. And there was no mention of him in the summary sent by the Nizhny Ministry of Security. What an unexpected bonus!

Just at that moment, the duty archivist comes over to me. 'Is everything all right?'

Should I thank her for giving me the extra file? I think better of it. She might take it away. 'So much to read and so little time,' I sigh. 'Is it possible to photocopy these files?'

The archivist explains the rules. Copying a file in its entirety is not permitted. Nor is copying testimony of people other than family members. She suggests that if I want to have material copied, I give her as many files as I can that afternoon and the rest the following day. The archive has only one copying machine, she explains, and there is a lot of paperwork to complete to enable me to export the documents from Russia without any difficulties with authorities.

I mark up the files as fast as I can. I am overcome by a profound sadness at the absurdity of the cases I see being constructed through the interrogations. All those wasted lives. But the task at hand keeps me focused. I notice that while the papers in the files have been reordered and renumbered, few pages are actually missing. And all the names are there—relatives, interrogators, denouncers. What a contrast to the blacked-out lines in files I have examined in the Australian archives.

Late that afternoon, when I am the only visitor left in the reading room, the chairman of the archive comes to check on my progress. He brings me a couple of volumes the Nizhny administration has published of previously secret documents which reveal what happened in Gorky during the purges. These might help me put my family's story in context, he says. He also mentions that the first 'book of memory' listing the names of those who perished in the purges is now in production and he asks me whether I have photographs of Manya or her father which might be included. I realise this is another local manifestation of Memorial's efforts to expose the secrets of the Soviet Union's sinister past and name its victims. I find a couple of photos of Manya in my bag and happily pass them over to be copied.

Emotionally drained and physically exhausted, I return to Olga Alekseyevna's cosy flat and sleep. The next day, I arrive at the archive just minutes after it opens. I work solidly all day, checking copies against originals, filling in words that did not come out clearly, writing notes from the pages that could not be copied. At closing time that afternoon, I walk out of the archive armed with my booty—132 photocopied pages and a writing pad full of notes. When it came to the crunch, I had managed to decipher the most difficult script. Ten years of Saturdays spent at Russian school in Sydney had not been in vain.

<hr />

Although I am due to leave Nizhny for Moscow that evening, there is still time for a final wander around town with Alyosha. Walking down the main street, Bolshaya Pokrovskaya, we see two square neon signs, one under the other. The first says 'Synagogue—No. 5a Gruzinskaya Street', in Russian and Hebrew. The second says 'Poker Machines—No. 7a Gruzinskaya Street'. Both have arrows pointing left through an archway.

'Please let's go take a look at the synagogue,' I say to Alyosha. 'My great-grandfather probably prayed there.'

Through the archway and down the road stands an ornate nineteenth-century building painted yellow and white in period style. A large man with a long black beard—the spitting image of Tevye from the musical *Fiddler on the Roof*—is talking energetically on a mobile phone in the yard. He turns out to be Rabbi Lypa Groozman. Directing us upstairs to see the room where the synagogue has recently been reopened, the rabbi tells us its history. Built in 1883 by local Jews and merchants visiting the Nizhny Novgorod Trade Fair, it was shut down in 1938 and the premises turned into metal and joinery workshops. Only in 1991 did a small group of Jews led by the rabbi succeed in having the synagogue returned to the community and reopened.

'Would this have been the synagogue where my great-grandfather Girsh prayed when he lived in Gorky in 1936 and 1937?' The rabbi confirms that there was no other.

Back in the centre of town, the streets are full of people making last minute purchases on their way home or simply window shopping as they stroll past the elegant facades, freshly painted in pastel colours. In the late afternoon sun, Nizhny has an air of lightness and optimism about it. I wonder if it had a similar feel in the mid-1930s, during that brief interlude when its people still dreamed of the future they were building; before fear and terror destroyed both it and them. Thinking of all those bronzed young Soviets in old propaganda movies, I hear the refrain of the rousing patriotic song:

Native land of fields and lakes and forests,
Nurtures beasts and fish and grain and trees
I can't think of any other country
Where a man can walk as tall and free . . .

Suddenly the music in my daydream is interrupted.

'A newspaper for Russian patriots, please subscribe,' an elderly woman thrusts a leaflet into my hand.

'Throw it away,' says Alyosha, 'she's crazy.'

It is an advertising flyer for the newspaper *Black Hundreds* published by the All-Russia Orthodox Monarchist Movement. Bearing the old Tsarist crest and the banner, 'For Faith, Tsar and Fatherland', it professes opposition to the 'present Judaeo-democratic semi-fascist regime' and appeals to those who have 'not yet chosen Pepsi, sneakers and "bucks" to join the battle for a united and indivisible Orthodox Russia'. Shades of the pogroms? These slogans are a modern variation of those proclaimed by the movement's turn-of-the-century antecedents at the time Girsh and Chesna left Russia for Manchuria. Some things never change.

'Well, at least there is freedom of expression in the new Russia and even the forces of darkness have learned about marketing,' I say, putting the leaflet in my bag as a souvenir. A block later, freedom manifests itself in a different form. This time it is a skimpily clad young woman who thrusts a leaflet into my hand. This flyer is for the Queen of Hearts Club, which invites the ladies of Nizhny Novgorod to a 'real male striptease' performed by 'a dark-skinned man from the shores of the Nile'.

From Black Hundreds to black sex—Nizhny in 1996 has it all! For all the optimism of the mid-1930s, I feel sure there had not been such freedom of choice.

———◦•◦———

After a quick farewell dinner with Alyosha and his mother, I show them the Onikul documents I found in the archives. I only have a couple of hours before my train back to Moscow.

'The house we went to in Oktyabrskaya Street was not the house your family lived in,' Alyosha says quietly after leafing through the papers. 'In fact, we were in the wrong street.'

'What? I know it was probably not the house they lived in—but it was definitely Oktyabrskaya Street.'

Alyosha shows me the address entered in Manya's very first interrogation:

Avtozavod, Sotsgorod, Oktyabrskaya Street, house no. 13, apartment 19.

In Russian, *Sotsgorod* is an abbreviation for 'socialist city'. That much I can work out.

'Sotsgorod was the residential area built near the Avtozavod for the workers in the 1930s,' Alyosha explains, 'that area we drove around, near Kirov Street. The Oktyabrskaya Street where your relatives lived had to be in that district.'

I am crestfallen. He continues flicking through the papers.

'All right. I've worked it out,' he says, showing me the address entry from Yasha's first interrogation record. 'The name was changed—back then—to Komsomolskaya Street. See, the address here. It reads:

Avtozavod, Sotsgorod, Komsomolskaya Street, house no. 13, apartment 19.

What a forensic eye for detail! Alyosha is not a scientist for nothing. 'If only we had seen these files before we went on our search,' Alyosha says. 'I think there is still a Komsomolskaya Street in the Avtozavod District. There is certainly a metro stop of that name and they usually go together.'

But unfortunately, there is no time to go back. Vadim will be here in half an hour to take us to the railway station. My precious files are spread all over the table and I still have to pack. Olga Alekseyevna suggests that I stay an extra day. She offers to call a friend who works at the railway to change my ticket immediately. But it is impossible. I am already locked in to leave Moscow for

St Petersburg the following evening. Alyosha promises he will go to Komsomolskaya Street in the next couple of weeks and send me a photograph if he finds the right house.

Nizhny is dark and quiet as we drive to the station. It has been raining and the road glistens. An image of the rustic wooden house in old Oktyabrskaya Street flashes through my mind but is pushed out by the stone monoliths I saw in Kirov Street. I figure the apartment block where the Onikuls lived in Sotsgorod probably looked much the same. That was the nature of 'socialist cities'. It made sense that they would have lived close to where they worked. Getting to and from the old town would have taken too long.

Before bunking down for the night on the night train back to Moscow, I leaf through the files I have copied. The amount of information they contain is overwhelming. There is much more than I ever imagined and far too much to absorb all at once. I am mesmerised by the biographical detail. Here at last I have the Onikul family history in their own words—from the *shtetls* in Byelorussia to their life in Manchuria and subsequently Gorky.

But the light from the small bulb above my bunk is too dim to keep reading. Besides, I am exhausted from the intense concentration and emotion of the past couple of days. I stow the bag with the papers in the metal box under my bunk, together with my camera, wallet and other valuables and lie down to sleep. The extraordinary developments of the last three days in Nizhny run through my mind.

I am disappointed not to have found the actual house where the Onikuls lived in Gorky. But I realise that it does not matter. I have seen enough of Nizhny to get a sense of what Gorky might have been like in the 1930s. And the material in the files is rich with information beyond all my expectations. I can now embark on a journey of discovery: who were these people and what drove them?

I drift off to sleep, my mind a jumble. I think about my grandmother Gita. The day after I got to Nizhny my mother telephoned from Sydney to tell me she had been taken to hospital with heart fluctuations. Thankfully, her condition has now stabilised. But she is eighty-five and I know her days are numbered. Still, I cannot imagine a world without her.

My mother was totally unmoved when I told her about the material I found in the archives. It is clear she thinks I should be back in Sydney with my grandmother rather than digging through old papers on the other side of the world.

If my grandmother knew what I was doing, I feel sure she would understand. She has always trusted me implicitly. I have not told her of my exploits with the former KGB or what I have discovered about her family's fate. After all these years, I imagine that it would only revive the pain. But I did show her the old photographs which I brought back from Riga in 1992, and she recognised many of the faces from Byelorussia and China.

By 1996, her memory is not always lucid. Sometimes she remembers old names and faces and relates stories as if they happened yesterday. At other times, she cannot make the connections. I am so grateful that at the beginning of 1991, on one of my visits back from Asia, I recorded a long conversation with her about what she remembered of her early life, bringing together many of the snippets she had told me over the years. Like the photographs from Riga, Gita's precious stories give a context to the information in the files and help me piece together the fragments of the Onikuls' lives.

CHAPTER 3

ON THE STEPPES OF
MANCHURIA

Question: *When and for what reason did you go to*
          Harbin?
Answer: *My husband's brother went to live in Harbin in*
          1908. After corresponding with him, my
          husband decided he would also go to Harbin to
          find work there. My husband, Girsh Morduho-
          vich Onikul, went to Harbin in 1909 . . .
          I followed him some months later. I did not go
          as far as Harbin, but to Hailar, where my
          husband had found work and a place to live.

THIS IS THE FIRST exchange in my great-grandmother
Chesna's record of interrogation by the Gorky NKVD in
June 1938. The biographical questionnaire that precedes
it records that Chesna was born in 1881 in the village of

Milehovo near Borisov in the Minsk province of Byelorussia. She was the daughter of small traders and was self-taught.

I never imagined that the files would provide so much valuable detail on aspects of the Onikuls' lives which were not strictly relevant to the charges they faced. Reading the photocopies of the NKVD files after my return from Russia, this is the material I focus on first. Before immersing myself in the detail of their alleged crimes, I want to get a picture of what the Onikuls were like as people and the lives they led in Hailar and Harbin.

I dig out the tape of the long conversation I recorded with my grandmother Gita back in January 1991, years before I had any inkling about the NKVD files. Now her account helps give life to the information they contain and the files add facts to Gita's story.

My conversation with Gita had taken place in her sunny room at the Montefiore Jewish Home in Sydney. It was not long after her eighty-first birthday and she had recently moved to the home from my parents' house for more companionship and care.

I ask her to start at the beginning and fill me in on her parents, their life in Byelorussia and then discuss her own life in Harbin and Hailar. Though initially nervous at the sight of the tape recorder, once Gita starts talking she is lucid, engaging and holds back little.

Gita pleads ignorance about life in Byelorussia. She was a six-month-old baby when her mother brought her and her two-year-old brother, Abram, to Hailar.

'Where from?' I ask.

'I don't know exactly. Some remote *shtetl* in some *gubernia* (province). Moghilev, I think. It's a pity I did not ask my mother more questions,' she sighs.

From my great-grandfather Girsh's file and my conversations in Moscow with Uncle Lyova, I now know it was the *shtetl* of Lukoml in the Senno district of Moghilev.

I have traced on a map the long journey the Onikuls made across the vast breadth of Russia into northern China. What a feat this must have been for a twenty-eight-year-old woman who had never ventured beyond the Byelorussian capital of Minsk—travelling by road and by rail, crossing borders and cultures, alone with two tiny children. Perhaps the difficulties helped prepare Chesna for the challenges that lay ahead.

By all accounts, Chesna was a strong and independent woman. Gita suggests that she inherited these characteristics from her mother, who single-handedly ran the family's small but lucrative grain business after her husband died, leaving her to bring up eleven children alone.

'I wish I'd made a copy of my grandmother's photograph which my mother used to have,' Gita says. 'She was wearing a wig and looked like a real aristocrat. Madame Klebanova.'

Listening to the tape, I have in front of me Chesna's photographs from Galya. Among them, I find a portrait of a formidable old dowager in a high-collared frock and an elaborate bonnet. 'A. Levinman French Photography Minsk' says the insignia on the back. The woman stares confidently at the world with piercing dark eyes, not unlike Chesna's. Later, when I show Gita the photo, she is amazed and confirms that it is the one she was talking about during our taped conversation.

As the youngest daughter of Madame Klebanova, Chesna stayed with her mother and married late—at twenty-five, which was old by *shtetl* standards. Chesna was not a conventionally pretty woman. My grandmother suspects her father Girsh married Chesna for money, rather than for love. She says they were 'an unequal couple', implying that Chesna married beneath her status.

Photographs of Chesna in her forties show a tall, handsome woman with straight, prematurely grey hair and strong features; a woman of character. Though self-taught, she was well-read in Russian as well as Yiddish. Her short, silver hair and upright posture are what I remember most about my great-grandmother from her visit to Harbin in the late 1950s. By that time she was in her late seventies.

From photos I have of Girsh, he was short and wiry, with a cropped moustache and twinkling eyes. Gita describes her father as genial and generous to a fault. Girsh would lend money to his friends, even when he could not afford it. He loved to chat and was forever doing deals. But as his generosity was greater than his wit, the deals often turned out to his detriment. 'A friend would come to borrow money and he would sign a cheque. Then he would have to pay off a bank loan,' Gita says. 'Of course, he tried to hide it from my mother.'

Meanwhile, Chesna ran the affairs of the family. She

made sure there was food on the table, the children were educated and well dressed and the small house was immaculate. Girsh was an observant Jew and student of the Talmud. Chesna respected his piety, but did not share it. Still, she kept a *kosher* home, and prepared festive meals on all the high holidays. But as in many of the other Jewish families in Hailar, her children grew up secular.

My grandmother does not know why Girsh chose to go to Hailar instead of staying in Harbin, like her uncle. It remains a mystery to everyone. By 1909, Harbin was bustling and prosperous with a Russian population of almost 30,000 and a thriving Jewish community of 5,000. Hailar was a trading post on the edge of the Mongolian steppes, where Mongol nomads came to sell their live-stock, skins and wool. Perhaps after the small Byelorussian *shtetl* from which Girsh came, Harbin seemed too big and too fast. On this question, his file casts no light.

All Girsh tells the NKVD interrogator is that from 1909 to 1916, he worked as the Hailar agent for the American sewing machine company, Singer—probably for its Russian franchise. After a few years, Girsh says he bought a couple of cows and moved into the dairy business selling milk, while continuing to fix sewing machines. Gita clearly remembers the huge Singer adver-tisement showing a beautiful young woman at her sewing machine which hung on the fence outside the Onikuls' small house during Girsh's Singer days: 'When I was little, I thought "Singer" was our surname,' she says.

'So did Chesna milk the cows?' I ask, imagining a scene where Girsh fixed sewing machines while Chesna ran the dairy.

'No way. My mother did not know how and did not want to. Either the housemaid milked the cows or a woman came especially to do it ... You must understand, my mother came from a wealthy background and such work was beneath her station.'

Still, there was nothing grand about the little house in which my grandmother grew up. 'It was a terrible house,' Gita says, 'simply terrible. There were only two rooms and not enough beds. My older brother Abram slept on chairs.'

I find photographs of the house in Chesna's album. They show a small white cottage, built of wood and adobe, so low that its windows sit almost on the ground. This was the house on First Street which Girsh rented when he first arrived in Hailar. Though far too small for a growing family, this modest abode ended up being the Onikul home for twenty-five years. Girsh had, in fact, been planning to build a new house and had even bought the timber. But it did not happen. Again, Girsh sacrificed his own plans to accommodate someone else, in this case his landlord whom Gita describes as 'a real crook'.

'Suddenly, without consulting my mother, my father bought the house in which we were living. Why? Because the landlord needed the money to return to Russia.'

How did Chesna feel, I wonder, living in the Russian quarter of this small frontier town, far from her relatives and anything familiar? The climate in Hailar was very trying—stinking hot in summer, bitterly cold in winter, with minus 45-degree frosts. In spring, the town was blasted by huge sandstorms, carried by the winds from the Gobi Desert. There must have been moments when she asked herself why on earth they had come to Manchuria at all.

Like many other subjects of the Tsarist empire, the Onikuls came to Manchuria because of the Chinese Eastern Railway, whose construction started in 1898.

It was part of a deal struck in 1896 between the governments of Tsarist Russia and Imperial China, following China's defeat by Japan a year earlier. In return for a secret defence pact against Japan, Russia gained an eighty-year concession to build and operate the railway across Manchuria, linking the Trans-Siberian Railway to Vladivostok. Russia's dreams of eastern expansion and railway imperialism were rolled into one.

Administered as an independent enterprise by a company of the same name, the Chinese Eastern Railway (CER) was Chinese in name only. The narrow extra-territorial zone granted to the CER along its route effectively became Russia's colony in Manchuria. CER headquarters were established near the small village of Harbin on the Sungari River and the distinctly Russian city that was built there came to be regarded as the capital of the Russian colony. The term 'CER' came to signify not just the railway and its administration, but the geographical location of the Zone. It was synonymous with 'Russian Manchuria'.

The CER drew people from the far reaches of the Tsarist empire in their tens of thousands to the largely wild and sparsely populated steppes of Manchuria. Engineers and labourers came to build the railway; clerks, guards and civil servants to work in its administration; entrepreneurs, merchants and traders to develop natural resources and provide goods and services in Harbin and other settlements along its route. Chinese 'coolies' were also brought from the southern provinces to work as construction labourers.

Believing that the rapid economic development of Manchuria would require private initiative and investment, the CER administrators and their patrons in the Russian Finance Ministry actively encouraged the migration of Jews and other minorities of the Tsarist empire. To this end, they deliberately created an environment of tolerance and equal opportunity. Settlers of various cultures and religious persuasions flocked to Manchuria—among them Jews, Poles, Tatars, Ukrainians, Armenians, Georgians and Lithuanians.

For Jews like the Onikuls, confined for over a century to the Pale of Settlement—the western border area of the Tsarist empire stretching from the Baltic to the Black Sea—Manchuria was the land of opportunity. The discriminatory policies of the empire did not apply there. Jews were not restricted in where they could live and there were no quotas on their number in schools and other educational institutions. Most importantly, there were no pogroms and little overt anti-Semitism, at least until the late 1920s.

Jews started coming to Manchuria from 1898 and played an early role in developing natural resources and commerce in the CER. Most settled in Harbin, though smaller communities also sprang up at the stations of Hailar, Manchuria, Mukden and Tsitsihar. By the early 1920s, the Jewish population was around 15,000. As well as establishing a range of community institutions, Jews played a prominent role in the commercial, cultural and public life of Russian Harbin.

In Hailar, the Onikul family quickly expanded. From the files, I learn that Manya was born in March 1911—at 'Station Hailar, CER'—the first Onikul child to be born outside Byelorussia. Yasha was born three years later. Letters home to Byelorussia must have painted an attractive picture of the opportunities Manchuria offered for a better life. Gita tells how a stream of relatives followed Girsh and Chesna to Hailar. Girsh's brother, Nohum, and his wife, Freida, came in 1914. According to the file of their son Sanya—the bonus file I obtained in Nizhny—they too ran a small dairy business.

Chesna's niece, Dora Tsirlin, came to visit from Bobruisk and ended up marrying Girsh's nephew, Yacov Kogan, who arrived with his brother from a *shtetl* near

Minsk. They became cattle traders. The names and details of these relatives recur in the Onikul interrogation records in Gorky—each time one of them was asked what family they still had living in Hailar. The lucky ones eventually migrated to Australia.

Hailar grew dramatically with the influx of refugees from the 1917 Bolshevik Revolution and the ensuing Civil War. By the 1920s, there were three schools, a hospital, a fire brigade, shops, bakeries, pharmacies, restaurants, small cafes, several churches, a Tatar mosque and a synagogue. A number of foreign firms had set up representative offices, buying and processing wool, skins and furs for export abroad. There were meatworks and grain mills, lumber and cement factories.

Hailar was a good place to bring up children. The photographs in Manya and Chesna's albums depict a happy, carefree, rural childhood—Manya and Gita rolling around in a haystack; the two of them with Yasha being taken for a ride in a horse and buggy in the summer heat. My mother says it was probably taken during a family outing to the river where Chesna would take all the children to play and picnic on the bank while she and the maid washed the clothes. Other photos show a teenage Manya clowning around or posing with school friends in front of a stone obelisk. My mother identifies the structure as the memorial to the 1905 Russo-Japanese War, which stood in the small town park across the road from the Onikul house.

'The school we went to was directly across the road from our house,' Gita tells me. 'At first it was just a primary school, later a high school was added. That's because so many good teachers arrived from Russia as refugees from the revolution. Some were very highly qualified, members of the intelligentsia . . . but there were also some spies among them. You know, people who supported the Soviets.'

At the age of seven or eight, Gita almost died of typhoid. She remembers lying in bed for weeks, fading in and out of consciousness. Girsh's friend, a former army paramedic, treated her with quinine but to no avail. Eventually, her mother took her, semi-conscious, to the hospital in Harbin. 'Everyone came to bid farewell with tears in their eyes,' Gita says. 'They did not expect to see me again. Even the doctor later told my mother that he didn't think I would live. But I recovered. I must have been very strong.'

Returning to Hailar with lots of new toys, Gita was the envy of the other children. 'Toys from Harbin—can you imagine? They were such a novelty!' But the illness took its toll. Gita points to her hearing aid and says her deafness is due to the excessive doses of quinine. She also lost a year at school and ended up in the same class as Manya.

Gita recalls that while her older brother Abram was in high school, he went off to study in the Soviet Union. She cannot remember when or where, only that the Bolsheviks threw him out because of his 'bourgeois class origins'. After that he went to work in Harbin, where he stayed with relatives.

In one of Yasha's interrogations, I find a little more detail, though no mention of Abram's expulsion:

> *My brother, Abram finished part of his high school educa-*
> *tion in Hailar and went to study at the Technicum in the*
> *town of Chita in 1923. He would come home for vaca-*
> *tions . . . When the Japanese occupied Hailar in 1932, my*
> *brother left and never returned. From that time, he lived*
> *in Vladivostok.*

Chita was a large town in Siberia, about six hundred kilometres west of Hailar along the route of the Trans-Siberian, and the Technicum was a technical high school.

In the absence of an NKVD file on Abram, Chesna's photographs are my best source of information. Gita describes Abram as generous, handsome and 'an adventurer'. His photographs bear out the last two qualities. One given to my grandparents shortly after their marriage shows a good-looking man of about twenty, with thick, dark hair and sensitive brown eyes. Abram has inscribed it with great flourish:

> *Treasure the copy but*
> *Don't forget the original*
> *Taken in Urga, Mongolia, August 1927*

Mongolia! Despite my extensive travels around Asia, I find this place exotic. The inscriptions on the backs of other photos of Abram in Chesna's album show him in Mukden, Harbin and Mongolia. One shows Abram in a field wearing jodhpurs and knee-high boots— *near the market, Ulan Bator, 20/XII/27* reads the inscription. Another has him standing with an older man in work clothes:

in memory of working with the head of the English joint stock company trading in furs and wool ... Ulia Sutay, 24 December 1926

This suggests that Abram actually worked in Mongolia, rather than just visited. It helps me understand another photo in Chesna's collection.

Taken in a studio, it shows Abram and three friends in Hailar. His friends are all dressed in European clothes—dark-coloured winter coats and caps. Abram is bareheaded and wears a light-coloured Mongolian jacket. Looking at that photo, I think of my own life and my wardrobe full of Eastern-style clothes. For Abram, it had been China and Mongolia. For me, Cambodia, Thailand, Vietnam. Though I know little about him, I suddenly feel a strong affinity with this man—he was a wanderer, like myself.

In comparison to his brother Abram, Yasha seems distinctly ordinary. Short and wiry, he is not particularly handsome but all who knew him describe him as a real charmer. In most of the photographs from Hailar, he is pictured as a student, wearing the military-style school uniform introduced by the Soviets in 1925 when they took over administration of the CER Zone. In one photo, he has a Soviet star pinned to the front of his school cap.

Born in 1914, the youngest of the Onikuls, Yasha finished high school in Hailar in 1931, just after the Japanese began their occupation of Manchuria. With prospects for further education seriously diminished, he helped his father in the milk business and studied English. Then he too left for the Soviet Union.

Manya was the academic achiever in the Onikul family. She gave her background to the NKVD interrogator in Gorky as follows:

> *. . . From the time I was born until 1928, I lived in Hailar . . . From 1920, I was a student . . . When I finished high school in Hailar, I went to Harbin to study at the Second Harbin Dentistry School. When I graduated at the end of 1930, I returned to Hailar to my father's house and worked as a dentist until 1933 . . .*

From Manya's academic records which I find among Chesna's papers, I gain some more clues and recognise that we have some things in common. From her final high school results, I see that Manya, like me, had a clear orientation towards the humanities over more technical subjects. She scored 'fives' (the top mark in the Russian system) for history, geography, English, philosophy and natural science. Still, she did sufficiently well in her ten other subjects to earn a certificate which qualified her 'to enter any institution of higher learning'. But she was no swot. Judging by her photo album, there was more to Manya's life than study. There are pictures of her with girlfriends and school friends and cuddling up with a handsome, young, dark-haired man.

At dentistry school in Harbin, Manya became more focused. She graduated in December 1930 'with distinction'– straight 'fives' in all subjects. Her diploma, issued by the Department of Public Education of the Chinese Republic, is a large and elaborate document, written in both Chinese and Russian. On one side it is topped with a portrait of the Republic's founder, Dr Sun Yat Sen, with the red and blue flags of the Republic on either side. Among Chesna's photographs, there are several group shots of Manya with her classmates in the laboratory, looking serious in white coats, with hair pulled back under sanitary hats. But other photographs of the time show a more carefree Manya—at soirées and outings, swimming in the Sungari River and promenading along its elegant embankment.

In the late 1920s, when Manya lived there, Harbin was at its most vibrant. With a Russian population of around 120,000, over twenty Orthodox churches and architecture reminiscent of St Petersburg, it was a conspicuously Russian city. The influx of artists, musicians and intellectuals who fled there from the Bolshevik Revolution endowed it with a rich, Russian cultural life. But streaks of art nouveau and the influences of its multi-ethnic population lent a modern accent and a cosmopolitan air. As well as the 300,000 Chinese who lived mostly in the adjacent district of Fujiadian, Harbin was home to Poles, Jews, Koreans, Japanese, Tatars and many others. Harbin had it all—fancy restaurants, fashionable stores, glitzy hotels and cafes on the main streets; gambling dens, opium rooms and bordellos tucked behind.

While a student like Manya would have had neither time nor money to participate in Harbin's high life, she could not have escaped its potent social and political mix. Young Russian students, born and bred in Harbin and other Manchurian towns, rubbed shoulders with former St Petersburg royalty, Jewish merchants from Siberia and poor White Army cavalrymen. Manya would have known students from Harbin's other tertiary institutions, including the Polytechnical Institute, the Pedagogical Institute and the Juridical Faculty. She probably picked up on the debates among the various political factions and saw the early signs of violence brewing on Harbin's streets as black-shirted young fascists and monarchists clashed with their pro-Soviet and Zionist counterparts.

The more closely I examine Manya's photos and contemplate her life, the more she fascinates me. There is something strangely modern about Manya; I have no trouble imagining her as my contemporary. The friends I see in her photographs seem like people I can relate to, pictured in situations I recognise, both at work and at play. Sometimes they look serious or soulful, sometimes they are clowning around. There is little difference between the clothes they wear and the retro style of the 1990s. A classic morning-after shot shows Manya in a kimono dressing-gown looking coyly at the camera. Who took it? I wonder. What was she really like? Did she have boyfriends? Who is the dark, handsome one who keeps reappearing in her photos? Who are all the people and what became of them?

I search for people who may have known her, but most have already died. My mother knew Manya—but she was only four years old when she last saw her. Two of my Hailar aunties are more useful. Gita's cousin, Ronia Onikul, and Ira Kogan, daughter of Gita's cousin Dora, were teenagers in Hailar when Manya was in her early twenties. Both are now in their seventies and live in Sydney.

Ira remembers that Manya's dental surgery was in a room at her parents' house. Both say she was sociable, good-humoured and outgoing. They liked her because she always had time for them as children. Looking through the photograph albums, they help me put names to some of the faces.

Did Manya have boyfriends? I ask them. Yes, plenty. They remember someone called Shmulevich, who used to come for her in his horse and cab. Manya apparently liked riding round in the cab much more than she liked its owner. Of all Manya's suitors, Chesna's favourite was Isaac Morduhovich, a handsome young man from a wealthy family, who came from Siberia during the Civil War. His family bred racehorses which ran on the tracks in Shanghai and Hong Kong. 'If only she'd settled down as her mother wanted, she might still be alive today.' If only . . .

If Manya was the brains of the Onikul family, my grandmother Gita was the beauty. Gita's beauty went far beyond her disarming smile and knowing dark eyes. She was gracious, good-natured and always saw the best in people. Recognising that Gita's strength lay in her looks and charm rather than her academic skills, Chesna and Girsh sent her to finish high school at Madame

Oksakovsky's school in Harbin. This was an exclusive establishment run in the old St Petersburg style, providing girls with an appreciation of art and aesthetics, morals and manners, as well as the usual school subjects. While studying there, Gita lived with relatives in Harbin, together with her brother Abram, who was working in Harbin at the time.

Being in Harbin opened Gita's eyes to the possibilities of a life more elegant and cultured than the one she had experienced in Hailar. She turned out a 'lady', but one grounded in the practical realities of life in a frontier town.

Returning to Hailar, Gita worked for a few months as a typist for the rich Jewish director of a fur company. She quit when she realised that he was checking her out as a potential bride. After breaking the hearts of a few other eligible young Jewish men, Gita, aged seventeen, succumbed to the entreaties of my grandfather, Motya Zaretsky, a cattle trader from Harbin. Tall and slim with grey eyes and a shock of chestnut hair, Motya was urbane, successful and twelve years older than Gita.

In our taped conversation in 1991, Gita talks at length about my grandfather and their courtship.

'You know the company he set up—Myasotrud— became one of the largest cattle trading firms in Manchuria. He used to come to Hailar to buy cattle from the Mongols—in massive quantities. He sent them to Harbin by the trainload. It was on one of these trips that we first met.'

Gita tells me how Ira Kogan's father, Yacov, already

married to Gita's cousin Dora, brought Motya along to Gita's seventeenth birthday party at the end of 1926.

'They arrived late because Motya had been out on the steppes all day. He said he could not come without a gift, so he and Yacov went to the pharmacist's house after the shop had already closed and asked him to reopen it so Motya could buy me a bottle of perfume. As I recall, it was very expensive perfume.'

Gita says that at the time, she was seeing somebody else and not in the least bit interested in Motya. But for him, it was 'love at first sight'. He wooed her shamelessly, showering her with gifts and attention. He organised a soirée to introduce her to his friends.

'I did not want to go but my father and Yacov persuaded me. So I sat there looking sullen. Still, I hear they liked me.'

On New Year's Eve, Motya invited Gita to the celebration at the fashionable Railway Club, with Dora and Yacov.

'I really didn't like him and was dreading that he would propose,' says Gita. 'I was so relieved when the cattle season was over and he finally returned to Harbin.' But Motya was not gone for long. He came back two days later and proposed.

'He got scared that someone else might catch me,' Gita laughs.

'And what was your response?'

'I remember exactly. I told him, "I don't love you, but I don't find you unattractive". I was so stupid at the time, so stupid . . .' Gita muses.

'So what happened?' I ask impatiently.

'Well, he could not stay in Hailar for long. You know how obsessive he always was about his work. But he would not take no for an answer.'

'But if you didn't love him, why did you say yes?' Gita says there was a fair bit of persuasion from her cousin Dora. But clearly, Gita was impressed by Motya's resourcefulness and determination.

'You know he was no ordinary man,' she says. 'By the time I met him he had already worked in New York, San Francisco and Krasnoyarsk. His business partners were all very substantial people in Harbin.' She lists their names. 'He did well for a boy from Kopys. What's more, he was a totally self-made man.'

Motya arrived in Harbin in 1912 as a teenager from Kopys, near Moghilev in Byelorussia, to work in his older brother's meat business. In 1915, he and a friend headed off in the hold of a ship from Japan to seek their fortunes in America. While his friend stayed on in New York, Motya returned to Harbin three years later, declaring that America was too much of a rat race!

My grandmother is right that Motya had also been in Krasnoyarsk. But only years later do I find out what he was doing there from his Public Security Bureau file in the Harbin archive. At the height of the Civil War in 1919, with foreign intervention forces swarming around Siberia, he spent six months as an English interpreter for the Trans-Siberian Railway. Once Soviet power was established, he worked for a year and a half as a cattle buyer for the huge Soviet trade cooperative Centrosoyuz. Perhaps this experience gave him some clues for the large cattle trading firm he would establish in Harbin in 1924.

In April 1927, Motya invited Gita to Harbin to meet his family. It was Russian Easter and the train was quite empty.

Travelling alone, Gita was nervous. 'I locked the compartment door and went to sleep without undressing. Then, in the middle of the night, halfway to Harbin, I heard someone at my door. It was dark. I was so frightened. Then I saw it was Motya. I recognised his flashing smile . . . I was so happy to see him. He had managed to catch my train at a station halfway to Harbin. How do you like that?'

'But I thought you didn't like him?'

'By this time I had come to terms with our forthcoming marriage and I did . . .' she answers and pauses whimsically. 'Do you think I was right?' The question is rhetorical. Her forty-seven-year marriage to Motya is legendary in our circle of *Harbintsy* for its romance and mutual devotion.

Gita goes on to tell me how she stayed in Harbin for several months with her uncle and got to know Motya's family. Gita came under pressure to get married in Harbin since Motya could not easily get away from his business. But she insisted that the celebration take place in Hailar with the blessing of her parents. When the couple returned to Hailar for the wedding, they brought a carriage full of new furniture and household goods for the home they would set up in the large house where Motya had his Hailar office.

Gita describes the wedding, which took place on 5 July 1927, as a simple but festive affair. Motya was a secular Jew and did not want to marry in a synagogue so a beautiful carpet was laid out in the Onikuls' backyard, with a wedding *chuppah* (canopy) decked with flowers. In the presence of the entire Onikul clan, Gita and Motya were married by Girsh's friend the rabbi, while neighbourhood children climbed the fences for a peek.

What a pity no-one thought to take a photo of this rustic idyll. Perhaps nobody guessed there would be no other occasion like it in the Onikul family. It was one of the last at which the entire family was together.

CHAPTER 4

COMING APART

As a student of international politics, I know that over the twenty-six years the Onikuls lived in Manchuria, the area experienced great political turmoil. The 1917 Bolshevik Revolution followed by Civil War, the Sino-Soviet conflict of 1929, and finally the establishment of the Japanese puppet state of Manchukuo in 1932 all left their mark. I have read tomes of turgid prose about the geopolitical consequences of great power rivalry in this 'cradle of conflict'. What I really want to understand though is how these events affected people's lives. I delve into the Onikul NKVD files in the hope of gaining some insights. But my first task is to learn to read between the lines of the NKVD interrogations.

One interrogation record I find in the file of my great-grandfather Girsh leaves me totally confused:

Question: *How many times were you subjected to arrest while you were living in Hailar?*

Answer: *At the end of 1919, I was once arrested by an officer of Baron Ungern's detachment. I spent about eight hours under arrest before being freed, thanks to the help of Police Inspector Kharitonov, with whom I had close relations.*

Question: *Why were you arrested?*

Answer: *I don't know.*

I first read about Baron Ungern-Sternberg in Peter Hopkirk's *Setting the East Ablaze*, a book about British spies and Bolshevik efforts to convert central Asia to their cause in the aftermath of the 1917 revolution. Known as 'the Bloody Baron', Ungern-Sternberg was a demented Balt, infamous for his barbarism against Bolsheviks and Jews during the Russian Civil War. Seeing himself as Genghis Khan reincarnate, his plan was to drive the Chinese from Mongolia before moving to liberate the Russian empire from the Bolsheviks. With Japanese backing, he succeeded in briefly occupying the Mongol capital of Urga in 1920 before the Bolsheviks captured and executed him a year later.

How astonishing to come across his name in my great-grandfather Girsh's NKVD file! It shatters my notion that, by coming to Manchuria early and being apolitical, the Onikuls somehow managed to escape the effects of the revolution and Civil War. Even a seemingly innocent bystander like Girsh got caught in the fray.

I know that among the hundred thousand Russians

who fled to Manchuria during the turbulent years of war following the Bolshevik Revolution, there were many militant White Guards and Cossacks. While the political status of the Chinese Eastern Railway (CER) Zone remained undetermined, it served as a major supply base for the White armies in their fight against the Bolsheviks. When I look deeper into the history, I learn that the frontier area around Hailar was the particular stamping ground of the Japanese-backed Cossack warlord, Ataman Semyonov. It was here that he raised his Special Manchurian Detachment for operations across the border into Transbaikal. I also discover that the troops of Baron Ungern, Semyonov's cohort until 1920, were often deployed to clear the frontier area of Bolsheviks.

Looking again at Girsh's answer, I realise that the 'arrest' he described was, in fact, his capture by one of Ungern's men. Why? Probably because he was a Jew. Ungern, like the Cossacks and many of the White Guard, was a bitter anti-Semite. For them, all Russian Jews were Bolsheviks who deserved to be punished as perpetrators of the revolution. Jews in White-controlled territory in Siberia were periodically pulled off trains and slaughtered by Cossack bands during the Civil War. Ungern's troops usually killed Jews on sight. The real question the NKVD interrogator should have asked Girsh was how on earth he had managed to escape from the 'arrest' alive?

But the interrogator had his own agenda:

Question: How many other times were you arrested?
Answer: Never.

Question: *When were you recruited as an agent of foreign intelligence?*

Answer: *Never.*

Question: *Whom did you know well among the Gendarmerie?*

Answer: *I knew…*

Question: *Whom did you know among the White Guards?*

Answer: *Among the White émigrés, I knew…*

Question: *All these people were fascists!*

'White Guards', 'White émigrés', 'fascists', 'foreign intelligence'. These Soviet labels and polemics pepper Girsh's records of interrogation and those of the other Onikuls. I know that the refugees escaping to Manchuria brought with them their politics and prejudices. But had life for ordinary people like the Onikuls really become so politicised? Or was that just how it appeared to the NKVD interrogators through the prism of 1930s Soviet paranoia?

To get the material in the files into perspective, I need a clearer picture of what life in Hailar and Harbin was like in those tumultuous times. What a pity I did not talk about it with my grandparents and their generation while they were still alive. I have the taped conversation with my grandmother, but her focus is very much on family life. Once again, I look to my extended family. My parents and their friends, children of the 1930s and 40s, contribute what they can remember from family stories. Some older relatives have better recall.

Then I remember Tima Litvin, a family friend in Israel, now in his eighties. The Litvins were a large Jewish family from the Siberian town of Irkutsk who, like the Onikuls, came to Hailar before the revolution. In Hailar, they traded in livestock and skins. Born in Hailar in 1920, Tima lived there through more than forty turbulent years, surviving personal tragedy and torment. At one time, he was a business partner of my grandfather Motya and he and his wife often visited us in Harbin. Since then, I have met him when he visited relatives in Australia and spent a couple of days with him in Israel. I have always found him quick-witted, amusing and loved his larrikin streak.

When I telephone him and tell him I want to know about life in Hailar, he is excited and happy to talk, delighted that I am taking an interest in this extraordinary story. I send him a long list of questions and a tape-recorder with which to record his answers. But he is frustrated by the technology and instead sends me ten closely typed pages of responses. After that, we talk again. Several times he calls me to add points he remembers later. Tima's remarkable recall of events, as well as fragments from others, help me put the picture together.

———◆———

Hailar's Russian community in the early 1920s comprised people of different ethnicities, religions and political persuasions. Among the former White Guards and Cossacks, there were those who refused to accept the

Soviet victory in the Civil War as final. Some Cossack units continued to mount raids across the border. But most Russians—both new settlers who had arrived after the 1917 revolution and old-timers like the Onikuls— accepted that the Soviets were in Russia to stay. They knew that one day soon the political status of the CER Zone would also be decided. They simply wanted to get on with their lives. Old settlers, Whites, Cossacks, Christians, Jews and Tatars lived side by side as neighbours. They traded with each other and sent their children to school together. But in spite of their best intentions, they would soon be caught in a dynamic beyond themselves. In the end, the struggle for control of Manchuria by rival powers—Soviet, Chinese and Japanese—would tear their community apart.

The first of three critical power shifts came in May 1924. The Chinese, who in 1920 had withdrawn recognition from Tsarist representatives and ended Russian extraterritoriality in the CER Zone, finally recognised the Soviet Government. After protracted negotiations, the two powers agreed that they would jointly administer the Zone under Chinese law. But in practical terms, the Soviets were in control of the administration of the CER, including the railway, schools, hospitals and other institutions.

A new Soviet administrator was appointed and a team of specialists arrived from the Soviet Union to take up key positions in the CER and to organise trade unions and workers' committees. Among them were agents of the Soviet secret security service, then known as the

OGPU. Their role was to ensure the political loyalty of CER staff, protect Soviet interests and gather economic, technical and political intelligence in a territory they regarded as a Soviet domain.

Within a year, the new Soviet administrator of the CER announced that only staff who had registered as Soviet or Chinese citizens would in future be employed by the CER administration. This was not an unreasonable requirement for what was effectively the civil service in Russian Manchuria. To preserve their jobs, almost 20,000 CER employees registered with the Soviet consulate. Many of them were jokingly called 'radishes'—Red on the outside, White on the inside. A small number took Chinese citizenship. Those who preferred to remain stateless 'émigrés' began to look for work elsewhere.

The invitation to register as Soviet citizens was not restricted to employees of the CER. Other Russian settlers who held old, now obsolete Tsarist passports were also encouraged to do so. Out of patriotism to the old Russia, refugees from the 1917 revolution and many early settlers chose to remain stateless émigrés or Whites. Though some took Soviet passports out of sympathy for the revolution, most, like the Onikuls, did so for practical rather than political reasons. They did not want to be stateless, particularly in the turbulent times in which they lived.

Registration with the Soviet consulate did not entitle these people to full rights as Soviet citizens or even the right to emigrate to the USSR. Though the little, brown clothbound books issued by the Soviet consulate were designated *passeport* in French, the Russian words that appeared on their front page simply said 'residence permit'. But this did not matter. Most holders of these passports had no intention of leaving Manchuria permanently anyway. They simply wanted the protection of the Soviet consulate while living in China.

By the late 1920s, China was politically divided, with left and rightist Nationalist regimes in Wuhan and Nanjing competing for authority against the internationally recognised warlord government in Peking. In Manchuria, real power lay with local warlord Chang Tso-lin, then backed by Japan's Kwantung Army based in Port Arthur on the Yellow Sea. The Kwantung Army's role was to protect the concessions Japan had won from Russia in southern Manchuria in the war of 1904–1905. But the army's expansionist aspirations were well known. It was strongly rumoured that the aim of the cross-border raids mounted against the Soviet Union by bands of White Russian militants was to provoke a conflict which the Japanese would feel moved to resolve.

It was against this backdrop that the Onikuls applied for Soviet citizenship, as did many Jewish families in Hailar, including the Litvins, Kogans and other Onikuls. The Onikuls did so at the consulate in the nearby town of Manchuria (Manchuli) sometime in the late 1920s. Because the passports were only valid for a year, they had to go back annually to have them renewed. Did the Onikuls consider taking Chinese passports? I ask my mother. Not for a minute. The Onikuls were Russians, first and foremost. They had arrived in Manchuria legally on Tsarist passports issued by the government of the day. Now that the government in Russia was Soviet, as was the administration in the CER Zone, they took the passports offered. It was not a big issue. The most important thing was not to be stateless. Their new son-in-law Motya Zaretsky had a Soviet passport from the time he lived in Krasnoyarsk and their elder son Abram had one from when he went to study in Siberia.

In light of this, I find some of the answers recorded by the NKVD in Gorky when the Onikuls were asked about their Soviet citizenship very curious. Chesna, for example, told the NKVD:

> *Until 1935, I, like everyone else in our family, was a Chinese citizen. In 1936, we took out Soviet citizenship and arrived in the USSR as Soviet citizens, on visas issued by the Soviet consulate in Harbin.*

Chesna was clearly talking about the time they received full citizenship that entitled the Onikuls to migrate to the USSR. But her answer about her previous citizenship being Chinese was simply not true. Likewise, a similar answer given by her nephew Sanya. To confuse things further, Yasha is recorded as saying that, prior to 1935, he had been an émigré. This is not true either. It is also at odds with a comment elsewhere in his file that as a child in Hailar, he was a member of the Pioneers, a Soviet-inspired youth group. It is unlikely that an émigré child would be a member of such a group. Somebody was not telling the truth—the question is who and why?

In 1929, the balance of power in Manchuria shifted again, this time at the initiative of the Chinese. The Nanjing-based Nationalist regime of Chiang Kai-shek had by then taken control of most of China, including Peking. It had been recognised by all world powers except the USSR. Manchuria's new warlord, the young marshal Chang Hsueh-liang, who had seized power after his father was assassinated by his former Japanese patrons, was now allied to Chiang Kai-shek. With Chiang Kai-shek's blessing, he moved to end Soviet control of the CER.

In May 1929, while Soviet and Chinese directors of the CER squabbled over the division of power, Chang sent Chinese police to raid the Soviet consulates in Harbin and other towns, including Tsitsihar and Manchuria station. Eighty people were arrested in the raid on the Harbin consulate, allegedly in the midst of a secret Comintern meeting plotting to overthrow the Nationalist government of China. Several months of diplomatic sparring followed. By mid July, diplomatic ties were severed, the Chinese had seized the railway and other Soviet establishments and arrested many senior staff. CER employees with Soviet citizenship were replaced by people with Chinese citizenship or émigré status. Arrests of CER staff, union and Komsomol activists in various towns, including Hailar, continued and soon reached more than 2,000.

Meanwhile, a special White Guard unit took over railroad security and militant White detachments took advantage of the hostilities to launch sabotage raids across the Soviet border. In November 1929, after six months of escalating cross-border clashes, the Soviet Army moved to defend Soviet rights. After quickly routing the poorly disciplined warlord troops, they occupied north-western Manchuria for a couple of weeks until agreement was reached to restore the previous order on the CER.

Hailar was in the heart of the action. Tima Litvin remembers Soviet planes flying over the town and dropping bombs on the outskirts. Panic reigned, as Chinese warlord troops rampaged through the town, looting and lighting fires, seizing trains and killing passengers and railway personnel. The Russian men of the town quickly organised a citizens' defence team, while women and children barricaded themselves in their houses. Soon all was quiet.

When the Red army walked into Hailar the following morning, people ran out to welcome them. Tima says he was among them and I assume that the Onikul boys—Abram and Yasha—were probably there too. According to the dates in Manya's file, she was at dentistry school in Harbin and would have missed the action. The Zaretskys were also in Harbin. They had gone there in early 1929 to take advantage of its medical facilities for the birth of my mother, and only came back a year later.

The Russian settlers were impressed by the professionalism and discipline of the Soviet soldiers and the speed of their operation. People talked of the army as 'our boys'. Tima says most of the time, the soldiers were on their best behaviour and marched around the street singing songs ridiculing Chiang Kai-shek as a 'bourgeois'. Still, they could not resist taking home some booty from the Russian bourgeoisie. Tima recalls 'the comrades' packing up all the dried fruit and the woolwashing equipment from the huge storehouse of the Naftanovich family, wealthy Jews, whose daughter Rachel was Manya's best friend. The positive impression of the Soviets was also marred when a number of Whites were deported to the Soviet Union and it later emerged that atrocities against civilians had been committed in raids on Cossack settlements in north-west Manchuria.

The third and decisive power shift in Manchuria came almost two years later. Japan's time had come. In September 1931, the Kwantung Army staged an explosion on the railway line near Mukden, which they blamed on Chinese soldiers and used as a pretext to occupy Manchuria over the next year. Harbin was taken in February 1932. The rest of the CER towns followed. Hailar was one of the last, taken on 5 December 1932. As part of the charade that the Japanese had come to assist the Manchurians against oppressive Chinese rule, in March 1932, the deposed last Manchu emperor of China, Pu Yi, was installed as head of the puppet regime of Manchukuo that would ensure Japanese hegemony for the next thirteen years.

This transformation of the political landscape marked the beginning of the end of Russian life in Manchuria and for the Onikuls, the break-up of their family.

When the people of Hailar heard the bombs and saw the billowing smoke rising from the Chinese garrison on the outskirts of town in December 1932, they knew the Japanese had arrived. Next, a bomb exploded at the flour mill near Hailar railway station. People scurried for cover. Children, my mother included, were hidden in cellars or darkened rooms. The Chinese army was quickly overwhelmed. When the Japanese troops marched into town the following day, some of their White Russian cohorts ran out to greet them. Tima Litvin remembers flags and lanterns with the slogan in Russian 'People rejoice, the sun has risen!' strung up along some of the fences.

At the Onikul house, the atmosphere was not so cheery. The night the Japanese bombing started, Abram disappeared from Hailar. Tima says he saw Abram at someone's *bar mitzvah* celebration several weeks earlier, then never saw him again. Ira Kogan, a nine-year-old at the time, remembers that Abram came with her uncle to grab her from school after the bombing of the flour mill. The next thing she heard was that Abram had escaped across the Soviet border in a railroad service car. Some time later, the family got a message that he was in Vladivostok. Why did Abram leave so hastily?

The district around Hailar featured prominently in Japanese military plans for Manchuria. It was to be the site of a huge underground base, large enough to house a whole division, surrounded by massive fortifications, with an airfield nearby. In his responses to my questions,

Tima Litvin writes that the construction work started with lightning speed:

> *First they build barracks and reinforced concrete bridges half a kilometre long. Hundreds of thousands of Chinese labourers are brought from the south to build a dam which draws three rivers into one. They each carry dirt in bamboo baskets on a yoke across their shoulders. The Chinese labourers are housed in barracks made of straw matting with galvanised iron roofs with no sanitation. Disease starts to spread. The sick roam the streets. At night a van comes around and they are thrown into it like dogs and taken away ...*
>
> *The police stop residents from going four kilometres beyond the town without a special permit. People are enraged. The Japanese don't stand on ceremony with their employees. At the slightest problem, they hit them across the face and shout 'Bakayaru'—you fool! Trenches are built from one end of town to the other and a 'war zone' is declared. All the cemeteries—Orthodox, Jewish and Tatar—fall into the 'war zone', so access is barred.*

When the army first arrived in Hailar, Japanese officers requisitioned accommodation in private houses around town, including at the Zaretskys. For the two or three months they were there, Gita and three-year-old Inna went to live with the Kogans, while Motya watched his new house-guests toss their fine china against the wall during sake drinking bouts. Luckily other relatives, who had Japanese military as long-term tenants during the occupation, found their behaviour considerably more circumspect.

As in Harbin earlier, the Japanese sought Russian assistance to control the Russian population in Hailar. They found willing collaborators among the militant anti-Soviet Whites and Cossacks. Some were recruited to work for the Japanese Military Mission, the Gendarmerie (*Kempeitai*) and other police agencies. These agencies also recruited Russian informers and secret agents and used Russian thugs to do their dirty work in protection and extortion rackets. Russian-speaking Japanese advisers were attached to all émigré organisations. The Japanese also took control of White Russian military units and trained them for intelligence-gathering and sabotage operations across the Soviet border. The political climate became increasingly oppressive, particularly for Soviets and Jews.

As part of the Japanese effort to drive the Soviet Union out of the CER Zone, CER employees and others with Soviet passports became the victims of harassment and arrest and the community started to become polarised between Soviets and White émigrés. From Manya's NKVD file, I learn that she left Hailar for Shanghai in October 1933, almost a year after the Japanese arrival, and later went on to the USSR. She tells her interrogator that until her departure she worked as a dentist.

Question: Why did you go to Shanghai in 1933?
Answer: Only because I was afraid that I would be arrested if I stayed in Hailar.

Question: *How did you know about your arrest?*

Answer: *I didn't. But Skuratov told me that it was no longer safe for me to stay in Hailar and that I should go to the USSR.*

No-one I ask from Hailar has any recollection of someone called Skuratov, but I guess he is somehow linked to the Soviet consulate or the CER administration. As for a reason for her possible arrest, I assume it has something to do with her Soviet citizenship.

The Japanese themselves were not driven by anti-Semitism, and publicly had good relations with the Jewish community. But their close association with the Harbin-based Russian Fascist Party (RFP) gave legitimacy to the latent anti-Semitism harboured by some Russians. It made people like the Onikuls, who were both Jews and Soviets, extremely vulnerable. In one of his NKVD interrogations, Yasha describes how a disagreement with a employee could result in detention by the Gendarmerie:

. . . In the course of an argument with my mother about a household issue, our domestic let loose a torrent of anti-Semitic abuse. When I found out about it, I dismissed her. As a result, first my mother, then I, was summoned to the Gendarmerie and detained for about three hours.

I was interrogated by a Japanese . . . He accused me of beating up [the domestic] . . . When I denied this, he slapped me across the face. Before he would release me, the Japanese beat me and ordered that I apologise to [her].

I later learned from an acquaintance that [the domestic] had informed the Japanese in some detail about our family, visitors to our house and other issues.

In March 1935, after protracted negotiations, the Soviet Union sold the CER to Japan for less than a quarter of the asking price. To get the Soviets to this point, the Japanese applied all kinds of pressure. CER employees were harassed and arrested. Japanese-sponsored bandits raided trains, robbing and murdering Soviet passengers. CER property was damaged and traffic disrupted. Payments for transportation of Japanese soldiers and material were constantly withheld. The Soviets realised that the CER had become unprofitable. With Nazi power on the rise on their western front, the Soviets were keen to remove an irritant that could lead to war with Japan. So they cut their losses. This eliminated Soviet influence in Manchuria for the next ten years and freed Japan to pursue its campaign of colonisation. The sale of the CER also left Russian settlers with Soviet passports in an extremely precarious position.

By this time, branches of the Bureau of Russian Émigré Affairs in Manchukuo (BREM) had been established throughout Manchuria, including in Hailar. Set up at Japanese instigation as a means of controlling the Russian émigré community, BREM worked closely with the Japanese Gendarmerie. It was headed by a succession of ageing White Guards and Cossacks and run by members of the RFP and their sympathisers. At one time, its leader was General Baksheev, a prominent

Cossack leader who lived for a time in Hailar. Quite a few Russians who held Soviet passports converted to émigré status by registering with BREM. Those, like the Onikuls, who chose not to do so often found themselves under surveillance and subjected to harassment, blackmail and arrest. In Girsh and Yasha's interrogation records, I find descriptions of several such instances.

Girsh tells how he was able to bribe his way out of arrest:

Question: *With whom did you have close relations among the employees of the Gendarmerie and police?*

Answer: *I had close relations with an employee of the Gendarmerie, Ivanov. He came to our house several times. When arrests of Soviet citizens started in 1935, I paid Ivanov bribes several times in order to avoid arrest. I also entertained him at the tavern and the restaurant. Two other employees of the Gendarmerie came with Ivanov . . . I also paid them bribes . . .*

Yasha was not so lucky. Once he was arrested and beaten in detention:

Question: *Why were you arrested by the Japanese authorities?*

Answer: *The first time I was arrested by the Japanese Gendarmerie—for what I don't know—and kept in detention for 7 or 8 hours. During my interrogation, they beat me and demanded that I confessed to being a member of the Komsomol.*

> *In spite of heavy beating, I gave them no evi-*
> *dence, even though I belonged to the Pioneers*
> *since 1924 . . .*

Another time, he was harassed, detained and put under
surveillance:

Question: *When else were you detained by the*
Gendarmerie?

Answer: *In November 1935, I travelled by train from*
Hailar to Harbin . . . During the course of the
eighteen-hour journey, I was interrogated seven
or eight times by the Gendarmerie (one Russian
and one Japanese). They asked where I was
going and why, and checked my Soviet papers
several times. As we were approaching Harbin,
I was warned that, on arrival, I would be taken
to the police bureau at the station. I was
detained there for about four hours. In the
interrogation, they asked 'Why have you come
to Harbin? Where are you staying? What do
you do? What do your relatives do? How long
have you been a member of the Komsomol?'
The next day I discovered I was under police
surveillance. At the same time, a policeman
started coming to the Zaretsky house, where I
was staying, asking when I would be leaving
Harbin. After ten days, I cut short my visit. On
my departure from Harbin, I was again inter-
rogated at the police bureau at the station. On
the train, the interrogations began again . . .

By February 1936, Yasha had had enough. He left Hailar to join Abram and Manya in the Soviet Union. Tima Litvin remembers Yasha coming to say goodbye on the eve of his departure and leaving with tears in his eyes because he did not really want to go. But he had developed a nervous twitch from the continual stress. Tima, who was also a Soviet, says he too had one or two encounters with the Japanese Gendarmerie. But nothing like the sustained harassment which Yasha described.

So it was that in 1936, after twenty-seven years in Manchuria, Girsh and Chesna found their family torn asunder: three of their children in the Soviet Union, driven from their home by fear of arrest by the Japanese; their daughter Gita and her family and they themselves living under threat in the puppet state of Manchukuo. The time had come to make a choice.

CHAPTER 5

FROM MANCHUKUO TO THE RADIANT FUTURE

Before departure 1936

THESE WORDS ARE neatly written on the back of a formal family portrait I find on the second page of my great-grandmother Chesna's photo album. Sepia printed on high quality paper, it shows Chesna and Girsh Onikul with my grandparents Gita and Motya Zaretsky, and my mother, Inna. Obviously taken in a studio, the photograph has a strangely solemn air.

'Where was this taken? What was the occasion?' I ask my mother, as we sit in her kitchen one afternoon in the summer of 1997.

Chesna and Manya's photograph albums and the files which I brought back from Nizhny Novgorod are spread out all over the table. Having seen the Onikul NKVD files for herself, my mother is amazed at the information they contain. Now that I am safely back from the 'evil empire', she is keen to help me put the pieces of the story together. The inscription on the back of this photograph jogs her memory.

'It was taken when my grandparents came to visit us in Harbin a few months before they left for the Soviet Union. It was *Pesach* (Passover), I remember. The whole house had to be turned upside down to make it *kosher* before they came. Special *Pesach* plates and cutlery were brought out, the kitchen scoured and the house cleaned to make sure there was no *chometz* (leavened grain) anywhere.'

Pesach always falls in the northern spring, so the photo must have been taken sometime in April 1936. The Zaretskys had recently moved from Hailar to their new home in Harbin. Although they were secular Jews, my great-grandfather Girsh was religious and all the rituals of the Jewish Passover had to be observed.

The Onikuls had decided to follow their two youngest children, Manya and Yasha, to Gorky. With their eldest son Abram living in Vladivostok and Gita and her family in Harbin, there was not much left for them in Hailar. My mother remembers hearing about the letters Manya and Yasha kept sending their parents, urging them to come to Gorky. Both had found good jobs and painted an inviting picture of a bright new future in the Soviet Union—their own country, far from the traumas of the Japanese occupation.

The photograph was taken during Girsh and Chesna's last visit to Harbin. My mother says her grandparents stayed with them for a couple of weeks before going back to Hailar to sell their house and pack up. During that time, she remembers the whole family going to Lifshitz's photo studio on Kitayskaya, the main street of the Pristan commercial district near their home.

As a farewell gift, her grandparents gave my mother a silver napkin ring and a tiny silver purse. Later that evening she pulls them out of the carved Chinese camphor chest to show me. Engraved on the purse are the words:

To Innochka from Grandma and Grandpa.

Inna remembers little about the Onikuls' departure, apart from her mother's tears and all the baggage that had to be loaded on the train at Harbin Station. Gita and Chesna had been shopping for days. Fabric for coats had been bought at Eskin Brothers and taken straight to the tailor, shoes and other items at Churin's department store, new china and kitchen utensils at Shved Co. She had never seen so many bags and parcels. All these purchases lent an air of excitement to the sadness of parting.

I find a few more details about the Onikuls' preparations for departure in the answers Girsh and Chesna gave their NKVD interrogators. While in Harbin, they collected their new Soviet passports and entry visas from the Soviet consulate. Getting these permits took a long time, but authorisation finally came through. On return to Hailar, they sold their house and their cows to a German whose name I cannot decipher. A Hailar policeman named Ivanov, the same one Girsh bribed to avoid arrest, bought their harmonium. In August 1936, after twenty-six years, Girsh and Chesna left Manchuria forever.

———◆———

There were many goodbyes at Harbin Station in the mid-1930s, as tens of thousands of Russians fled the oppressiveness of the Japanese occupation. With the economy in decline and crime on the rise, life in Harbin had lost its previous charm. The political polarisation of the community and the rise in anti-Semitism exacerbated the malaise. Many left for the safety of the international settlements in Tientsin and Shanghai, including more than half of Harbin's Jewish community, who were out-raged at the wave of kidnapping, extortion and murder perpetrated by Russian thugs with fascist links and masterminded by the Japanese secret police.

The Soviet Union's sale of the Chinese Eastern Railway (CER) to Japan in March 1935 prompted a massive exodus. Over 30,000 Russian families with Soviet passports left Manchuria for the Soviet Union. Most of them were employees of the CER who had worked on the railway and the CER administration, in schools, hos-pitals and other institutions. Quite a few were born in Manchuria and had never seen Russia. They headed for their 'homeland' with excitement and anticipation. The departures were festive occasions. Crowds waved goodbye from the platform as overloaded trains pulled out of the station, some decked with red flags and banners with slogans like 'Mother Russia—receive your children!'

'Did the Zaretskys think of leaving?' I ask my mother.

'It was never on the agenda,' she replies.

Both my grandfather and his older brother, Ruvim, were well respected in the Harbin business community as old settlers who had established a name for themselves in the meat and livestock business. While Ruvim operated a successful retail outlet at the Harbin market under the name Brothers Zaretsky & Co., Motya was a wholesale cattle merchant. In 1934, he had completed the construction of a two-storey apartment block in Diagonalnaya Street near the Sungari River.

Though its construction had been interrupted by the great 1932 flood, in 1935 he finally moved his family from Hailar into one of the four apartments. Now Motya was preoccupied with his business, while Gita had her hands full with children. Apart from my mother, she was looking after two teenage relatives from Hailar, Ronia Onikul and Ira Kogan, who were going to school in Harbin. Motya's aged mother and one of his sisters also lived with the Zaretskys. When she had free time, Gita amused herself with *mah jong*, tea parties and the occasional operetta.

'But what about the Japanese occupation?' I ask.

All Inna recalls from the time is that the British school she was attending closed and she went to the new Soviet 'pink' school, so called because of the distinctive colour of its splendid building. I later learn that, in the face of the

Japanese arrival, my grandfather and his partners had liquidated their large cattle business, Myasotrud, and Motya assumed a low profile role in the partnership with his brother.

———◆———

'Did you know that Manya went to Shanghai before she went to the Soviet Union?' I ask my mother, showing her the relevant part of Manya's NKVD interrogation. It comes as a complete revelation. But being four years old when her aunt left Hailar, my mother could hardly have been expected to know. Besides, Manya did not stay in Shanghai for long. As she told her NKVD interrogator in Gorky:

> In October 1933 I went to Shanghai and stayed with friends, the family of Ruvim Alexandrovich Poliak. I worked for a short time at the Women's Studio as a dentist. At the end of 1934, I left Shanghai for Vladivostok . . . I stayed in Shanghai no more than ten months before going to the USSR.

Further in the interrogation Manya describes Poliak as a wool merchant and explains that she left Hailar for Shanghai after being warned of possible arrest. She says she did not go directly to the USSR because her parents did not yet have Soviet entry papers and she did not want to lose contact with them. I search Manya's file for more information about her time in Shanghai, but this brief mention appears to be all there is.

Shanghai, once called the 'Paris of the East' with its rich mélange of nationalities and lifestyles, has long captured my imagination. First opened to the west as a 'treaty port' by the British in the 1840s, by the 1930s it had grown into the most dynamic commercial centre in the far east, complete with vice, espionage and political intrigue. Cosmopolitan, glamorous and exotic, Shanghai was a city of extremes and contrasts: dire poverty and gross abundance; hope and despair; a place where everything could be bought and sold.

Growing up in Sydney, I met many Russians from Shanghai among our family friends. They all seemed sophisticated and spoke good English. Some fled there in the early 1920s from the Bolshevik Revolution. Others came in the 1930s to escape the strictures of Manchukuo. Among my own friends were children of European Jews who found refuge from the Nazi Holocaust in Shanghai. The stories of life in Shanghai's extraterritorial enclaves— the International Settlement and the French Concession —and the ghetto of Hongkew were always full of colour and movement. Set against the backdrop of the banks and trading houses that lined the Bund waterfront, opulent villas, glitzy nightclubs, sleazy bars and slick cafes, they seemed so much more exotic than our Harbin story.

Shanghai was international. Harbin was Russian and provincial. 'Why didn't we come from Shanghai?' I ask my mother, as if there was something she could have done to change it. 'It was so much more romantic!'

'Yes Shanghai had high-life,' she replies, 'but Harbin had culture.' I know she means culture with a capital 'c' and there is little point debating the issue. Still, I am delighted that through Manya, I have acquired a Shanghai connection.

Though Manya's stay in Shanghai was brief, I am intrigued by its mystery. Why did she really go there? What did she do? Why did she leave? There has to be more to it than the answers revealed in her interrogation. Did she really leave Hailar because she was afraid of being arrested, as she told her NKVD interrogator? Or was this a line proffered under pressure of interrogation to rationalise choosing to live in a city driven by capitalist excess?

When I ask my Hailar aunties, Ronia Onikul and Ira Kogan, whether Manya went straight to the Soviet Union when she left Hailar, both say she went to Shanghai first. We are sitting around my kitchen table in Sydney where the two of them have been helping me identify some of the faces in Manya and Chesna's photograph albums.

Ronia flicks back to a small studio photograph of Manya with an attractive young woman whom she had earlier identified as Manya's close friend Rachel Naftanovich. 'They went together,' she says. On the reverse side of the photograph are the words:

from Manya and Rachel
Harbin May 1933

Manya and Rachel probably spent time in Harbin en route to Shanghai and this was a photograph Manya sent to her parents, Ronia suggests. She remembers that the Onikuls were friends with Rachel's parents, who were wealthy Hailar cattle breeders, and their daughters grew up together. She points to Rachel in quite a number of the Hailar photographs with both Gita and Manya.

Ira has a sudden recollection of hearing as a child that Manya may have followed a boyfriend to Shanghai. She speculates that it was Isaac Morduhovich, the son of the horse-breeding family whom Chesna had hoped Manya would marry. Perhaps this memory is the remnant of Ira's childish fantasy? Who can ever know?

No-one I ask is able to cast any light on the identity of Ruvim Alexandrovich Poliak, with whom Manya stayed. It is true there were many Russian Jews in China named Poliak. The Women's Studio, where Manya said she worked in Shanghai, also draws a blank. I can only assume it was some kind of establishment for women, with a polyclinic attached.

Later, while looking through notes I made from pages of the Onikul NKVD files which the archive had not allowed me to photocopy, I find another snippet of information about Manya in Shanghai which leaves me totally perplexed. It is a few lines extracted from the NKVD interrogation of an opera singer in Gorky named Karmelinsky, who is described as a confessed Japanese spy. He alleges that while living in Shanghai, Manya:

... had links with the White bandit newspaper 'Shanghaiskaya Zarya' and was a member of the so-called 'Women's Studio', which existed on the premises of this newspaper. It was widely used for espionage purposes by various foreign consulates. I know from my own life abroad that the 'Shanghai Studio' was an espionage organisation, which the White Guards used for various foreign consulates.

I know that by the mid-1930s, Shanghai had a Russian community of about 25,000, with their own churches, synagogues, shops, cafes, clubs and varied political persuasions. *Shanghaiskaya Zarya* (Shanghai Dawn) was the most widely read Russian émigré daily. It was owned by the same proprietor as the *Zarya* in Harbin and another variant in Tientsin. As I understand it, they were all mass appeal émigré papers which steered clear of contentious ideological debate. Still, in the context of Stalinist polemics, that might still have qualified the *Zarya* as 'White bandit'. I am bemused by what sort of 'studio' might have been attached to a newspaper.

Karmelinsky's description conjures up an image of a smoke-filled journalists club where diplomats, businessmen, artists, journalists and spies gathered to drink, trade gossip and do deals; much like the press clubs I've visited in Hong Kong and Washington, I imagine. But where would a dentist surgery fit? Shanghai Studio or Women's Studio —none of the Shanghai Russians I ask has heard of it.

Leafing through the *Far Eastern Economic Review* in the Summer of 1977, I stumble across a review of a book on the history of the former Russian émigré community of Shanghai by a Chinese scholar and manage to track down a copy. It turns out to be in Chinese, but my linguist father obliges with a translation. The book provides a comprehensive study of Russian life in Shanghai, its key businesses and cultural institutions. But there is no mention of any studio. I am beginning to resign myself to the fact that this studio will remain a mystery.

Still, Shanghai beckons me. I am suddenly engrossed by media reports on the economic and cultural resurgence of this great city. I long to see it for myself and to discover what vestiges still remain of its cosmopolitan past.

In 1998, the fates which seem to be drawing me to unravel my family's history conspire again. In hindsight, it is clear that the pivotal event is a chance meeting with a Chinese scholar at the ancient Van Mieu Temple of Literature in Hanoi. The string of coincidences, fortuitous journeys and friendships that follow over the next two years help resolve some of the mysteries of Manya's time in Shanghai.

It is a May evening in Hanoi where I am just about to conclude my two-and-a-half-year assignment. Chatting with a couple of guests at an official function in the picturesque Van Mieu temple courtyard, I am asked about my family background. My answer, which naturally mentions Harbin, is overheard by a Shanghai professor who once taught at Harbin University. In the course of our conversation, it emerges that the author of the Chinese book I found about Russians in Shanghai is his colleague at the Shanghai Academy of Social Sciences. Another of his colleagues is a specialist on Jews in China. 'Come and visit and I will introduce you to them both.'

Miraculously, this happens just four months later when a new business role takes me to Shanghai for a few days. It is the first of many visits over the next two years. The two academics become my friends and play a vital role in helping me to put together my family mosaic.

Wang Zhicheng, the Russian expert, has spent years immersed in Russian émigré collections in the Shanghai Library, as well as the Museum of Russian Culture in San Francisco. A true Slavophile he uses the nickname 'Sasha'. Together we spend hours wandering the avenues of the former French Concession where Russians lived in the 1930s. Still lined with plane trees and a few remaining old villas, the area has retained its distinctive Parisian air. Sasha shows me the remains of Russian life here—the Russian shopping district on Avenue Joffre, the schools where Russians sent their children, the former Russian hospital, and a couple of former Orthodox churches. One is now a restaurant, the other houses the stock exchange trading floor.

Using old business registers, police files and old and new maps of Shanghai, Sasha helps me track down the landmarks of Manya's life. He identifies Ruvim Alexandrovich Poliak, with whom Manya stayed, as a prominent member of the Russian Jewish community.

On a later visit, he takes me to the tall Sun Court apartment block in Weihaiwei Road in which Poliak's family once lived. The studio where Manya worked remains a mystery.

Pan Guang, the prolific dean of the Jewish Studies Centre, shows me around the main Jewish locations, including former synagogues, art deco apartment houses and the grand old Jewish Club, which is now part of the Shanghai Conservatorium of Music. A consummate net-worker, he also suggests some contacts I should make among his list of former Jewish residents of China. Two of them, women who grew up in Shanghai and live on opposite coasts of the United States, unwittingly lead me to answers about Manya's time in Shanghai.

In May 1999, the writer Rena Krasno takes me to the Hoover Institution Archive at Stanford University to see a collection of books and papers which belonged to her father, the former editor of a Jewish magazine in Shanghai. Among them is an extraordinary Russian album of photographs, *Russians in Shanghai,* which was published in 1936 by a Russian Shanghailander, Captain Jiganoff. Leafing through it, I come across a page headed:

The Women's Professional School
(formerly the Women's Studio of the newspaper
'Shanghai Zarya')

Below is a photograph of the building in which it was located.

I am stunned. The heading alone puts much of what I had read in Manya's file into perspective. The accompanying article explains that the Women's Studio was established in 1933 by the newspaper's management and in 1935 moved to larger premises and became the municipality's Professional School. The studio's original purpose was to provide Russian women the opportunity to learn a trade or craft which would 'help them earn a crust in the long term'. It offered such courses as dressmaking, millinery, manicure, hairdressing, cooking, typing, French and English.

The studio must have been a real blessing for the thousands of women who fled Russia after the Bolshevik Revolution with no practical skills and little prospect of employment other than taxi-dancing or prostitution. It is conceivable that such a studio might have had a small clinic where Manya may have fixed teeth. So much for the nest of spies Karmelinsky describes in his alleged evidence against Manya.

Interestingly, I find Karmelinsky's photograph in the pages of the same Jiganoff album when I am back in the Hoover Archive a year later. Having heard from a Russian friend that Karmelinsky was a variety artist in Shanghai, I have a hunch that his photograph may be among those of the dancers, musicians and young ingénues I saw last time. Sure enough, as I flick through the pages, my eye falls on a photograph of a moon-faced Pierrot. Underneath is the name Alexander Zaharovich Karmelinsky.

My contact with the second American woman, Lily

Klebanoff-Blake, in New York is prompted by the fact that she has the same surname as my great-grandmother Chesna. We swap information via email about the Byelorussian roots of our respective families and their lives in China, but reach no conclusion. Only when Lily expresses surprise that my family stayed in Harbin when most Jews moved to Shanghai in the 1930s, do I bring up Manya—my Shanghai connection. I mention that she lived with the family of Ruvim Alexandrovich Poliak, in case Lily knows of them.

By the time I arrive in New York in June 2000, not only has Lily arranged for me to meet Poliak's grand-daughter, but also a close friend of her mother's, Elia Poliak, who knew Manya in Shanghai. This really is serendipity.

Elia Poliak is a charming and elegant New Yorker in her mid-eighties. Over morning coffee in a lower Manhattan bistro, we unravel one connection after another. It emerges that Elia is the cousin of Rachel Naftanovich, the friend with whom Manya went to Shanghai. The reason the two of them stayed with Poliak is quite simple—he was Rachel's uncle, a Siberian Jew who had lived in Shanghai since 1915.

'I knew Manya through my cousin Rachel,' Elia tells me. 'We used to see each other in Shanghai.' She describes Manya as a brunette with big black eyes, who was not very tall and wore her hair cut short. 'She was very pleasant . . . affable and attractive . . . I don't often remember people but I remember her well,' says Elia.

I show her a studio photo of Manya in an elegant black dress with short hair fashionably slicked back to reveal her dark eyes and high cheekbones.

'Yes,' says Elia. 'That's how she looked when I knew her.' I always thought the photo had a Shanghai look about it.

Next I show Elia a photograph of the tall apartment block in Weihaiwei Road which Sasha identified as the place where the Poliaks lived. She immediately confirms it is where Rachel and Manya stayed when they first got to Shanghai.

'When they first arrived they did not have much money, apart from what their parents sent them. They stayed with Poliak, as many of his relatives did when they first got there. But the girls soon found jobs and moved into a rented room together.'

Elia knows that Manya found a job as a dentist, but does not remember where. I ask her what kind of person Manya was. Serious? Lively? Did she have a boyfriend?

'I don't know,' Elia laughs. 'She struck me as serious and very unassuming.'

Her answer surprises me. In all the accounts I have heard of Manya while she lived in Hailar, Harbin and even in the Soviet Union, she comes across as spirited and outgoing. These qualities also come across in her photos. I try to draw Elia out.

'Don't forget that at the time she arrived in Shanghai, she was very young, as we all were. She was in a new city. And for the first time in such a great big city. Even people who came from Harbin found Shanghai huge by comparison, and Manya came from Hailar. Maybe she felt a bit lost? She was alone, without her family; though she did have Rachel, her friend from childhood . . .'

It occurs to me for a moment that Elia's insight might also help explain why Manya decided to leave Shanghai for the Soviet Union. Perhaps she felt alone and vulnerable, even a little intimidated by its intensity? Perhaps she realised it was not somewhere she could ever entice her humble parents from Hailar?

Elia is unable to explain Manya's reasons for going to the Soviet Union but she knows others who went from Shanghai, both in the mid-1930s and at the end of the war in 1945. What drew them? For some it was the promise of Russian culture—language, literature, ballet, theatre, opera. For others, it was a yearning for their homeland. From what she knew, they all ended up living in dreadful conditions and eventually lost all contact with friends in Shanghai.

Elia is staggered to hear of Manya's fate in Gorky.

'How tragic. What horror—to die like that for no rhyme or reason.'

So, what happened to Manya's friend Rachel? Elia tells me she stayed in Shanghai and got married, though her husband was tragically killed in a plane crash. After the war, she went to Brazil, where she died in the early 1990s.

Though Elia does not know many details about Manya's time in Shanghai, hearing her talk about my relative is immensely reassuring. Here at last is a living person who knew Manya in Shanghai. It gives her life in that city a validity beyond the NKVD file.

I know that Manya's decision to go to the Soviet Union prompted the rest of her family to follow. What I don't understand is why they chose to go to Gorky. Why not to Moscow, where they had relatives? Why not Leningrad, the centre of art and culture? For that matter, why not Vladivostok, where Abram was living?

The facts, as my mother knows them, are simply that Manya found work in Gorky and the others followed. Manya's NKVD file does not say much more than that. She tells her interrogator that, after leaving Shanghai in October 1934, she went to Vladivostok to stay with her brother Abram for a couple of months, then to Moscow where she lived with her mother's sister, Feiga Tsirlin. In April 1935, she went to Gorky and found a job as a dentist at the Gorky Avtozavod (GAZ) polyclinic. Yasha's file throws a bit more light on the subject. Asked how his sister ended up in Gorky, he explains that while she found work in Moscow, she could not get a residence permit or find a place to live.

I have certainly read about the severe overcrowding in Moscow as masses flocked there after the 1917 revolution. At first they came in search of new opportunities and employment; later, to escape the famine that swept the countryside. By the mid-1930s, Moscow's population had swelled to four million. In 1933, the government introduced internal passports and a system of urban registration as a measure of social control. This meant that only those granted a residence permit in a city had the right to live there.

To get to the bottom of the Gorky connection, I turn again to my extended family, using the information in the files to jog their memories. My mother tells me that Feiga Tsirlin, the aunt with whom Manya stayed in Moscow, is Ira Kogan's grandmother.

Not surprisingly, Ira proves to be a fount of knowledge on the Tsirlin family. She first met them as a child in the late 1920s, when her mother took her from Hailar to visit her grandmother in Moscow. She visited the younger Tsirlins again several times after she and her family moved from Harbin to the Soviet Union in the early 1960s.

When I ask her why she thinks Manya went to Gorky, she has a simple answer: 'She went because her cousins, the Tsirlins, were there already and probably helped her find a job.' Ira explains that Feiga's son, Mark, and his wife, Fanya, went to work at the GAZ in the early 1930s when its foundations were still being laid. By the time Manya arrived, the plant had been up and running for about three years.

Just as one family member had followed another from the *shtetls* of Byelorussia to Manchuria a quarter of a century earlier, so their children followed one another to Gorky in the 1930s. Manya followed the Tsirlins in April 1935. Her cousin Sanya Onikul, the eldest son of Girsh's brother Nohum, followed her from Hailar the same year.

In answer to a question during his NKVD interrogation in 1938, Sanya tells how his education at the Industrial Technicum in Harbin was cut short when the Japanese closed the school. When his cousin Manya wrote to him saying he would be able to find work and study at the GAZ, he came to live with her in Gorky and found a job as an electrician.

According to their files, Manya's younger brother Yasha followed in February 1936 and went to work at the GAZ as a technical interpreter of English. Finally, Girsh and Chesna arrived in August 1936. For the first time in their lives, the old couple did not have to work but were supported by their children.

When I saw the scale of the GAZ plant during my visit to Nizhny Novgorod in 1996, I realised that it was no ordinary car factory. I subsequently learn that the GAZ—which until 1956 was also known as the Molotov Avtozavod in honour of Stalin's deputy—had been one of the model projects in Stalin's massive industrialisation program in the 1930s.

The GAZ was built with the assistance of America's leading car manufacturer, Henry Ford, on the blueprint of his Detroit plant. It was the USSR's first real automobile plant, with assembly lines on the latest American model. Ford had seized the opportunity to sell American equipment and expertise to the Soviets and to help them develop an automobile market at a time when America was going through an economic depression. Ironically, the portrait of this quintessential capitalist is said to have hung for a time alongside those of Marx and Engels at the GAZ plant. The first car produced at the plant, the GAZ-A, was a rebadged Model A Ford.

The GAZ project brought thousands of workers to Gorky from all over the Soviet Union. It also brought American and other foreign engineers and workers eager to take part in the great 'socialist experiment'. When the general secretary of the British Trades Union Congress, Sir Walter Citrine, visited the GAZ in 1935, it already had 25,000 workers in the plant, a medical staff of 500 and 12,500 workers still involved in construction.

How exciting it must have been for the young Onikuls to be working in the midst of all this activity, helping to build the 'second America'! It was a far cry from sleepy old Hailar. As a technical interpreter of English in the department building mechanical work-shops for the GAZ, Yasha may even have worked with some of the American advisers who had come to help get the GAZ plant up and running. Did he and Manya see themselves as part of the Socialist vanguard, I wonder, transforming backward Russia into a modern Soviet state?

From Manya's file I see that from 1935, she was a member of the Komsomol. I wonder whether she joined because she was a true believer or from political expedi-ency? I know that Komsomol members got access to better accommodation, resorts, goods and services. But my sense is that Manya was probably a patriot, ready to make sacrifices today in order to build a better tomor-row—the 'radiant future' of which Soviet leaders so often spoke.

As for life in the Avtozavod's 'socialist city'—the Onikuls were apparently very happy there, whatever my own views about its aesthetics. As Chesna told relatives, she was most impressed with the large two-room apartment Manya and Yasha had been able to secure. With high ceilings and a sunny outlook, it was a marked contrast to the cramped low adobe house the Onikuls had left behind in Hailar. And it was luxurious by comparison to the one-room apartment Chesna's sister Feiga shared with her daughter's family and any relatives who came to visit in overcrowded Moscow. There were certainly benefits to living in a 'company town' where the enterprise built everything from scratch.

Apart from accommodation, the GAZ also had its own recreation facilities, clubs and a large theatre where films were screened and local and visiting artists performed. Girsh would have been disappointed that there was no synagogue in walking distance. But he probably understood that, like his own children, the Soviet paradise they were building was secular. At least while he was alive, the synagogue in old Gorky functioned.

Girsh and Chesna were sad to have left behind their extended family in Manchuria and worried how they were faring under the Japanese occupation. But both had relatives in Moscow, who had moved from Byelorussia in the 1920s after the Bolsheviks ended Jewish confinement to the Pale of Settlement. On Chesna's side there were the Tsirlins and Klebanovs; on Girsh's side the Rayaks. The train ride from Gorky to Moscow was only fourteen hours. Uncle Lyova Rayak remembers meeting Manya and Yasha in Moscow quite a few times and Girsh and Chesna at least once after their arrival in Gorky. According to Chesna's file, it was probably in November 1936.

Having Mark and Fanya Tsirlin in Gorky was a practical bonus for the younger Onikuls. Both were engineers who had worked at the GAZ since its establishment and now held senior positions. Fanya was highly regarded as a specialist in automobile paints, having been sent for training to the Ford plant in Detroit, as well as to Paris and Berlin. The Tsirlins could give their Manchurian cousins good advice on who was who and how things worked at the GAZ.

Ira Kogan remembers her first visit to the Tsirlins in Gorky in the early 1960s, not long after moving from Harbin to Alma Ata. Mark and Fanya were both still working at the GAZ. By this time, Fanya was director of the paint workshop with two thousand staff. Her skills were in high demand by members of the Soviet elite who wanted her personal supervision in the tinting of their new Chaika convertibles.

Ira describes the three-room apartment in which the Tsirlins lived as 'sheer luxury by Soviet standards'. Like many of the old apartments built for senior managers in the Stalin period, it had large rooms and high ceilings, as well as a good kitchen and bathroom. She remembers that it was located in a tall apartment block on a broad avenue with a *gastronom* (food shop) conveniently located on the corner.

'Whereabouts in Gorky was it?' I ask her.

'In the Avtozavod Sotsgorod—Kirov Street.'

I have no doubt that it was apartment 15, no. 23—the address of Chesna's place of residence which I had looked for with my friends in Nizhny. I had seen in Sanya's file that he too had lived at that address. So it was to the Tsirlins that Chesna and Sanya had moved from Oktyabrskaya Street after the arrest of the other Onikuls. How dangerous it must have been for the Tsirlins to take in the relatives of arrestees in those paranoid times. Blood certainly is thicker than water.

Did the Onikuls meet up with Abram, I wonder, after they came to the Soviet Union? There is no evidence among the files or photos to suggest that they did. Vladivostok *is* a very long way from Gorky, even further than Harbin, particularly when the short cut through Manchuria was no longer available. But at least they were in the same country and were able to resume correspondence. Among Chesna's photographs, there is one Abram sent his parents in April 1937. Much stouter and with considerably less hair than in the photographs taken in China, he is dressed in a uniform and has signed it 'from your son, the *pogranichnik*' (border guard). He must have finished his studies at the university and found a job. In one of the interrogation records, there is a mention that along with Manya and Yasha, Abram helped to support his parents financially.

I look through Manya and Chesna's photographs for a picture of the whole family in Gorky but cannot find one. In fact, the only photos from that time are a few of Manya—one with her cousin Tenya Tsirlin in Moscow, one in medical attire at her desk in Gorky, the one with her doctor lover, and a series of photos taken in the Crimea, over a period of two weeks in October 1936.

The Crimean series appears to be photographs of a group excursion. Most have numbers, place names and dates written in white. It is probably Manya's annual vacation with other young workers from the GAZ. The place names are from a number of popular tourist spots around Yalta: the Nikitinsky Botanical Gardens; the Palace at Alupka; Kuchuk Lambat. Most of them still feature in my *Lonely Planet* guide to Russia. The photographs remind me of the Intourist groups I have seen, travelling around the Adriatic in the 1980s. It is that unmistakeable Soviet chic—men in ill-fitting suits, women in floral-printed cotton dresses wearing socks and sandals.

There are only two photos in the whole series that capture Manya's spontaneity. The first shows her with three other women, all dressed in kimonos, sitting on the sand with the Black Sea crashing onto the shore behind them. Any minute now they will throw off their kimonos and jump in for a swim, rejoicing to have at last escaped from the rest of the group.

The second is a group shot—almost a tableau—taken on a wall in Alupka against the backdrop of a tall white mountain. Manya stands centre stage, wearing a thin cotton dress with bell-shaped sleeves which flow gently round the contours of her body. With a beatific smile, her left hand shielding her eyes from the sun, she gazes into the distance.

Perhaps she is reflecting on the eighteen months that have passed since she first arrived in Gorky? She has managed to get most of her family out of occupied Manchuria. Far from the reaches of the Japanese, they are safe and secure and together at last. Now they can all rebuild their lives in their own country. Perhaps Manya's eyes are fixed on the 'radiant future'?

CHAPTER 6

BLACK RAVENS IN OCTOBER

WHEN DID MANYA realise that the radiant future she saw was an illusion; nothing more than a mirage shimmering in the distant burning sun? Within one year of her trip to the Crimea, she and her family were caught in the terror that engulfed the Soviet Union in 1937. From one October to the next, her hopes and dreams were shattered.

Reading the history of the purges it is evident how, month by month, the vortex of Stalin's Terror spiralled out to swallow more and more innocent people. I can see this with the benefit of hindsight. But how far could those living in the midst of it see? When did Manya and the others begin to comprehend what was going on around them?

In the Onikul interrogations, I find snippets of information about their lives in that fateful year. Other fragments come from relatives' memories. My only way of finding credible answers to my questions is to put this information together with what I have read about key political developments—and to use a little imagination.

———————

Manya is in Vladivostok with her older brother, Abram, when the event that precipitates the purges takes place in December 1934. The murder of Leningrad's popular Communist Party chief, Sergei Kirov, allegedly causes outrage among the Soviet public. According to the newspapers, the people demand that the culprits be severely punished. By the time Manya moves to stay with her aunt in Moscow later that month, the witch hunt has begun.

Kirov's murder is linked to an alleged long-range plot to kill other Soviet leaders, including Stalin himself. It is used as a pretext to arrest Stalin's suspected Party opponents, including his former Politburo members, Zinoviev and Kamenev. A connection is also found to Stalin's exiled adversary, Leon Trotsky. Soon Party members across the country are being purged for alleged involvement in 'Zinoviev-Trotsky terrorist organisations'. More arrests are being planned, though few people realise this.

In society at large, Stalin's portrait is everywhere, together with his proclamation that, 'Life has become better, life has become happier.' And perhaps it has. Bread rations ended in 1935 and there is a new spirit of celebration as the taboos imposed in the late 1920s on 'bourgeois' activities and 'un-proletarian' behaviour are lifted. Now, the urban masses are encouraged to enjoy their leisure and consumer goods, if they can find them. The Soviet Union is going to be modern, just like the United States, with mass-produced processed foods like ice-cream and frankfurters. Eau de Cologne and champagne are back in vogue. Sentimental musical films play to packed theatres. Special dance platforms are built in public 'parks of rest and culture' and Grandfather Frost comes in from the cold.

It is in this atmosphere that Manya, having found a job and a place to live in Gorky, writes to her family in Hailar encouraging them to join her.

By August 1936, the Onikuls have all arrived—just in time for the first Moscow show trial. No-one could miss the news in August 1936 that Kamenev, Zinoviev and their co-conspirators have been found guilty of Kirov's murder, as well as other crimes, including a plot to kill Stalin. Complete with confessions from the accused and colourful orations from Public Prosecutor Vyshinsky, their highly theatrical public trial is widely reported in the newspapers. Excerpts are broadcast on the radio and shown as movie newsreels.

Do Manya and Yasha see through the charade? Why would they? Like most people at the time, they have no reason to mistrust Comrade Stalin and the Soviet justice system or to suspect that the confessions of the accused may have been extracted through untoward methods. They would be stunned to hear of treason so close to the top of the Party. At most, they might put it down to the final playing out of rivalries among old Bolsheviks. At work, they attend meetings to discuss the need for vigilance and must be surprised to hear that one of the conspirators, Smirnov, was once the director of their very own GAZ.

But by the end of the year, public attention has shifted to the new Soviet constitution, which has been circulating widely for public discussion before being adopted in November 1936. It promises an impressive array of civil and political rights and freedoms. For many people, including Jews like the Onikuls who hold stark family memories of discrimination in the Pale of Settlement, this document is a reason to rejoice.

And rejoice they do. Nineteen-thirty-seven is welcomed with fanfare and frivolity. The newspapers report that, in Moscow alone, a quarter of a million New Year fir trees were lit up as a symbol of the country's 'happy youth'. Just two years earlier such trees, along with Grandfather Frost, were still banned as reflections of old traditions. Like all major enterprises, the GAZ organises New Year's Eve parties for its staff, with music and dancing—perhaps even jazz which has again come into its own. I imagine the younger Onikuls are there. At midnight, all raise their glasses in the first new year toast—'To Comrade Stalin! To our Motherland! To our radiant future!'

But before January is out, the Soviet public is confronted with its second Moscow show trial. Again, treason and conspiracy are exposed at the very top. Again, the accused are senior Party figures. This time, they are convicted for treason and 'wrecking' the economy at the behest of Germany and Japan. Most of them are executed. People are taken aback that among the alleged conspirators is Yuri Piatakov, a close associate of Sergo Ordzhonikidze, the People's Commissar for Heavy Industry. Ordzhonikidze is much admired for his role in developing Soviet industry during the first Five Year Plan. The GAZ project is considered to be one of his triumphs. In February 1937, he dies suddenly, apparently from a heart attack. Years later, it emerges that he was probably murdered at Stalin's direction.

I imagine that these events are of great interest to the young Onikuls. Their cousins, the Tsirlins, have always been full of praise for Ordzhonikidze. They worked quite closely with him from the early days of the GAZ and he was instrumental in sending Fanya Tsirlin abroad for training.

As for the news that Japan is one of the foreign powers behind efforts to damage the Soviet Union, this comes as no surprise. Back in Manchuria, Manya and Yasha had heard rumours that the Japanese were training some of the militant White Russians to conduct sabotage operations in the USSR. But they never imagined that the Japanese could have agents so close to the top. Now they speculate whether a war with Japan is imminent in the Far East.

From the Onikuls' NKVD interrogations, I learn the names of other people from Harbin and Hailar whom they have met in Gorky; indeed, it seems to be a standard question in the interrogators' repertoire. Manya has become friends with two women from Harbin—Leah and Vera. She tells the interrogator they met briefly while she was studying dentistry in Harbin. There, Leah worked in a millinery and Vera, for the Chinese Eastern Railway. Both arrived in Gorky in 1935, around the same time as Manya, and were working as clerks at the Moscow-Kursk railway station in Gorky.

'We visited each other,' the interrogator records Manya saying. I guess that means they were quite close. From my own experience of living abroad, I recognise how people who move in quite different worlds at home are often drawn together in a new environment by their common background. In Gorky, these women are all former *Harbintsy*.

One of Manya's acquaintances from Harbin whose name catches my attention is the opera singer, Karmelinsky. Manya tells the NKVD she recognised him in Gorky where he was working at the opera theatre. Previously, he sang in the Harbin opera, and toured clubs in other major centres in Manchuria. She cannot remember his name and patronymic.

Another name that appears in the files of most of the Onikuls is Bendikov. A one-time neighbour in Hailar, Chesna tells her interrogator that he was at school with her son Abram. Though by Manya and Yasha's descriptions, the Onikuls have little in common with Bendikov, he visits them in Gorky for a couple of days in 1936.

On 23 March 1937, Manya turns twenty-six. The same day, the newspapers trumpet the completion of the massive Volga Dam—another feat of Soviet mastery over nature. Now that the Soviet people are being encouraged to enjoy themselves, I imagine that Manya's birthday is an occasion for celebration. Sociable and well liked by all accounts, Manya invites friends around for a special dinner, prepared by her mother Chesna.

I envisage Yasha pouring champagne to toast his sister's health and Manya's doctor friend arriving with roses and 'Red Moscow' perfume. Originally created in honour of the house of Romanov before the Bolshevik Revolution, the fragrance was renamed in 1925 and became a long-time favourite of Soviet women. I know it because Yasha brought some for my grandmother when he visited Harbin in the late 1950s. When it was finished, she gave me the empty bottle to play with.

After dinner, the young people continue their revelry at the GAZ club. Having lived for a while in Shanghai, I expect Manya to be a good dancer.

I wonder how Manya manages to have a private life, living in a two-room apartment with her parents, a brother and a male cousin? Intimacy is difficult enough for married couples under those conditions, let alone for secret lovers. Even if Manya's lover is estranged from his wife, as the story has it, he may still have to live with her. If there are children, it may be even more complicated. Since the mid-1930s, the Party has frowned upon divorce, especially for those in senior positions. The pro-family Mothers' Assistance Law adopted in mid-1936 outlaws abortion, raises family subsidies and makes divorce more difficult.

There is a chance, of course, that Manya's lover has come to work on the GAZ project alone, leaving his family in another city. For Manya's sake, I hope so. Her life was all too short as it was.

As the spring of 1937 unfolds, the newspapers are full of stories about 'enemies of the people' being uncovered in the senior ranks of the Communist Party. Examples of corruption, nepotism and elitist behaviour are reported in great detail. Stalin's speeches from the Central Committee Plenum in February point to Trotskyite sabotage and espionage in many enterprises and party organisations. This is the explanation given for the many shortages people are experiencing—everything from bread to ladies' stockings and galoshes. In Gorky, the Onikuls hear that 'enemies' among senior apparatchiks at the GAZ have been unmasked and expelled from the Party. But this is still far removed from their everyday reality.

In the second half of 1937, reality comes closer. Early in June, there is a shock announcement about treason in the Red Army. Eight senior military leaders, led by deputy Defence Commissar, Marshal Tukhachevsky, have been arrested for conspiring in a military plot in collaboration with Germany. And all this while the country is strengthening its defences against fascist aggression and preparing for war! Tried in camera, the eight are shot the next day.

The purge now begins in earnest. Starting at the top, it moves right through the ranks of the Red Army, then through the Party, with expulsions and arrests across the Soviet Union. Soon the ripple effect is felt in Party organisations—in trade unions and the Komsomol.

Leaders are arrested and greater vigilance demanded. It is the duty of every member to help root out 'wreckers' and traitors and to unmask 'enemies of the people'!

As a member of the Komsomol, Manya no doubt has to participate in the Komsomol meetings at the GAZ, perhaps to unmask a traitor or expel a comrade. I imagine she would find group victimisation and public scapegoating distinctly distasteful. Likewise, being put on the spot to give an opinion on something from which she is far removed. I wonder if she is brave enough to speak up for what she believes. Or does she, like so many others, have to bear the shame of losing courage in the face of peer group pressure: preparing to say what she thinks, but finding that her mouth turns dry and mumbling something non-committal?

Perhaps Yasha also gets a taste of workplace meetings and 'self-criticism' sessions where hidden enemies in the ranks are revealed through 'collective discovery'. I wonder if, in his work as an interpreter, he picks up on the new sense of tension regarding foreign influence and notice that almost all of the American and other foreign workers have gone home.

Thanks to his annual vacation, Yasha gets some respite in July 1937, at the very time when the witch hunts reach their frenzy. According to his NKVD file, he goes to the Caucasus, to the mineral springs resort in Pyatigorsk. Popular as an elegant resort among fashionable society in the nineteenth century, this is the place where the famous Romantic writer Michael Lermontov met his untimely death in a duel.

By the time Yasha gets back to Gorky, the 'black ravens' are circling by night. For Russians, the raven is a symbol of doom and foreboding. The nickname 'black ravens' is given to the ugly black vans in which the NKVD arrive to take away their prey. Each night, between 11 pm and 3 am, people lie awake, anxious to hear where the 'black raven' will pull up. Ironically, these 'black ravens' are manufactured at the GAZ, mounted on the same chassis as bread delivery vans.

I picture Manya telling Yasha about her sleepless nights and how she has noticed people disappearing. Patients fail to turn up for their dental appointments. When the nurse rings their workshops, she is told that the people no longer work there. In at least one case, she is told straight out that the patient has been arrested as an 'enemy of the people'. Manya finds it inconceivable, but dares not say so—even to her nurse. The climate of distrust is all-pervasive. One never knows who might turn out to be an informer.

When he gets back to work, Yasha experiences the disappearances for himself. I imagine him visiting an engineer to follow up on a translation he delivered before going on vacation, only to find a subordinate sitting in his place. 'Where is Comrade Frolov? Is he on leave?' He is simply told that Frolov has 'moved on'. Only later might he discover that Comrade Frolov was denounced as a 'foreign spy' by the same subordinate now sitting in his chair—picked up while walking in the street. What is unnerving for the Onikuls is that these people are no longer senior apparatchiks. They are just ordinary people like themselves.

Spies, traitors, enemies of the people are found everywhere! The media are whipping the population into a frenzy of spy mania. The deputy Public Prosecutor, Lev Sheinin, has written a play, *The Confrontation,* about the unmasking of spies. It is being performed in theatres around the country to standing ovations.

For the Onikuls, things are getting uncomfortably closer to home. At the end of July, the local Gorky newspaper *Gorkovskaya Kommuna* runs an article warning men against sexual entrapment by foreign spies. It gives the example of an engineer who was seduced by a pretty young woman, recently arrived from Harbin. She turned out to be a Japanese spy! This article gives rise to considerable speculation among the Onikuls. Was the woman really a Japanese spy? Who was she? Did they know her?

The report must ring alarm bells for Manya. Russian friends who grew up in the Soviet Union tell me of the striking impression Harbin women created when they first started arriving in the Soviet Union. With their stylish clothes and Chinese art objects, they seemed to be truly exotic creatures. Soviet children used to rummage through their refuse for 'treasures'—fragments of their broken china. Against the drabness of their own existence, it is little wonder that some Soviets mocked these Harbin women as 'pampered princesses'.

Manya is astute enough to pick up quickly on such resentment, particularly the veiled envy of many of the women. This might explain the change I notice in Manya's dress style. The photographs taken in China show her dressed simply, but with flair. In the few from the Soviet Union, she has adopted Soviet chic—socks, sandals and the obligatory beret—to look just like the rest of her female comrades. In the midst of 'spymania', Manya realises that her past life in Manchuria and China makes her vulnerable to denunciation as a Japanese spy. She needs to be even more careful not to stand out.

In the climate of growing fear and suspicion, the Onikuls no doubt maintain a low profile and stick more closely together. Now the young ones regularly come home for dinner, each bringing more stories of arrests and denunciations. Priests around Gorky are arrested and churches closed. Girsh wonders whether the synagogue will be next. They notice yet another apartment in the block with seals on the door—parents arrested, grandmother evicted and children sent to orphanages.

How is it that a year that had started so positively can deteriorate to this extent?

Do the Onikuls hear on the grapevine of some *Harbintsy* who previously worked on the Chinese Eastern Railway being arrested as Japanese spies? Does Manya, as a member of the Komsomol, feel moved to defend such arrests, arguing that perhaps these people *were* spies? Does she remind the family of the danger the Soviet Union faces from aggressors on all sides?

While none of the Onikuls would dare ask openly why on earth they came back to the Soviet Union, I am sure the thought crossed each of their worried minds.

When my great-grandmother Chesna visited us in Harbin in 1957, everyone was conscious of what a traumatic time she had lived through, both during and after the purges. Though it was twenty years after the events, no-one dared ask her to talk about what happened.

But one afternoon, of her own accord, she took my mother aside and told her the story in secret. Inna remembers that the conversation took place by the window in my grandmother Gita's bedroom while she was out and I was sleeping.

'Why did she tell you and not Gita?' I ask my mother.

Inna's hypothesis is that Chesna could not bear it— Gita was too close.

Chesna told my mother how, by the end of 1937, the whole family was living in the grip of terror. Reluctant to burden each other with their fears, they often ate in silence. At night, each lay awake, listening for the 'black raven' on the streets outside. Would it stop or would it drive past?

On 2 October 1937, the 'black raven' stopped.

Chesna heard it pull up. Then the boots on the stairs. It was just after midnight. She had heard the noise once before and been relieved when no knock on their door followed. This time the knock was unmistakeable.

Then the commotion started. Manya ran into her parents' room to dress. Chesna threw on a dressing gown and shook her sleeping husband awake. Yasha opened the door in his nightshirt with Sanya behind him. They were faced by four NKVD men in uniform, flashing their purple identity cards—the *chekists*. With them was a neighbour, looking tired and drawn—representing the residents' committee.

'Onikul, Yacov Grigorievich, Onikul, Maria Grigori-evna . . .' the *chekist* shouted, 'you are under arrest. Your papers, please.'

There was no mistaking that the black raven had come for them.

The *chekists* proceeded to ransack the apartment, emptying drawers, pulling books from shelves, turning the Onikuls' life on its head. Chesna set about packing warm clothes for her children, as Girsh sat weeping. She remembered Yasha telling him there must be some mistake and that they would soon be released.

In Yasha and Manya's files, I find receipts for the items the NKVD confiscated—their passports and GAZ identity passes, Yasha's military service card, Manya's Komsomol card, eighteen foreign language books, a bunch of group photographs and personal letters.

It was all over quickly. Yasha and Manya were pushed into the black van in full view of the neighbours who were woken by the noise. The *chekists* liked to have witnesses to prove that the arrests were conducted with full Soviet legality. Chesna remembered how young and vulnerable Manya looked, with messed-up hair and huge dark eyes.

Left alone in the debris of the search, Girsh, Chesna and Sanya stood weeping and hugging each other. Then Chesna started to put the place back in order.

'There's been a mistake and they'll soon be released,' Girsh repeated Yasha's words over and over.

Four nights later, on 7 October, the 'black raven' returned. This time, all three of them had small bags with warm things ready.

'Onikul, Grigory Abramovich'—Girsh's Russian name was Grigory.

The *chekists* did not bother with another search. They even forgot to confiscate Girsh's passport. Chesna watched them march Girsh down the stairs, a sad old man. She wondered if she would ever see him or her children again.

CHAPTER 7

JAPANESE SPIES IN GORKY

SPETS KORPUS, *GORKY PRISON* was the new address for Manya, Yasha and Girsh; it's where they were taken after their arrests in October 1937. This information appears at the very front of their NKVD files. All three cases were handled by the Third Department of Gorky NKVD's Directorate of State Security (UGB), which was responsible for counter-intelligence.

In each of the files, a case officer filled in their personal details and the charge against them: Article 58.6 of the Criminal Code—espionage. Their arrests were authorised by two levels of the NKVD hierarchy and sanctioned by the military procurator. Soviet legality—which at the time required judicial oversight of NKVD arrests—was observed. In form, at least.

Yasha's file looks to be in order. It was opened four days before he and Manya were arrested on 2 October, with an order for search and arrest dated a day earlier. Manya's file, on the other hand, is a complete jumble. While her arrest order is dated 2 October, it appears her file was opened and arrest authorisations given five days later. This is one of many such discrepancies I will discover.

In Russian, *spets korpus* means 'special building', but it carries an association that is much more menacing. Perhaps it is because the prefix *spets* is attached to many Soviet words that hold sinister connotations: *Spetsnaz*—the special forces of the KGB or *spetsposilenie*—a special settlement for political exiles.

This case proves to be no different. The *Spets Korpus* at Gorky Prison was reserved for the NKVD's political prisoners. This is the building I was craning my neck to see in the prison yard in Nizhny in 1996. It is the building I later read about in Victor Herman's book, *Coming Out of the Ice*.

An American arrested in Gorky in the 1930s, Herman spent time in the very same *Spets Korpus*. In his book he describes how prisoners were crammed into dim cells and sat silently for days around a huge cauldron of excrement. Waiting. Waiting and waiting for the night they would be called for interrogation.

On the fateful night, the guard would call the prisoner through the hatch in the door by initial only: 'O, get ready' and unlatch the heavy iron door. Then, the prisoner would be led in total silence along the padded corridors of the *Spets Korpus*, past rows and rows of tiny cells and out into the yard. Locked tightly in the back of a 'black raven', the prisoner was driven to NKVD head-quarters on Vorobyova Street—that same four-storey limestone building my friend Alyosha pointed out to me in Nizhny in 1996, the 'Vorobyovka'.

There, each night, the NKVD interrogators practised their dark art of extracting confessions—beating and tor-turing their victims in hideous ways. Herman describes a single 'transfigured scream' he heard on his first visit to the Vorobyovka:

> *a stupendous howl of exquisite agony with relief mixed into it ... beyond gender—but a perfectly human sound ...—and on either side of it ... a perfect silence.*

He describes how by day, the citizens of Gorky would divert their eyes from the NKVD building as they walked by, apparently by order of the authorities.

By late 1937, the purges had reached a crescendo. A year after his appointment, the new NKVD chief, Nikolai Yezhov, was well on the way to earning his reputation for presiding over the worst excesses of the purges. The Soviet leadership had ordered a mass oper-ation of repression, with centrally planned quotas for arrests. Targets were set for each region and city, speci-fying how many were to be executed, how many to be interned. Beatings and torture were sanctioned as a means of extracting confessions.

In Gorky, as in the rest of the Soviet Union, the NKVD was working overtime to root out 'enemies of the people'—counter-revolutionaries, agents of foreign intelligence and anti-Soviet elements. Gorky Prison was full to overflowing. The testimonies of former NKVD officers in Gorky, made public in the 1990s, paint a gruesome picture of what was going on. I read a few extracts in one of the volumes given to me by the chairman of the archive in Nizhny.

The deputy chief of the NKVD's Third Department (counter-intelligence), Primilsky, is quoted as saying:

> ... *In the period 1937–38, I conducted unwarranted arrests of innocent Soviet citizens on the orders of the Gorky NKVD Chief Lavrushin and [his deputy] Listengurt. Perverted methods of investigation were widely practised in the NKVD's Third Department.*
>
> *Lavrushin was in charge of all the criminal work related to unwarranted arrests (authorisation of arrests and searches etc). He instituted a system of beating prisoners over the head.*
>
> *Listengurt ... set himself the goal of maximising the number of arrests. He motivated his subordinates by telling us that we were falling behind other regions and had to close the gap.*

When I find the names of both Primilsky and Lavrushin on the indictments of all three Onikuls, a chill runs down my spine.

Other NKVD officials speak about the widespread falsification of cases and the use of 'physical pressure' to extract confessions. This included various forms of beatings, as well as the *stoyka*, where a prisoner was made to stand up for hours during interrogation or under guard day and night. Then there were the 'conveyor belt' sessions, where a prisoner would be interrogated non-stop for days at a time, deprived of food and sleep. The aim was to break the prisoner—physically, mentally and emotionally—to the point where they were prepared to sign anything.

I know that in this environment, NKVD investigations had nothing to do with establishing facts or prosecuting crime. In this context truth was irrelevant. Getting a prisoner to confess was the real purpose of the interrogation process. Of course, the purpose of the sessions was also to obtain 'facts' to use against other victims and names to add to the ever-expanding list of suspects. But these objectives were secondary.

Still I search for logic, studying each record in forensic detail, comparing it with others in the same file, then in others. Surely, there must be some reason to explain how and why the Onikuls got ensnared in this madness?

I read and reread the three Onikul files, struggling to master the unfamiliar Soviet vocabulary and legal terminology. Examining the three files together, I start to discern a pattern in the NKVD's investigation process.

Yasha, Manya and Girsh each have three records of interrogation in their files. In some of them, dates are missing or appear to have been written in by another hand. Each record has the prisoner's signature at the bottom of every page and is countersigned by the interrogator on the last page. In each case, the first interrogation begins with detailed biographical questions. Sometimes there are follow-up questions, sometimes not. Then the investigator confronts the prisoner with the charge of working for Japanese intelligence. In all three cases, this is invariably met with a denial.

All three Onikuls are asked similar sorts of questions: What citizenship did they hold in Manchuria? What encounters did they have with the Japanese Gendarmerie? What ongoing contacts do they have with family and friends in Manchuria? They are also asked whether they know certain people from Manchuria who further on in the files are described as spies. The same names recur— Panfilov, Baksheev, Bendikov, Grigerman. Somewhere in the last interrogation, each Onikul is asked to name other *Harbintsy* they know in Gorky.

In each file, the records of interrogation are followed by the indictment, which sets out the charges that have been 'proved' against each person. Then comes the sentence in the form of an 'Extract from Proceedings'. Most of the files also contain excerpts from other people's records of interrogation which mention or incriminate the Onikuls in some way. Yasha's file also contains letters of appeal to the NKVD, protesting his arrest and incarceration and seeking a review of his case. At the end of all the files are documents from the mid-1950s, when the files were reviewed after Stalin's death.

One curious thing I notice in all three records is the complete confusion of Harbin and Hailar. The interrogators appear to make no distinction between the two places. Even when the prisoner is recorded as speaking about Hailar, the indictment reads as if all the action took place in Harbin.

I guess it must have been difficult for the NKVD interrogators to make sense of all the places the Onikuls talked about. I have read that, in the late 1930s, many of the interrogators were poorly educated and ill-trained. It is unlikely that those dealing with the Onikuls would have travelled much beyond Gorky or, at most, Moscow. What hope did they have of comprehending the complex geographies and exotic lives of the people they were dealing with?

Harbin, Hailar, Manchuria the town, Manchuria the province, Manchukuo—to the interrogators, they were one and the same: places that generated Japanese spies and enemies of the people. For most of the interrogators, life was black and white. It was probably easier that way.

Yasha's first interrogation is dated the day after his arrest and is conducted by Lieutenant Driven, the chief interrogator of the counter-intelligence department of Gorky NKVD's Directorate of State Security (UGB). I wonder why they thought twenty-three-year-old Yasha was so important as to warrant such a high level interlocutor.

I notice that though the record is written in Driven's erratic hand, the date and the details have been filled in neatly by another. In fact, further in Yasha's file I come across information which suggests the interrogation took place almost two weeks later.

Driven's early questions are unremarkable: When did Yasha arrive in the USSR? Where from? What was he doing in Hailar before his departure? Yasha's answers are similarly straightforward, with the exception of one about his citizenship. The answer recorded is that, prior to taking Soviet citizenship in June 1935, Yasha had been a 'stateless émigré'.

This makes no sense. In 1935, Yasha may have obtained the Soviet passport which enabled him to migrate to the USSR. But, like the rest of his family, he was registered as a Soviet citizen much earlier. I know from my mother and relatives who lived in Hailar that none of the Onikuls were ever stateless émigrés or 'Whites', as the use of the term in Yasha's record implies.

After the question on citizenship, Lieutenant Driven turns up the heat:

Question: To which foreign counter-revolutionary organisations did you belong?

Answer: I did not belong to any foreign counter-revolutionary organisations.

Question: You are lying, but we will return to that
question later. How many times were you
arrested by organs of the Japanese Gendarmerie
in Manchuria?

Yasha explains that he was never arrested, but relates in some detail the two instances when he was detained and harassed by the Japanese Gendarmerie. The first was in December 1934, when he and his mother were summoned to the Gendarmerie over Yasha's dismissal of a domestic. The second was in November 1935 when agents of the Gendarmerie interrogated him on the train between Hailar and Harbin and detained him at Harbin station because of his Soviet papers.

'Those were the only occasions I came into contact with the Gendarmerie,' Yasha concludes. 'That's not true,' says Driven and moves on to the accusation:

Question: *Tell me straight: when, where and under what circumstances were you recruited as an agent of foreign intelligence?*

Answer: *No-one ever recruited me as an agent of foreign intelligence.*

Question: *You are lying. It is clear from the evidence that you were recruited as an agent of Japanese intelligence and came to the USSR with a mission of a counter-revolutionary nature. Give me evidence on this question.*

Answer: *I categorically declare that I was never recruited as an agent of Japanese intelligence.*

This is the end of the record. As stipulated on the interrogation form, Yasha signs at the bottom of every page. At the end of the record his signature and that of the interrogator appear under the words:

> *Recorded from my words accurately and read by me.*
>   *Y. Onikul*

Manya's first record of interrogation, the one which I read on my first day in the Nizhny archive, is undated. Lieutenant Driven's name has been crossed out and replaced by that of Sergeant Ryabkov—this recurs in several of Manya's records. Having taken down her biographical details, Ryabkov gets straight to the point and accuses her of coming to the USSR to spy for Japan. Manya denies the charge categorically. And that is it. By comparison with the probing that Lieutenant Driven gave Yasha, Ryabkov seems mild-mannered. Perhaps he was still learning the ropes.

Girsh's first interrogation—also with Lieutenant Driven—is dated 8 October, the day after his arrest. The record is brief. After a few opening questions—How long did you live abroad? What did you do there? How long have you had Soviet citizenship? How many times were you arrested?—Driven moves to the accusation:

Question: *When were you recruited as an agent of foreign*
intelligence?
Answer: *I was never an agent of foreign intelligence.*

All three Onikuls were confronted with the charge of espionage in the interests of foreign intelligence—Article 58.6 of the Criminal Code. All three categorically denied it. The interrogators had to work harder to extract their confession.

———

Judging from the dates on the files, two months passed between the time of the Onikuls' initial interrogations in early October 1937 and the next round on their specific cases. What happened to them in the meantime? Were they simply left to sit in their stinking cells? Were they subjected to tortures and coercions? This remains unrecorded.

From their files, it appears that Manya and Yasha were required to assist Lieutenant Driven with the investigation of another man from Hailar, named Bendikov. Three documents I find in their files give some insight into how the NKVD went about collecting 'evidence' to expose him as a 'Japanese spy'. All three documents are records of interrogation written by Lieutenant Driven. Manya's is dated 14 October, Yasha's a day later. The third is a typed but unsigned copy of Yasha's interrogation but I find it in Manya's file.

'Do you know Bendikov? ... Tell all that you know about him,' Manya and Yasha are each asked. The answers recorded are remarkably similar—even in the turns of phrase they use.

Each says they know Bendikov from childhood in Hailar and describe him as coming from a 'White Guard' or 'White bandit' family, mixing in 'White Guard' circles and generally being regarded as anti-Soviet and anti-Semitic. They say that while studying at the Juridical Faculty in Harbin, Bendikov joined 'the Russian Student Society', which they describe as a 'fascist' or 'White Guard' organisation. Manya says Bendikov's mother told her in 1929 that she wanted to go and live in the USSR, but that her son would never agree. Yasha tells how Bendikov suddenly started mixing in Soviet youth circles and, to everyone's surprise, departed for the USSR in 1935. No-one had expected this of such a 'White bandit'.

Was Bendikov a Japanese spy? Both Manya and Yasha deny any such knowledge, though each admits that the Bendikov house in Hailar was used by the Japanese Gendarmerie and their Russian associates. For Lieutenant Driven, this is probably enough 'evidence' to pin Bendikov as a Japanese spy. Manya admits to knowledge of Bendikov's association with Baksheev, whom Driven had labelled a 'known Japanese agent'. She also admits that Bendikov wrote to her seeking contact details for a number of people whom Driven had also described as 'Japanese agents'.

Something about these documents does not ring true. I know that records of interrogation are summaries rather than verbatim transcripts. Still, these records contrast sharply with others in Manya and Yasha's files. Apart from the uncharacteristic use of Soviet polemic, there are factual inconsistencies. Would Bendikov's mother, described by Yasha as anti-Soviet and anti-Semitic, really have discussed such a sensitive issue as her family's attitude towards the USSR with Manya, a Jew with Soviet papers?

Looking at further records in her file, I also notice that Manya gives quite different answers when questioned about some of the same people. All she knows of Bendikov, for instance, is that he went to school with her brother Abram.

Most telling are the signatures on the final page of Manya's record. In all other records, Manya signs her name immediately at the end of the text. In this record, her signature sticks out in the middle of the page, several lines below the text. A little way below it, is Driven's signature. Curiously, his designation, which usually appears on the final page of a record, is missing; below it are two more completely unintelligible scrawls.

Was Manya forced to sign a false record? I know from the published accounts of former NKVD officials that such practice was quite widespread in Gorky at the time, as in the rest of the country. Some prisoners were beaten till they signed records that bore little resemblance to their words. Others were forced to sign blank pages, which were later filled with whatever 'evidence' was required. As head of the investigation, Driven had the power to amend records and invent evidence.

My guess is that, one way or another, he coerced Manya into signing some blank pages—hence the strange position of the signatures—then used the typed copy of Yasha's interrogation to fabricate Manya's record. The additional signatures may have belonged to some subordinates he had invited to witness his interrogation technique.

A curious exchange in Yasha's record makes me think his record was probably also tampered with. His last point about Bendikov reads as follows:

In 1936, when my father, Onikul G.M., was leaving Hailar for the USSR, Bendikov's mother sent with him a plain watch, which was inscribed 'To Baby from Me'.

Question: *Apart from this watch, did Bendikov have other watches?*

Answer: *Yes, he had both men's and women's watches.*

This meaningless digression makes no sense in terms of what comes before it and what follows. But the next question and answer about Bendikov's involvement with Japanese intelligence takes the record to the bottom of the page. Was Yasha just rambling to fill in time? Or was Lieutenant Driven filling in space? Perhaps Yasha was also forced to sign a blank page and Driven fabricated both records? Information I discover further on in Yasha's file about the dates of his interrogations confirms my suspicion that, at the very least, his records were altered.

In a file note written during the review of the Onikul cases in 1956, I learn that Bendikov was arrested in November 1936 for treason. He was convicted and shot as a Japanese spy a year later. Bendikov's brief mention of the Onikul family in an interrogation on 20 August 1937, which I find in Girsh's file, was probably used to justify their arrests two months later. The 'evidence' from Lieutenant Driven's records of interrogations with Manya and Yasha, inconclusive as it was, was probably used to help seal his fate. This is how the NKVD built its cases: putting words into one person's mouth to implicate another; twisting information from case to case.

So where did the 'evidence' about Manya, Yasha and Girsh come from?

It is clear from their indictments that all three of them were 'exposed' by the 'evidence' of one of their Hailar compatriots, named Panfilov. I find copies of his record of interrogation of 19 October 1937, again written by Lieutenant Driven, in all three files.

Asked whether he knows the three Onikuls from Hailar, Panfilov replies that he was at school with Yasha and also knew Girsh and Manya. The details he gives about them are straightforward and mostly accurate.

'That's all I know,' he says.

'That's not true,' the interrogator protests:

Question: *We are aware that you know of the Onikul family's involvement with Japanese intelligence. Do you admit it?*

Answer: *I don't know whether they were agents or not, but I know that they were close to a Japanese agent, Baksheev.*

Question: *I demand that you give honest evidence on the question of the Onikul family's involvement with the Japanese.*

Answer: *I admit that I heard from Baksheev, Grigerman and Bendikov, at different times when I was in Harbin, that the Onikul family stood in good stead with the Japanese because they had links with the Japanese Gendarmerie. Apart from that, I know that Onikul's son-in-law, Zaretsky, who currently lives in Hailar, is*

> *a prominent cattle merchant, White bandit*
> *and, I heard he is a member of the Fascist Party.*
> *I don't know anything else about Onikul.*

I am astonished. This flimsy, unsubstantiated exchange was all the evidence the NKVD required to arrest and imprison all three Onikuls. Now I can see where the allegation about my grandfather came from. A fascist and a 'White bandit' to boot! Clearly, Panfilov never knew him.

From a file note written during the review of the Onikul cases in March 1956, I learn that Panfilov was arrested in Gorky on 22 May 1937. He was charged with involvement in counter-revolutionary organisations—the Russian Fascist Party and the Russian Student Society; and of being a Japanese spy, who had allegedly arrived in the USSR in 1935 with the purpose of espionage. On 16 October 1937, three days before he was interrogated about the Onikuls, Panfilov had already confessed to these charges. He was subsequently shot.

Panfilov's 'confession' made his evidence 'fact'. These 'facts' then provided the basis for subsequent interrogations of people from Hailar. The same names of alleged spies from Hailar come up again and again in the Onikul interrogations—Panfilov, Baksheev, Grigerman, Bendikov—along with the invention about Zaretsky.

In Manya's case, Panfilov's 'evidence' is compounded by that of another compatriot—the opera singer, Karmelinsky, described in her indictment as a 'Japanese spy'.

In an extract from his interrogation dated 28 November 1937, I find the strange allegations about Manya's involvement with the organisation he variously calls the 'Women's' or 'Shanghai' Studio:

> *... I know from my own life abroad that the 'Shanghai Studio' was an espionage organisation, which the White Guards used for various foreign consulates. In Gorky, Onikul M.G. [Manya] confirmed this herself in one of our conversations.*
>
> *Onikul, M.G. came to Gorky after I did. She sought me out in the theatre and after this, we met several times ... In one of our conversations, she asked me whether I knew what the 'Shanghai Studio' represented. I told her I did. She then told me that she had come to the USSR with a mission from this studio.*
>
> *Inviting me to visit their house more often, Onikul M.G. said that she wanted to link her espionage activities with mine. As I didn't know her very well and didn't want to expose myself to risk by being linked with her in espionage activity, I declined her proposition. Soon after that I left for the town of Kirov and never met Onikul M.G. again.*

In contrast, Manya mentions Karmelinsky only once, almost as a postscript at the very end of her final interrogation in December 1937. It was probably prompted by the interrogator to get Karmelinsky's name into Manya's record:

> *. . . I should add that among those who came to Gorky from Harbin, I also know Karmelinsky—I don't remember his name or patronymic. I met him in Gorky, where he worked at the opera theatre. When he lived in Harbin he also worked in the theatre and used to perform in various clubs around Manchukuo. When we met, we did not discuss anything out of the ordinary.*

Given that the Women's Studio was nothing more than a professional school, as I later discover, it seems bizarre that Karmelinsky's lurid allegation can serve as evidence against Manya.

Again, the critical factor that turned fiction into 'fact' was Karmelinsky's confession. A memo in Manya's file written in March 1956, when her case was being reviewed notes that Karmelinsky admitted to being a Japanese spy within a week of his arrest in August 1937. Karmelinsky may, in fact, have had little input into the 'evidence' on Manya. A broken and tormented man, he probably just signed what was put before him.

In December 1937, the Onikul cases resumed in earnest. The 'evidence' the interrogators had gathered from the Onikuls' compatriots provided a basis for their next questions. But confessions were what they were really after.

Manya's interrogation on 4 December begins where the first one in October left off—with her life in China. She talks about growing up in Hailar, studying dentistry in Harbin and returning to work in Hailar for a while before moving to Shanghai in 1933 and then to Vladivostok. Asked why she went to Shanghai, Manya explains that someone named Skuratov warned her she might be arrested if she stayed in Hailar and advised her to go to the USSR.

Question: Why didn't you go straight from Hailar to the USSR, but to Shanghai?

Answer: I didn't go to the USSR only because my parents did not have Soviet passports and I did not want to break ties with them. So I went to Shanghai.

Question: You are lying. We have evidence that the reason you went to Shanghai was that you did not want to go to the USSR. Do you confirm that?

Manya holds her ground. After a few questions about her stay in Shanghai and her journey to Vladivostok on the ship *Hua Shan*, the interrogator moves to explore Manya's relations with the people named by the confessed 'Japanese spy' Panfilov as Japanese agents in Hailar—Baksheev, Grigerman and Bendikov.

The interrogator presses Manya about Baksheev in particular. The name Baksheev is familiar to me. General Aleksei Baksheev was a Cossack leader who lived in Hailar and headed the Japanese-sponsored Bureau of Russian Émigrés Affairs (BREM) in 1937–38.

He was executed in Moscow as a Japanese collaborator after the Second World War. Chances are the Baksheev in question was a relative.

Manya says she knows that Andrey Baksheev used to work for the Whites. She also heard rumours in Hailar that he worked for Japanese intelligence. But she is careful: 'Whether or not Baksheev is an agent of Japanese intelligence, I personally don't know.' Manya says she met Baksheev once or twice. She cannot remember where—perhaps he came to buy milk—but she had never spoken to him.

As for Grigerman, Manya says she knew him from high school in Hailar, while Bendikov had been at school with her brother Abram. 'That's all I know about them. When I went to Shanghai, they both stayed in Hailar.' This comment on Bendikov is such a contrast to the tortured answers Driven had recorded in Manya's earlier falsified record.

The interrogator's last question for the session is about my grandfather Zaretsky being a member of the Fascist Party. This is the question which had so alarmed me when I first saw it in her file in Nizhny Novgorod. Manya denies the charge.

In her next interrogation two days later, on 6 December, the focus shifts to her life in the USSR. Manya briefly relates how she had spent time in Vladivostok and Moscow before coming to work in Gorky in April 1935. The interrogator moves quickly to what was probably one of the most uncomfortable questions Manya had to answer:

Who do you know among the Harbintsy *who came to Gorky?*

She must have known that this would give the NKVD a new list of victims—that is, if they had not been fingered already. Manya names two women she knows from Harbin—Leah and Vera—and two men she met at the GAZ, one of them a patient at the dental clinic. Each name in the record is followed by a brief pen portrait of the person, evidently based on Manya's responses to questions. It is impossible to know how many of the names Manya volunteered, and how many were thrown at her for comment.

Manya's last point about Leah is that she had not been aware of Leah's links with the Japanese Gendarmerie in Harbin. This is clearly a line the NKVD were pursuing. Leah was, in fact, arrested as 'an agent of foreign intelligence' the day before Manya. This I discover from the 1956 file note. In her interrogation, Leah describes Manya as a friend from Gorky and 'a dedicated Soviet citizen'. Leah was sentenced on 1 April 1938 to ten years in a corrective labour camp for 'counter-revolutionary activities'.

Yasha and his father Girsh were also interrogated on 6 December—both by a Sergeant Utkin, who I notice was present at Lieutenant Driven's interrogation of

Panfilov in October 1937. Utkin was clearly getting quite an exposure to the prisoners from Hailar.

He starts with the point Lieutenant Driven left hanging in October: What was Yasha's involvement with Japanese intelligence? Twice he accuses Yasha of being a Japanese agent who arrived in the USSR with orders for espionage. Twice Yasha rejects it.

Utkin then moves onto familiar ground—the names from Panfilov's 'evidence': Do you know Baksheev? Do you know the Grigerman brothers? Do you know Bendikov? Do you know Panfilov? Yasha says he knows them all from Hailar. He met Baksheev a number of times in the street; the Grigerman brothers, he knows socially; Panfilov, he knows from high school. As for Bendikov, Yasha says he knows him from Hailar and the USSR, and that Bendikov once came to visit him in Gorky.

Utkin goes back for another round:

Question: *The investigation is aware that you are an agent of Japanese intelligence and were on good terms with all the above-mentioned people, with whom you were linked in joint spying activities.*

Answer: *I repeat that I am not a Japanese intelligence agent and never had espionage links with any of these people.*

Question: *You continue to give false evidence, denying your involvement in the Japanese intelligence service. The investigation categorically proposes that you stop your obstinacy and give honest evidence.*

Answer: *I maintain that I was not recruited as a Japanese agent.*

Utkin changes tack: What relatives does Yasha have left in Harbin? Yasha lists them. Utkin continues:

Question   *Which of them belong to counter-revolutionary organisations?*

Answer: *None of my relatives belong to any counter-revolutionary organisations.*

Out comes the now familiar allegation that my grandfather, Zaretsky, is a member of the Russian Fascist Party (RFP).

Answer: *Whether or not Zaretsky is a member of the RFP, I don't know.*

Utkin gives up on Yasha. Clearly no confession is forthcoming.

———•◦•———

The same day, Sergeant Utkin interrogates Girsh, the sixty-two-year-old father of the family. His interrogation starts with Girsh's relations with the 'military-political police' in Manchuria. With whom did he have close relations? Girsh names Ivanov and a couple of others who worked for the Japanese Gendarmerie in Hailar. He says they came to his house on a couple of occasions. After the Japanese Gendarmerie started arresting Soviet citizens in 1935, Girsh paid them off in order to avoid arrest.

But Utkin isn't satisfied. He insists that these were not the only people linked to the Gendarmerie with whom Girsh had close relations. He demands Girsh answer the charge.

Answer: *I confess that I failed to mention the former police inspector Kharitonov . . .*

This is a name from Girsh's very first record of interrogation. Kharitonov was the policeman who helped free him from 'arrest'—or more accurately kidnap—by Baron Ungern's troops back in 1919, thirteen years before the Japanese took over the military police in Manchuria. One can understand Girsh forgetting to name him. But his use of the words 'I confess' seems indicative of a weakened spirit.

Another 'confession' comes in answer to the next question. Asked to name people with whom he had 'close relations' from the White Army, Girsh lists five, among them Andrey Baksheev, who, according to Manya's testimony, may have come to their house to buy milk.

'All these people are fascists,' says Utkin.

'I have to confess that all these people are fascists,' Girsh repeats.

After a brief detour into what Girsh was doing while living in Hailar and which of his relatives remain there,

Utkin returns to the Japanese Gendarmerie. Was Girsh arrested by them before his departure for the USSR? Out comes an extraordinary tale.

Girsh tells of being arrested by the Japanese Gendarmerie at Manchuria Station, the last station before the Soviet border. He was kept under arrest for eight or ten hours and his passport detained for two days. While in detention he was asked questions of a personal nature. They were particularly interested to know where he was going. Why? Which relatives remained in Harbin and Hailar? After giving 'exhaustive answers', Girsh was released.

Question: *Did you sign the record of your interrogation?*
Answer: *Yes I did.*
Question: *Who interrogated you?*
Answer: *I was interrogated by one of the military police, a Japanese.*
Question: *What language was the record written in?*
Answer: *The record was written in Japanese.*
Question: *Can you read Japanese?*
Answer: *No, I don't know Japanese.*
Question: *So you signed a record of interrogation without reading it and not knowing what was written in it?*
Answer: *Yes, I signed the record without reading it.*

Girsh's scratchy signature sits at the end of the line. Underneath is Sergeant Utkin's bold one. The construct Utkin is building is becoming clear.

At Girsh's next interrogation, the following day, Utkin makes it explicit.

Question: *The investigation has established that, during the time you were under arrest at Manchuria Station, you were recruited as a Japanese intelligence agent and received orders for espionage. The investigation proposes that you give frank and detailed evidence about your recruitment as a Japanese agent and the orders you received.*

Answer: *I have to confess that, during my arrest at Manchuria Station, the Japanese policeman proposed that I undertake espionage work for them in the USSR. After I rejected his proposition, he threatened that he would not let me leave Manchuria. In response to his threat, I agreed to spy for them and to carry out all the orders I was given.*

This is the answer that seals Girsh's fate. It is underlined in red and sidelined in the margin.

The scenario that follows reads like a script from a bad 1930s spy movie. Girsh says he told the Japanese police that he was going to live in Gorky, where his son and daughter worked at the big automobile factory. The Japanese instructed him to collect information about the factory including what it produced apart from cars. Girsh's main task was to receive Japanese agents sent into the USSR. He was told he would recognise them by the password, 'I bring you regards from my daughter'. He was then to pass on the information he collected.

Girsh admits that he signed an agreement, but cannot say what was in it because it was written in Japanese. Which agents came to see him in Gorky? None other than Bendikov! What information did Girsh give Bendikov during his visit? None. He had not yet had a chance to gather any material.

Perhaps it is true. Perhaps Girsh *had* been arrested by the Japanese Gendarmerie at Manchuria Station. Perhaps he *had* agreed to their proposition in order to get out of Manchuria, knowing full well that once he was across the border, he would be out of their control. But it seems unlikely.

Girsh was travelling with his wife, Chesna, and all their possessions. If they had been arrested and detained for three days, the Onikuls would have had to unload all their goods from the train and to find accommodation. Manchuria was a town where they had friends. There was also a Soviet consulate. The story would have filtered back down the line to Hailar in a matter of days, and eventually found its way to Harbin.

But no-one had ever heard it. When Chesna was asked about arrests by the Japanese during her interrogation in July 1938, she made no mention of it. Even more telling is the fact that her investigators did not raise it with her either.

So how did Sergeant Utkin get Girsh's confession? Was Girsh beaten? Was he tortured? Did Utkin present him with the record, written in advance and appeal to his sense of honour—promising the old man that his wife and children would be spared if he confessed. Was Manya tortured before his eyes or did the interrogator simply threaten to do so to the sound of anguished screams from the room next door?

The exchange in the record about the family suggests the family connection may have been one of the weapons used:

Question: *Did your sons and daughter know that you were a Japanese agent?*

Answer: *I can't say whether anyone in my family knew that I was a Japanese agent because I did not tell any of them about this. But it is possible that one of them may have suspected.*

I try to imagine Sergent Utkin. Was he young and awkward, the khaki trousers of his uniform tucked into highly polished boots, shouting and full of bravado to conceal his ignorance and fear? Perhaps he was middle-aged and dishevelled, smelling strongly of vodka, which he drank to dull his sense of what he had become. The image of Girsh I see more clearly: a tired old man with blood seeping from the wounds on his head. Physically abused and emotionally harangued, his hand shook as he signed the absurd record:

Recorded from my words accurately. Read by me.

Onikul

After that, there were no more interrogations for any of the Onikuls. The NKVD had extracted the confession they were after.

⬧━⬧

Indictments on all three Onikuls were finalised by the Gorky NKVD's Directorate of State Security (UGB) within three days of Girsh's confession. Each one was signed off by Driven and Primilsky of the NKVD's Third Department and authorised by Gorky NKVD chief Lavrushin and the regional procurator. The accusation against each of them was identical. Each was charged that:

> ... *while living in Hailar [in Girsh's case, Harbin], [he/she] was recruited as an agent of Japanese intelligence and was sent to the USSR with the purpose of espionage——i.e. crimes pertaining to Section 58.6 of the Criminal Code of the RSFSR.*

In each case, the NKVD's investigation established certain facts. Common to all three is that, while living in Hailar, they had 'close relations with White émigré-fascists and employees of the Japanese intelligence service'—variously Baksheev, Bendikov, Grigerman. All three Onikuls had been 'exposed' by the 'evidence of the executed spy, Panfilov' and in Manya's case, also that of 'Japanese intelligence agent Karmelinsky'. Girsh's indictment says he 'admitted his guilt totally'. Yasha and Manya's note that they had not.

The facts 'established' in the individual indictments are spurious. Manya's highlights four points: her 'close relations with the prominent Japanese agent recruiter Baksheev' in Hailar; her 'membership of the Women's Studio at the fascist newspaper *Zarya* in Shanghai; her 'written correspondence with the fascist and prominent Harbin livestock merchant, Zaretsky'; and her links with 'Japanese agents, Bendikov and Karmelinsky'.

Highlighted in Yasha's case are the statements that he was 'a stateless émigré' until 1935 and that his brother-in-law, Zaretsky, was allegedly a member of the 'Russian Fascist Party'. He was also linked with alleged Japanese agents in the USSR, including Bendikov and others, whose names had not even appeared in his records of interrogation. Curiously, the brief biography of Yasha in the indictment refers to him as 'a former UGB agent—a double agent'.

Girsh's indictment reflects the absurdity of his confession.

Considering the charges proved, the Gorky NKVD's UGB referred all three matters to the UGB of the NKVD of the USSR for priority review. A month later, the verdicts were returned. By order of a Special Session of the NKVD of the USSR, on 7 January, Manya and her father were sentenced—'to be shot'. Three days later Yasha was sentenced to ten years in a corrective labour camp. The sentences were authorised at the highest level by Yezhov, the People's Commissar of Internal Affairs and Vyshinsky, the Procurator of the USSR.

Manya and her father were executed on 14 January 1938.

In Victor Herman's book, I find a description of the execution ritual. Four executioners clad in black leather with straps crisscrossed over their chests arrive in the dead of night to walk the accused from their cell to the prison yard. Three carry bayonets pointing upwards, one carries a revolver pointing to the ground. Rubber gag pushed into the mouth, the accused is made to kneel on the ground. Then, against the noise of backfiring automobiles, the executioner with the revolver shoots a bullet into the prisoner's head.

CHAPTER 8

THE RAVENS RETURN

Dearest Mama
How happy I was today to receive your postcard after
4 months' silence. You can't imagine how hard it's been.
Just those couple of words from you have livened me up
enormously . . . We are all well. Motya is working as
before. I am busy with housekeeping and with Inna. She
is studying hard and is a good ice-skater . . . In general,
everything is fine but I worry that you write so rarely.
Please have Papa write a few words too . . .

When my grandmother, Gita, sent this postcard from
Harbin to her mother Chesna in Gorky in December
1937, she had no idea what had happened in the four
months since Chesna's last letter. But she sensed that all
was not right with her father. She noted the new return
address on her mother's card—Kirov Street, rather than

Oktyabrskaya Street—and addressed hers accordingly. Still, the card never got to Chesna.

Intercepted at the Gorky Avtozavod post office on 20 December 1937, the yellow *Carte Postale* with Manchukuo stamps lay buried in the NKVD's files until it was released to me in 1992 by the Ministry of Security of Nizhny Novgorod. With it is another card from Gita to Chesna, dated 26 May 1938. It refers to letters various relatives in Harbin had received from Chesna that month. Obviously some mail was still getting through. Again the message ends with the plaintive line: 'Please ask Papa and the children to write a few lines. I am worried.'

Gita's second postcard was intercepted at Gorky on 10 June 1938. Just three days earlier, an investigation file on Chesna was opened at the Gorky NKVD by the same Lieutenant Driven who played the key role in the investigations of Chesna's husband and children. Like them, Chesna was to be arrested for espionage under Article 58.6.

On 14 June 1938, the 'black raven' stopped at the Tsirlin apartment in Kirov Street, where Chesna and Sanya had been staying since their eviction from Oktyabrskaya Street after the arrest of the others. Chesna told my mother later that she knew it had come for her. She was just surprised it had taken so long. Chesna was taken to Gorky Prison, to the same *Spets Korpus* where her loved ones had been held. In the eight months since the arrest of her family, not much had changed.

Some things, however, were different. Where the others endured several interrogations, in Chesna's file, I find only one brief record. It is dated 20 June 1938, six days after her arrest. The questions are straightforward: When and why did Chesna go to Harbin? What work did she do there? When did she take Soviet citizenship?

Chesna explains how her husband intended to follow his brother to Harbin in 1909, but ended up in Hailar. She followed Girsh directly to Hailar, where they lived until 1936. She did not work but was supported by her husband. On citizenship, Chesna's answer reads: 'Before 1935, I, like everyone else in my family, was a Chinese citizen. We took Soviet citizenship in 1936 . . .' Yasha's interrogator recorded him as saying he was a 'stateless émigré'. Neither is true. The family had originally come to Manchuria on Tsarist Russian passports and taken Soviet citizenship in the late 1920s or early 1930s.

Asked to name close friends in Hailar, Chesna replies that she didn't have many friends and visited people infrequently. Nevertheless, the interrogator lists the names of a few people Chesna allegedly 'knew well among the Russians'—her next door neighbours, the Spirkins; and Ivanov, a Hailar policeman who bought Girsh's harmonium before their departure from Hailar. Almost as an afterthought—probably prompted by her interrogator—Chesna adds:

Apart from them, I knew as a person, Bendikov, who went to school with my son Abram. But Bendikov went to the USSR in 1935. After we arrived in Gorky, Bendikov dropped by our apartment at the beginning of 1937, though I was not home as I had gone to Moscow. He did not visit us again.

Bendikov had, in fact, been arrested in November 1936. But establishing an association between Chesna and Bendikov, however garbled, was clearly important to the interrogator's case.

The two final questions are about the Japanese:

Question: *Were you repressed by the Japanese while living in Hailar?*

Answer: *No.*

Question: *At the time of your departure for the Soviet Union, were you recruited by Japanese intelligence for espionage work in the USSR?*

Answer: *No-one ever recruited me for espionage activities. There is nothing more I can say on this question.*

And that is the end of the interrogation. Twenty years later in Harbin, Chesna told my mother how two *chekists* tried to make her confess by throwing her, a frail fifty-seven-year-old woman, backwards and forwards between them for a whole night. She did not give in. Her denial that she was recruited by the Japanese at the time of her departure from Hailar stands in sharp contrast to Girsh's agonised confession. The fact that the interrogator does not pursue the point also refutes its veracity.

Chesna's indictment is similar in form to the ones I

read in the other Onikul files. But hers is an extremely sloppy document. Undated, it is full of factual inaccuracies and errors in terms of dates and place names. There is no mention at all of Hailar—it has become Harbin. The indictment charges that Chesna:

> ... *while living in Harbin, mixed in White émigré circles until 1935; was a Chinese citizen. Arriving in the USSR in 1935, Onikul established close links with those sentenced to the 1st category as agents of Japanese intelligence, ie. crimes pertaining to Section 58.6 of the Criminal Code ...*
>
> *She did not admit her guilt to the charges, but did confirm her links with the Harbin policeman, Ivanov.*

As supporting evidence, the indictment mentions Chesna's 'close relations with White émigré and Japanese agents, Bendikov and Ivanov'; the fact that her daughter and son-in-law Zaretsky still live in Harbin where he is a member of the 'counter-revolutionary Russian Fascist Party'. It notes that her husband Girsh, 'a Harbin businessman', is a confessed Japanese agent, who, along with her daughter, was sentenced to 'the first category' (ie. execution), while her son was sentenced to ten years imprisonment.

Like the earlier Onikul indictments, Chesna's is authorised by Major Lavrushin, the NKVD chief of the Gorky region and countersigned by the procurator. Handwritten in bold pencil under Lavrushin's name is a four-word recommendation:

Exile 5 years Kazakhstan

A nondescript half-page document contains Chesna's sentence. It is headed:

Extract from decree No 36
Meeting of the Special Troika of the Gorky Regional
Directorate of the NKVD of 20 October 1938.

On the right-hand side of the page it sets out the case heard against Chesna and notes that her husband had been convicted as a Japanese spy. On the left-hand side it reads:

Decreed:
Onikul, Chesna Abramovna, is to be exiled to Kazakhstan for a term of five (5) years, commencing from 14 June 1938. To be deported by convoy to exile in the city of Alma Ata.

These 'Special Troikas' were three-man tribunals, empowered to administer summary justice at a regional level, bypassing the usual legal procedures. Troikas had been introduced by the regime during various times of crisis, including the Civil War and the collectivisation campaign in the 1930s. They had been re-established in mid-1937 to expedite sentencing from the mass arrests across the USSR. Each troika was headed by the regional NKVD chief and had a representative from the Party Committee and the Procuracy. This meant that in Gorky, the head of the troika was the same Major Lavrushin who had authorised Chesna's indictment. Not surprisingly, he had accepted his own recommendation.

———•••———

On 14 June 1938, the day of Chesna's arrest, her twenty-two-year-old nephew, Sanya, was sacked from his job as an electrician in the mechanical workshop at the GAZ. In his record of interrogation, I read how Sanya returned to work from a rostered day off to find he had been 'dismissed'. An accident had occurred during his absence with one of the machines in his service area. This, he was told, demonstrated his 'negligent attitude towards his responsibilities'.

The number of 'accidents' in Soviet enterprises had risen sharply in the late 1930s under the strain of ever-increasing targets. But these could not be put down to a failure with the system, poor materials or faulty workmanship. As Stalin's trusted Commissar for Transportation, Lazar Kaganovich, put it in 1937: 'Each accident at an enterprise has its own name, patronymic and surname'. This one was Isaac Naumovich Onikul.

Two weeks later, on 27 June, Sanya was arrested and taken to Gorky Prison—to the same *Spets Korpus* where the others had been held. The charge against him was that he came to the USSR from Harbin to conduct espionage and 'wrecking' activities under Article 58.6.

From his indictment, it emerges that Sanya's fate was sealed by the 'evidence' of a man from Harbin named

Chudner, who had himself been arrested as a Japanese spy. A very long extract from Chudner's record of interrogation on 8 June 1938 appears in Sanya's file. Its polemical language and wild assertions remind me of the other fabricated records I have seen in Manya's file. Though Chudner says he only met Sanya in Gorky, there is no angle about him that he does not cover.

Chudner starts with Sanya's life in Manchuria, painting it in vivid detail and anti-Soviet colours, which bear scant resemblance to reality. He describes Sanya's parents as prominent émigré cattle merchants who mixed with 'White bandit traders'. He says that in Harbin, Sanya attended the Commercial High School, had many anti-Soviet friends in Zionist and émigré circles and spent most of his free time at the synagogue or Zionist club. In Hailar too, Chudner alleges, most of Sanya's friends belonged to 'White bandit' organisations. Even my grandfather Zaretsky, whom Chudner says Sanya admired, has lost his previous 'fascist' label and become 'a prominent White bandit'.

Though Chudner claims he and Sanya were 'firm friends' since both had relatives arrested by the NKVD, he has no qualms about relating alleged comments by Sanya that in Stalin's time were tantamount to treason—comparing life in the USSR unfavourably with his former life in Harbin and saying 'his relatives, who were arrested as enemies of the people, were innocent, while those who arrested them were guilty'.

Though he did not work with Sanya, Chudner says he had heard from 'a student' that Sanya had a negative attitude to work and that his carelessness with equipment had caused a number of accidents and explosions. As he knows Sanya to be a 'competent electrician', Chudner suggests these incidents must have been acts of deliberate sabotage, reflecting Sanya's 'hatred towards the USSR'. His conclusion is that Sanya had been 'trained by the Whites in Manchuria for subversive activities in the USSR or, at the very least, as someone who at the appropriate time could always become a Japanese agent'.

In Sanya's file, I also find two statements the NKVD obtained from his superiors to support their case about Sanya's 'subversive' activities at the GAZ. They are far from conclusive. One of them describes Sanya as 'a suspicious character', referring to three accidents which occurred over two years while he was on duty. The other describes the accident for which Sanya was sacked as 'not a big deal in itself, but one that *could have* led to an explosion'.

What did Sanya himself have to say on the matters in question? As in Chesna's case, his file contains just a single record of interrogation. Prepared by the same investigator, it is dated July 1938 with no day filled in. In the biographical section, Sanya tells how, after finishing school in Hailar, he went to study at the Technicum in Harbin. After the Japanese closed it down, he came to Gorky in August 1935 at the suggestion of his cousin, Manya, who wrote to tell him he could get a job at the GAZ and also study.

Asked about the social position of his parents, Sanya explains that his father was a small cattle agent and his mother sold dairy products from their rented house. Curiously, on the question of citizenship, he says that before taking Soviet citizenship in 1935, he and his family were all Chinese citizens. This is the same line I had seen in Chesna's interrogation. Once again, it is untrue.

Chudner's 'evidence' against Sanya provides the script for the NKVD interrogator as he moves into the accusations. Starting with Sanya's alleged association with White émigrés and Zionist youth, which Sanya denies, the interrogator builds one accusation on top of the other:

Question: *Mixing among White émigré youth in Harbin and having counter-revolutionary inclinations, you came to the USSR to conduct counter-revolutionary subversive activities. Tell the investigation about this.*

Answer: *I already said I had no contact with White émigré youth and was never involved in counter-revolutionary subversive activities. I came to the USSR to continue my education and to work.*

Question: *You are lying. You came to the USSR to conduct subversive counter-revolutionary espionage work, which you did at the Avtozavod. Give evidence on this question.*

Answer: *I repeat that I was never involved in any subversive activities at the Avtozavod.*

Question: *You were recruited as an agent of Japanese intelligence and sent to the USSR to conduct subversive-espionage activities. For this reason*

> *you contacted one of the Japanese agents in*
> *Gorky, Onikul M.G. [Manya], and conducted*
> *your enemy activities at the Avtozavod. Give*
> *evidence.*

Answer: *I was never recruited by anyone for subversive*
espionage activities. I came to stay with Maria
Grigorievna Onikul because she was my relative.

The interrogator gives up. Clearly no confession would be forthcoming.

Asked whom he knows among the *Harbintsy* in Gorky, Sanya names Chudner and another man, both of whom he met in 1936 at the Engineers and Technicians Club at the GAZ. He says he did not know them in Harbin and saw them only three times in Gorky. Their conversations had mainly been about work and study and had never touched on any political issues. It is hardly the 'firm' friendship Chudner had described.

Sanya's indictment, which is undated, charges that:

> *... while living in Harbin, he was recruited for espionage*
> *activities and sent to the USSR with orders for subversive*
> *activities and espionage in the interests of Japan.*

It notes that Sanya has not admitted his guilt, but that the case against him is proven by the evidence of the 'Japanese agent' Chudner and the statements of his superiors at the GAZ.

The rest of the document is a complete jumble of errors and untruths. It alleges that Sanya's parents in

Hailar are still Chinese citizens, linked to 'Japanese espionage circles' through my grandfather Zaretsky, an 'active member of the Russian Fascist Party in Harbin' who is now described as 'their son-in-law'. It says Sanya arrived in the USSR 'together with' Yasha, Girsh and Manya, who were all convicted as Japanese spies; and that he established links with a number of other Japanese spies, including Bendikov, a name which had never appeared in Sanya's interrogation. Clearly the 'evidence' uncovered in the earlier Onikul cases was now being extended here.

Sanya's sentence issued by the Special Troika of the Gorky Directorate is dated 20 October 1938:

Onikul, Isaac Naumovich—TO BE SHOT
Personal effects TO BE CONFISCATED.

Underneath is a handwritten note:

Shot 5 October 1938 in Gorky

Perhaps it is a slip of the pen and is meant to read 5 November. But the possibility that Sanya was in fact shot before the sentence was issued is not inconceivable.

Either way, it is indicative of the chaos in which the NKVD was operating and the arbitrary way they dealt with people's lives. By mid-1938, more people were being arrested than the interrogation system could cope with. Camps and prisons were overflowing. The Terror was out of control.

By the end of the year, action to restore order was taken at the highest Party and government level. On 17 November 1938, the Communist Party's Central Committee and the government's Council of People's Commissars issued a joint resolution on 'arrests, procuratorial supervision and the conduct of investigations', whose text has become available in the post-Soviet period.

Distributed widely among NKVD, Procuracy and Party officials across the USSR, it is a damning document. The resolution acknowledges that during 1937–38, the NKVD made significant inroads to inflict a 'crushing defeat on enemies of the people' and 'agents of foreign intelligence services, who had infiltrated the USSR from abroad in great numbers'. Among these, it specifically mentions 'Harbintsy'. But the resolution goes on to say that because 'simplified investigative and trial procedures' were used in the NKVD's mass operations, the NKVD had been penetrated by enemies of the people and foreign spies who were 'consciously perverting Soviet laws and carrying out mass unjustified arrests'.

The 'deficiencies' for which the NKVD is criticised include mass arrests conducted without proper investigation; extracting confessions out of prisoners without obtaining corroborating evidence; sloppy records of interrogations written as summaries well after the conclusion of the investigation; omitting testimony which might refute any facts in the indictment; and records undated and unsigned by one or other party. I had noticed many of these 'deficiencies' in the Onikul files. For its part, the Soviet procuracy is criticised for not taking action to stop these 'violations of revolutionary legality' and simply rubber-stamping NKVD decisions.

The resolution orders that mass arrests are to cease and special troikas to be abolished. The Procuracy would henceforth sanction all NKVD arrests and supervise all investigations, which were to be conducted strictly in accordance with the Criminal Trial Code. Those who failed to comply would be severely punished.

This resolution struck at the very heart of the NKVD. No matter that the Terror of 1937–38 had been sanctioned, if not ordered, by the Communist Party's supreme body, the Politburo. There had been excesses. Now the Politburo was taking control. It did not mean that the Terror would end—but it would become more orderly.

NKVD chief Nikolai Yezhov, the chief architect of the repression, received the blame. Within a week of the decree's issue, Yezhov had resigned and was replaced by Stalin's man from Georgia, Lavrenty Beria. In April 1939, Yezhov was arrested and accused of spying. He was executed a year later. Meanwhile, the 18th Communist Party Congress, held in March 1939, officially repudiated the 'excesses' of the purges.

With Yezhov's fall came the removal of all his deputies, department heads and close associates. Documents I find in the Onikul files from the 1950s show that the key figures from the Gorky NKVD, who had presided over most of the investigations—Lavrushin, Primilsky and Driven—were all convicted as 'enemies of the people' for 'violation of Socialist legality'. According to one of the volumes about the purges which I was given at the Nizhny archive, Gorky's regional NKVD chief, Lavrushin, was executed in 1940 and Primilsky, the deputy of the counter-intelligence department, was sentenced to ten years imprisonment. Driven was not sufficiently senior to have his fate recorded in official publications.

One would think that following this exposure of the NKVD's gross transgressions, measures would be taken to somehow make amends to the victims of this massive miscarriage of justice. At the very least, those unjustly condemned and incarcerated in prisons and labour camps of the Soviet Gulag should have been immediately released and compensated, and those already dead be rehabilitated.

It did not happen. Too many thousands had been shot already and it would have been difficult to release so many witnesses of the NKVD's illegal practices without admitting Stalin's monstrous crimes. Nevertheless, some cases were reopened and reassessed in the post-Yezhov period. I discover from my great-grandmother Chesna's file that hers was one of them.

In April 1939, just as Comrade Yezhov was arrested, Chesna's case was under review by two bodies—the

Gorky NKVD's newly created Investigations Branch and the office of the regional procurator. Each concluded that there was no case to link her to espionage activity under Article 58.6. Under the circumstances, each decreed that 'pursuant to Article 204 of the Criminal Trial Code', the case against Chesna be dropped and that she be 'immediately released from detention'. This decision, confirmed by the head of the Gorky NKVD, was passed on to the head of Gorky Prison.

But Chesna was unlucky in her timing. She had unfortunately left Gorky Prison quite some time ago. In December 1938, she was deported 'by convoy' to serve out her five years exile in the central Asian republic of Kazakhstan. Years later she described to my mother how one day, without explanation or warning, she was taken from Gorky Prison, wearing the same clothes in which she had been arrested six months earlier. Packed with other prisoners into a stinking cattle car masquerading as a goods wagon, she had endured the gruelling rail journey from Gorky to the Kazakh capital of Alma Ata, with little food and practically no water.

From the pages and pages of internal NKVD correspondence in Chesna's file, it is clear that the Gorky NKVD was faced with a real problem as some of the regulations laid down by the joint resolution of 17 November 1938 had been contravened. The saga I read in the correspondence gives an insight into the massive bureaucratic buck-passing and bungling that occurred as the Soviet machinery of repression shifted gear.

Chesna had been sentenced to five years exile by a Special Troika in October 1938. However, by the time she was advised of the troika's sentence two months later, troikas had been abolished by the joint resolution. The Gorky NKVD explained this situation to NKVD central headquarters in Moscow in a memorandum in June 1939. They had apparently advised Gorky Prison that Chesna's sentence should not be implemented, while advice was sought from the appropriate agencies on how her case should be handled in the context of new NKVD procedures.

Unfortunately, by the time Gorky Prison received this request, Chesna had already been deported 'into the jurisdiction of the NKVD in Alma Ata'. Gorky NKVD asked Moscow central to confirm the Investigations Branch's decision that the case against Chesna be dropped and that she be released. They also asked Moscow to issue an order to the Alma Ata NKVD to release Chesna immediately.

Moscow NKVD did just that, adding that, in the event of Chesna being moved to another settlement, Alma Ata NKVD was to forward the order to the appropriate location. On 13 August, the NKVD in Alma Ata sent a memo marked 'Urgent—Release' to the NKVD in the town of Kzyl-Orda, in southern Kazakhstan. It said simply:

We are forwarding the decree of the Gorky NKVD regarding the release from detention of Onikul C.A. for implementation.

But the NKVD in Kzyl-Orda would have nothing of it. On 21 August, they sent a memo to the NKVD chief in Gorky confirming that Chesna was serving the term prescribed in her original sentence in a place called Zhosaly. They refused to accept Gorky NKVD's revised decision of April 1939 as a basis for Chesna's release from detention because they had no advice 'that the earlier sentence had been revoked'.

For Chesna, things went downhill from there. In September 1939, the Gorky NKVD chief decreed that after a second review of her case, the troika's sentence was to be left in force and Chesna was to remain in Kazakhstan. The decision of April 1939 ordering her release was to be regarded as 'inoperative'.

Somewhere along the line, Chesna found out about the April 1939 decision ordering her release. In her file, I find two letters of appeal which she wrote by hand on pages torn out of an exercise book in April 1940. One is addressed to the Gorky NKVD chief; the other to the NKVD in Moscow. Referring to earlier correspondence, Chesna's letter to the NKVD in Moscow reads:

As I consider myself to be guilty of nothing, I appealed to the Supreme Soviet and to you. The answer I got from both places was that I only needed to appeal to the Procurator of the Gorky Region, which is what I did. As I received no written reply, my relative [probably Fanya Klebanova] went to see him personally. He told her that I had been freed as of 9 April 1939. As I have still not been advised of this, I am appealing to you to take account of

*my situation—alone in my declining years, ill and helpless
and in a remote region—and to issue the directive which
is in your power about my release.*

Her letter to the Gorky NKVD is even more succinct:

*According to information from your investigator,
Comrade Nikolaev, I was freed by a decision of 9 April
1939. Regardless of this, I have still not been informed
of this decision and remain in exile in Kazakhstan at
Zhosaly. I request that you issue a directive about my
release.*

Chesna's appeal sent the Moscow NKVD into a flurry.
Clearly not everyone had been advised that the decision
to release her had been overturned. One memo went out
questioning why Chesna was still in detention a year
after they had instructed Alma Ata to let her go. Another
confirmed that, after a second review of Chesna's case,
the April 1939 decision about her release was to lapse and
the sentence of the troika to remain in place.

What brought about this turn of events? Why did the
NKVD apparatchik in provincial Kzyl-Orda decide to
challenge the order from Moscow to release a tired old
woman? What made the Gorky NKVD chief counter-
mand a decision by his own organisation and the regional
procurator which he had sanctioned earlier? Perhaps this
was an instance where the machinery of processing political prisoners was still rolling to old production schedules
too cumbersome to stop? Maybe too much time had

passed and it was easier to simply leave Chesna where she was? Or was it that her husband's confession and the conviction of her children as Japanese spies had caught up with her?

Whatever the reason, Chesna paid the price. She served out her five-year sentence in the town of Zhosaly, alone in the hot and dusty steppes of Kazakhstan, digging potatoes from dawn till dusk until her hands were numb. By June 1943, she had done her time.

But bad timing caught Chesna again. With the Soviet Union at war, political prisoners were forced to remain in confinement, even if they had completed their sentences. So Chesna stayed in exile for another two years.

Years later, her relatives asked her how she survived it all.

'A human being is stronger than stone,' she replied.

CHAPTER 9

'ALL HARBINTSY ARE SUBJECT TO ARREST'

I HAVE LONG been familiar with the fate of the millions of Russians who perished as victims of Stalin's 'Great Terror'. I remember struggling with the Russian version of Aleksandr Solzhenitsyn's *Gulag Archipelago* at university in the early 1970s. As a student of Soviet politics, I was appalled by the horror of it all, but never thought to draw a direct link with my own family. The Terror was something that happened to 'them—over there'. We were different. We were 'Russians from China'.

While at university, the poem 'Requiem' by Anna Akhmatova, one of Russia's greatest poets, left an indelible imprint on my mind. It gave voice to the numbed grief of all the women standing in lines for hours outside prisons across the USSR, lips blue from cold, waiting to hand over parcels for loved ones whose fate they did not know. But I never connected such images with the grief of my great-grandmother, Chesna. Now I know that she too had stood in lines at Gorky Prison until she ended up on the inside herself.

When I started reading Eugenia Ginsburg's book, *Journey Into the Whirlwind*, about her eighteen years in Stalin's prisons and Siberian labour camps, I found it so gripping, I could not put it down. But did I relate it to the journeys of Yasha and Chesna or perhaps Abram? Not for a minute. I saw the references Ginsburg and Solzhenitsyn made to people from the Chinese Eastern Railway (CER) in Manchuria being arrested as Japanese spies but these too left no personal impact. After all, none of my relatives had ever worked on the railway.

Some twenty years later, when I discover that the Onikuls were arrested and punished as Japanese spies, I struggle to understand the reasons. Why had these people, who had gone to the Soviet Union as loyal citizens, full of hope for the future, been pinned with such a label? From what I know, they had in fact left Manchuria because their life had become too difficult under the Japanese occupation. What in their behaviour could have made them 'enemies of the people', 'traitors', 'Japanese spies', I wonder?

I keep looking for logic where there is none. In Nadezhda Mandelstam's memoir of the purges, *Hope Against Hope,* there is a passage which quotes Anna Akhmatova's reaction to friends who, hearing about yet another arrest of a friend or acquaintance, continually ask, 'What for?':

What do you mean 'what for'? It's time you understood that people are arrested for nothing!

Perhaps I should pay more attention to these lines.

Nevertheless, a pattern seemed to be emerging. When I started asking other Russians from China about relatives or friends who had gone to the Soviet Union in the mid-1930s, I heard that most of the 'returnees' had been caught in the purges. For a long time, information was scant. In many cases, people had simply 'disappeared'. Some had been arrested and sent to labour camps; this often had to be deduced from cryptic messages such as, 'uncle has gone on a long vacation in Siberia'. Still others died mysteriously. On the rare occasion that official explanations for death were given to relatives in the Soviet Union, it was invariably attributed to 'heart failure' or 'lobar pneumonia'.

Only when survivors started to emerge from the camps after Stalin's death did they start to tell of *Harbintsy* and other Russians from China being shot or sent to labour camps as 'Japanese spies'. Clearly this was linked to the fact that the Japanese were occupying Manchuria. But what was behind it?

The answer lies in Operational Order No 00593, issued by NKVD chief Nikolai Yezhov on 20 September 1937. With the collapse of the Soviet Union, this order was uncovered in the depths of the archives of the Ministry of Security in Moscow in the early 1990s. Its text was first published by Memorial in Moscow in the early 1990s and picked up by the Russian émigré press around the world some time later. [See page 449 for full text.]

The order relates specifically to 'so-called *Harbintsy*'. In Russian, the word *Harbintsy* simply means 'people from Harbin', used in the same way as 'New Yorker' or 'Muscovite'. But in his order, Yezhov redefined it to mean all 'former employees of the Chinese Eastern Railway and returnees from Manchukuo'. A preamble, written in his name, notes that some 25,000 *Harbintsy* had arrived in the USSR and were working in railway transport and industry. It goes on:

> *Operational intelligence materials have revealed that the overwhelming majority of* Harbintsy *who have arrived in the USSR are former White officers, police, gendarmes and members of various émigré fascist spy organisations etc. The overwhelming majority of them are agents of the Japanese intelligence services, which over a number of years, has sent them to the USSR to conduct terrorist, subversive and espionage activities.*
>
> *... In railroad transport and industry, for example, some 4,500* Harbintsy *have been repressed for terrorist, subversive and espionage activities over the last year. Investigations of these cases have revealed a carefully planned and executed operation by Japanese intelligence to organise on Soviet territory a subversive-espionage base from among the* Harbintsy...

Yezhov instigated a comprehensive operation to liquidate all such 'agents', starting on 1 October 1937.

'All *Harbintsy* are subject to arrest', the order states. It could have stopped there. But it goes on to elaborate thirteen categories, so comprehensive that they could apply to any Russian who had ever lived in Manchuria or elsewhere in China.

The first category covers all those working in transport or industry who had been 'exposed or suspected of committing terrorist, subversive, espionage and wrecking activities'. Then all the obvious political categories are listed: former Whites who had arrived during the Civil War and who served in the White armies, former members of anti-Soviet political parties, Trotskyists, members of émigré fascist organisations. Bracketed in this last category are groups ranging from the truly reactionary like the Black Ring or the Brotherhood of Russian Truth to ones that were simply anti-Soviet, like the Russian Student Organisation and even the YMCA.

Other categories include employees of the Chinese police and armed forces—both before and after the Japanese occupation of Manchuria; those who previously had Chinese citizenship; owners and co-owners of various enterprises in Harbin—'restaurants, hotels, garages, etc'; employees of foreign companies—primarily Japanese, but also White Guard firms'. Singled out by name is the well-known Churin Company, whose Harbin department stores had been established well before the 1917 Bolshevik Revolution.

The arrests of the *Harbintsy* were to take place in two steps. First to be arrested were all those working in the NKVD, the Red Army, transport sectors, defence and strategic industries and the electrical power plants of all industrial enterprises. Second were all other

Harbintsy working in Soviet establishments, state and collective farms. Any *Harbintsy* working in the transport sector and industrial enterprises who managed to escape arrest were to be immediately sacked. Investigations of those arrested were to be carried out as a matter of urgency.

The order prescribed two levels of punishment for arrested *Harbintsy*. All those involved in 'subversive-espionage, terrorist, wrecking and anti-Soviet activities' fell into the first category. They were 'to be shot'. All other, 'less active *Harbintsy*', were to be confined in prisons or camps for a period of eight to ten years.

The regional NKVD and procuracy were to decide the category into which the arrested *Harbintsy* fell on the basis of intelligence material and investigation. Every ten days the regional NKVD chief was to send lists of people in each category to the NKVD central headquarters in Moscow for confirmation. After confirmation by the NKVD chief of the USSR and the chief procurator, the sentences were to be carried out 'immediately'.

Towards the very end of the order is another point which catches my attention:

> *The operation against the* Harbintsy *is to be used to recruit qualified intelligence agents, taking measures to ensure that double agents are excluded from the secret service.*

The operation was to be concluded by 25 December 1937, though it was later extended by almost a year.

This shocking document explains everything.

I begin to understand that the particular lines of questioning taken by the NKVD interrogators in Gorky with the Onikuls had not been driven by anything the Onikuls had *actually done*. The aim was to pin them into one or more of the thirteen arrest categories.

This is why seemingly ordinary dealings between the Onikuls and White émigrés were turned into crimes and why the NKVD interrogators persistently tried to link them with White Guards and fascists.

This is the reason for the many questions about arrests, the police and the Gendarmerie; why Girsh was reprimanded for failing to remember the policeman who rescued him from Baron Ungern's brigand; why the policeman to whom Chesna had sold a harmonium featured in her indictment; and why Chesna and Sanya were saddled with Chinese citizenship.

It is also quite clear why the interrogators used Harbin and Hailar interchangeably. To them, the distinction was irrelevant—their prisoners were all *Harbintsy* and *Harbintsy* were Japanese spies. In the face of such chilling logic, for the Onikuls and other *Harbintsy* like them, there had never been any way out.

What prompted Yezhov to issue this order about the *Harbintsy* in September 1937? Perhaps it was true that Russians from Harbin and other parts of Manchuria had been sent to the Soviet Union by Japanese intelligence as spies and subversives? It was. Some had. Just as Soviet agents had been sent into Manchukuo and Japan.

Even before the Japanese occupation of Manchuria in 1931, Cossack and White Guard units were intermittently mounting cross-border incursions into the Soviet Far East to gather information, incite the local peasant population against their commissars, to set off explosions or try to seize a border post. Many of them were caught. Others were seized in the course of Soviet raids into Manchuria.

When the Japanese took over, they used White operatives to collect intelligence on the disposition of Soviet border troops or to provoke incidents which would test Soviet readiness. Ill-prepared, many of the hapless troops met tragic ends. Quite often, their cover was blown by Soviet agents planted in key émigré organisations in Manchukuo. In Harbin, the Japanese Military Mission ran special intelligence training courses to prepare agents for intelligence work in the Soviet Union.

There is no question that the Japanese and their White Russian collaborators in Harbin would have seen the mass departure of Soviet citizens from Manchuria after the Soviet Union sold the Chinese Eastern Railway (CER) in 1935 as an opportunity to plant some 'agents' in their midst.

Did it follow from this that the 'overwhelming majority' of 'so-called *Harbintsy*' were former White officers, members of the police, Gendarmerie and various émigré fascist spy organisations who had arrived in the Soviet Union with the purpose of spying for Japan? Most probably not. Most of them were ordinary workers of the CER railway and administration, including engineers, clerks, teachers and doctors. Having lost their jobs in Manchuria, they set off to build new lives in their 'homeland'. They were joined by others who saw dim prospects for Russian life in Manchuria after the central artery of the CER was severed and wanted to escape the Japanese occupation.

Yezhov's massive operation against the *Harbintsy* was dictated by the logic of Stalinist paranoia.

In the xenophobia that gripped the Soviet Union from the mid-1930s, the mass migration of Russians from Manchuria raised suspicions. Arriving in their 'motherland' full of hope for a new tomorrow, it was only a matter of time before their Manchurian past caught up with them. To the Soviets, these people were tainted by their life among foreigners and White émigrés. The Japanese occupation of Manchuria simply heightened suspicions that they had been recruited as spies.

At the February–March 1937 Central Committee plenum, Stalin spoke of war preparations against the Soviet Union being made by its enemies—Germany, Poland and Japan—and demanded that measures be taken to eliminate a potential 'fifth column' and agents of foreign intelligence. A remark about returnees from the CER by one of Stalin's trusted commissars, Lazar Kaganovich, set the stage for the subsequent mass operation against *Harbintsy*:

Of course it's bad to wrongly draw the conclusion that all who have arrived are bad people. But unfortunately, there are an awful lot of spies among them.

By mid-1937, hysteria about enemies of the people and foreign spies striking at the heart of the Soviet regime had reached fever pitch. The Harbin order came among a raft of other directives for mass arrests.

Key among them was NKVD Operational Order No. 00447 of 30 July 1937, which initiated a nation-wide operation against 'kulaks, criminals and other anti-Soviet elements'. Worded so loosely that anyone could have been picked up in its net, the order came with specific quotas for the number of people to be arrested in each region, how many of them were to be shot, how many to be sentenced to eight to ten-year terms in labour camps and prisons. The quota for the Gorky region was 4,500 arrests, 1,000 executions and 3,500 internments. It was this order that re-established 'special troikas' to expedite 'justice', unencumbered by judicial procedure. The operation's original target was 268,950 arrests in four months, but it was extended to November 1938 and led to the arrest of over 750,000 people, more than half of whom were shot.

From late July 1937, orders were also issued for a series of 'national operations', aimed at liquidating the 'potential intelligence base' of enemy states. The NKVD's operations against Germans, Poles and the *Harbintsy* (also referred to as the 'Harbin-Japanese' operation) were classed as the three key 'national' operations. A range of other 'nationalities'—Koreans, Latvians, Estonians, Finns, Greeks, Iranians, Chinese, Romanians, Macedonians, Bulgarians and Afghans—were targeted later. Although there were no quotas set for the national operations,

Memorial researchers have calculated that by mid-November 1938, almost 350,000 people had been arrested under their guise.

From a simple geographical designation of residents of a remote town in Manchuria, the term *Harbintsy* had suddenly acquired the status of a nationality, and a suspect one at that. By 1937, it was synonymous with 'Japanese spy'.

———•——•———

Yezhov's order had instructed the mass operation against the *Harbintsy* to commence on 1 October 1937. The Gorky NKVD wasted no time. Yasha and Manya Onikul were arrested just one day later, on 2 October 1937; their father five days after them. Sanya and Chesna, who had missed out in the first round, were picked up eight months later—either under an extension of the operation or as relatives of 'enemies of the people'.

In the space of one fateful year—October 1937 to October 1938—a family of five had been destroyed: three of them shot, one sent to labour camp, and an old lady to serve her exile on the steppes of Kazakhstan.

I have often pondered just how many Russians from China were victims of Stalin's purges or the operation launched by Yezhov's hideous order. It was not a statistic I ever expected to find. Even estimates for the number of Russians who returned to the Soviet Union after the CER sale varied anywhere from between 20,000 and 100,000.

Nevertheless, I decide to ask the question. I had established a correspondence with a researcher at Memorial's Research and Information Centre in Moscow, Sergei Larkov, who had helped me clarify a number of issues about the Onikul cases. Given the gargantuan work Memorial was undertaking to document all aspects of the Stalinist repression, I figured they might have calculated this gruesome statistic.

In March 2002, I email my query: Is it known how many people were arrested under the Harbin order and how many were shot?

I am not surprised when Larkov responds that he is not aware of any such statistics and thinks it may be 'practically impossible to separate the *Harbintsy* from the mass of people arrested in autumn of 1937'. But he undertakes to consult his colleagues. A month later I get another answer:

> . . . *I was wrong about the number of* Harbintsy *repressed [under the NKVD's so-called 'Harbin Operation']—such information does exist!*
>
> *According to unpublished research by A.B. Roginskii and O.A. Gorlanov of Memorial's Research and Information Centre, . . . 48,133 people were investigated by extra-judicial process [ie arrested] . . . and 30,992 of them were sentenced to be shot.*

Larkov later confirms that, with few exceptions, the remaining 17,141 were incarcerated in camps and prisons.

Right: At seventeen, Gita Onikul was a classic beauty. This is the photograph she inscribed to her fiancé, Motya Zaretsky, several months before their marriage in 1927.

Left: Manya Onikul had a certain 1930s glamour.

Even as a youth, Abram Onikul had an adventurous spirit.

Yasha Onikul, pictured in his school uniform in Hailar in the early 1930s.

An elegant Gita in Harbin in 1930.

Sanya Onikul, Manya's cousin who followed her to Gorky, pictured in the early 1930s.

Left: 'Treasure the copy, but don't forget the original', Abram wrote on the back of this photograph which he sent to Gita and her husband Motya from Mongolia in 1927.

Above: Abram Onikul, in a Mongolian coat, with friends in Hailar.

Gita and Motya Zaretsky made a handsome couple. Their 47-year marriage was legendary for its romance and mutual devotion.

Harbin in the 1930s was a distinctly Russian city. This postcard shows a cafe and clothing store on Kitaiskaya, the main street of the commercial Pristan district.

Manya, with her friend
Rachel Naftanovich,
photographed in Harbin
in 1933 on their way to
Shanghai.

Manya in Shanghai in 1934.

Manya (front row, sixth from the left) with fellow students at the
Harbin Dentistry School.

'Before departure 1936'. Chesna and Girsh Onikul, on their last visit to Harbin before they left for the Soviet Union; with Gita, Motya and Inna Zaretsky.

Harbin Station was the scene of many goodbyes as thousands left for the Soviet Union after the sale of the Chinese Eastern Railway to the Japanese in 1935. *Photo courtesy of Ira Magid.*

Manya in her office at the Gorky Avtozavod Hospital with a fellow doctor in the mid 1930s. Was he her lover?

Manya (third from left) with friends on the beach in the Crimea in 1936.

Manya (seventh from right), sightseeing with fellow workers in Alupka during a vacation in the Crimea, gazes into the 'radiant future'.

Japanese troops on a Harbin street not long after the occupation of the city in February 1932. *Photo courtesy of Elena Taskina.*

Harbintsy watching the Soviet Red Army parade in the square outside St Nicholas Cathedral after the Soviet takeover of Harbin in August 1945. *Photo courtesy of Elena Taskina.*

CHAPTER 10

THE SURVIVOR

WHEN THE NKVD interrogators in Gorky accused him of being a Japanese spy and asked who had recruited him and when, Yasha was completely taken by surprise:

> *I was amazed at this totally undeserved and fictitious accusation. I had only one answer—I never had and never could have been recruited by any Japanese. I was working loyally for the Soviet secret service.*

These words are repeated in four handwritten letters I photocopied from Yasha's NKVD file in Nizhny. Two of them are addressed to the NKVD chief of the USSR, Lavrenty Beria himself. The other two to lesser NKVD deities. In each one, Yasha protests his conviction as an 'enemy of the people' and appeals for an urgent review of his case, skilfully intertwining the facts with patriotic rhetoric.

His appeals were all written between May 1939 and March 1940 from the Ivdel Lag prison camp in Sverdlovsk province, where he was sent to serve his ten-year sentence. Having read the first two letters, I realise the texts are practically identical, with a point added here and there.

I already know from material I had received from the Russian government back in 1993 that Yasha's brother Abram worked for the NKVD as a Chinese interpreter somewhere in the Far East. But I have never heard anything of the sort about Yasha. Nor has anyone else in the family. His letters tell an astonishing tale.

Perhaps to compensate for his 'foreign' origins, Yasha starts each appeal by affirming his proletarian roots and his early commitment to the Soviet cause. Describing himself as the son of an 'impoverished Byelorussian peasant', Yasha says he grew up in Hailar in the Chinese Eastern Railway (CER) Zone, where his father was forced to go in search of work in 1909. He claims he was one of the first to join the Pioneers youth group in Hailar when it was established in 1925 along with the railway workers' union. I calculate that at the time, he would have been eleven years old. Strangely, no-one I speak to from Hailar remembers such a youth group, but perhaps they were too young.

Then comes a startling revelation:

From 1930, I worked for the Soviet secret service in Hailar, as did all my family. I can say, without exaggeration, that the work we did ... was serious and, under the circumstances, extremely dangerous ... But I paid no attention to this and worked willingly. I considered it to be my duty. I was happy that, though living outside the Soviet Union, I could help to build Socialism ... In 1935, we had to reduce our work significantly because the Japanese authorities were already suspicious and had put us under surveillance. That was why my brother, Abram Grigorievich, left the CER Zone and moved to Vladivostok in 1932 when the Japanese occupied Manchuria. It was also why my sister, Maria Grigorievna [Manya], left for Gorky in 1934.

Yasha relates how he was harassed by the Japanese Gendarmerie several times in 1935. After that, it became too dangerous for him to do much secret work. The following year, he and his parents left Hailar for Gorky to join his sister Manya, who, he wrote, 'had also worked for the Soviet secret service in Hailar'. Yasha names a number of staff of the Soviet consulate in the border town of Manchuria who were familiar with his family's work and could vouch for their 'honesty and commitment to the Soviet Union'.

Yasha recounts how not long after he arrived in Gorky and started working at the Avtozavod (GAZ) as an English technical interpreter, he was summoned by the head of the NKVD at the plant. The man knew of his work for Soviet intelligence in Hailar and proposed that Yasha become a 'secret agent of the NKVD at the GAZ'. Yasha says he agreed and worked 'without reprimand' until the moment of his arrest:

I was proud of all the achievements of the USSR and was ready to assist in whatever way I could. I was happy to destroy enemies of the Soviet people, both internal and external. All this is not unsubstantiated. I proved it in my work for Soviet intelligence, first in Hailar and then at the Gorky Avtozavod.

My stomach turns. If what he says is true, I doubt that Yasha would have had the option of saying no.

Yet on 2 October 1937 Yasha was 'suddenly arrested'. When the investigators accused him of 'spying for Japan' at two brief interrogations on 16 October and 6 December 1937, Yasha says he rejected 'this totally undeserved and fictitious accusation' and told them he had only ever worked for Soviet intelligence. No concrete evidence against him was provided.

All my requests for the interrogators to provide even the most paltry facts on which I could have been suspected of espionage for the Japanese went unanswered. The charge levelled at me was an evil fabrication which I categorically denied. It was not supported by any evidence at my two interrogations.

Yasha claims that throughout his five-month detention in Gorky Prison, he was expecting to be called for further investigation:

I was certain that in the process, the investigators would be convinced of my innocence. But in February 1938, with

no indication that the investigation was over, I was
deported to the NKVD Ivdel Lag (labour camp). Only on
arrival there did I learn that I had been sentenced by the
Special Board of the USSR NKVD on 24 December 1937
to ten years for counter-revolutionary activities.

I had read in Solzhenitsyn's *Gulag Archipelago* how prisoners were unloaded from the freight cars at their destination and made to kneel beside the railway tracks while their sentences were read out to them. It seems the same happened to Yasha.

Located in the Ural Mountains near the town of Serov, the Ivdel Lag camp was one of the vast network of camps which the Chief Directorate for Corrective Labour Camps (Gulag) had established across the Soviet Union in the 1930s. In a comprehensive Russian-language handbook on the *System of Corrective Labour Camps in the USSR* published by Memorial in 1998, I discover that more than half of Ivdel Lag's population were, like Yasha, political prisoners and its main industry was processing timber from the surrounding forests.

In his appeals, Yasha writes that he worked as a tree feller and was, on average, exceeding his norm by ten to twenty percent. But a month after his arrival, he fell ill with an abscess of the psoas, a muscle used for flexing the hip joint. This resulted in two operations, after which he was put in the invalid group. By the time he wrote his last appeal in April 1940, Yasha had spent twenty-two months under hospital treatment. With a contracted hip joint he could not bend his leg and walked with crutches.

Yasha's first appeal in May 1939 makes no mention of his family. But subsequent letters indicate that he was getting information about his mother from somewhere. While he keeps repeating that he knows nothing of the fate of his father and sister, he expresses concern about Chesna's situation, adding more detail each time. He writes that Chesna had been exiled to Zhosaly in south Kazakhstan and claims she was unfit for any kind of labour and unable to support herself due to ill-health. In his final appeal, he complains that all the Onikuls' belongings were confiscated after Chesna's arrest, though confiscation had not been part of her sentence. Such information could only have come directly from Chesna or someone close to her.

Yasha's appeals follow the age-old Russian tradition of petitioning a higher authority to intervene and redress an injustice. In Tsarist times, peasants petitioned noblemen and the Tsar. In Soviet times, workers petitioned commissars and Comrade Stalin. Invariably the last two paragraphs of Yasha's letters are masterpieces of patriotic rhetoric. They also reflect an acute awareness of the politics of the purges:

> To this day, I don't know why I and my family, honest Soviet workers, devoted to the Soviet Union to the marrow of our bones, have been so unfairly punished and find ourselves in the ranks of enemies of the people. I think my arrest can only be the result of evil slander by a real enemy of the people.
>
> For this reason, I request your urgent intervention to

expedite the review of my case and my release from confinement so that I, on a par with all the Workers of the USSR, can rejoice in the Victory of Socialism.

It seems Yasha had heard about the November 1938 decree ordering the NKVD to curb the excesses of the purges and about the outrage expressed at the March 1939 Party Congress. His reference to slander by a 'real enemy of the people' echoes many of the speeches which decried innocent Party members falling victim to real enemies.

Yasha's appeals leave me speechless. Can it be true that he and the entire Onikul family worked for the Soviet secret service? Manya? Her parents? Or did Yasha invent the story as a way of getting himself out of the camp?

If it is true, why is there no mention of it in any of the Onikul records of interrogation? Why didn't they raise it as a defence at the time? Then I remember some points which mystified me earlier: Yasha being described as 'a double agent' in his indictment; Manya saying she left Hailar in 1933 after some unknown 'Skuratov' warned her to go to the USSR because she might be arrested by the Japanese. It is entirely possible that the Gorky interrogators omitted the details from their records simply because these 'facts' were at odds with the cases they were building. What else did they leave out, I wonder?

It is difficult to distinguish fact from fiction. The fact that the letters of appeal were written by Yasha himself gives them significant credibility. It is notable that he repeatedly mentions only two interrogation sessions, while three records with discordant dates appear in his file. Yet I know that Yasha is also manipulating facts to build a case to secure his own release.

Perhaps Yasha did work for the NKVD at the GAZ? Maybe this is what saved him from sharing Manya's fate? Why else was Manya executed while Yasha got ten years when neither of them had confessed? There is also the obscure point in Yezhov's Harbin order about using the operation to 'recruit qualified intelligence agents'. Had Yasha been identified as a useful asset?

⬥

Yasha's first letter of appeal in May 1939 prompted quick action by the secretariat of the new NKVD chief Beria. Within two weeks, it had been referred down the line to a subordinate NKVD department for review and urgent advice. Then the matter got lost in the bureaucratic morass for almost a year. But in the turmoil in which the Soviet security agencies found themselves at the time, this was hardly surprising.

In the Nizhny archive in 1996, I had not been able to photocopy the pages and pages of inter-agency corre-spondence which Yasha's appeals provoked. But I took detailed notes. Juxtaposing these with Yasha's letters, I now manage to piece together what happened.

In April 1940, the NKVD in Gorky was at last instructed to review Yasha's case and to report their conclusions back to Moscow 'as a matter of urgency'. Among the issues they were asked to establish was:

> *Whether Onikul ... has, in fact, worked as a secret agent for the NKVD in Gorky and, if so, what material he provided.*

In the meantime, Yasha's physical condition was deteriorating. In follow-up letters he sent to the NKVD in June and July 1940, Yasha writes that over the past two years, he had been having treatment for his leg in the camp hospital and was also suffering from kidney stones. He says he sees no prospect of improvement under prison camp conditions and asks for 'urgent review of his case so that he can recover from his illness and again be useful to the USSR'.

In August 1940, the Gorky NKVD sprang into action. Internal memoranda flew in all directions: checking at which address Yasha lived before his arrest, getting references on him from former neighbours and work colleagues, checking with the Ivdel Lag camp on his medical condition and whether there was any 'compromising material' on him.

In one reference letter, a colleague at the GAZ confirms that Yasha worked as an interpreter and writes that he understood the Onikuls came to the USSR from China 'because the political situation there was apparently rather turbulent'. He remembers that, at the meeting where Yasha was admitted into the trade union, he spoke about his background 'reluctantly and in a muddled way'. He also mentions that Yasha was on close terms with Tsirlin, the head of one of the electrical workshops, 'who was his relative'.

A man who lived in the apartment next to the one the Onikuls once occupied in Komsomolskaya (formerly Oktyabrskaya) Street confirms that 'a family from China' lived in number 19. Wisely, he tells the NKVD that he does not know their surname and never spoke to them. A reference from the NKVD at the Ivdel Lag camp advises that Yasha was in charge of supplies in the medical section of the camp, had a good attitude to his work and had not received any reprimands. But there is nothing in the file to establish whether or not Yasha worked for the NKVD in Gorky.

Finally, in January 1941, the Gorky NKVD issued a ruling on the review of Yasha's case. It repeats all the original charges from Yasha's indictment in 1937 and notes that his father and sister were convicted as Japanese spies and that his father had confessed to the charge. It concludes:

> *Bearing in mind that Onikul is a socially dangerous element*
> *I DECREE THAT:*
> *the decision of the Special Session of the USSR NKVD of 1938 should remain in force and that his complaints are unfounded.*

The decree is signed by Lieutenant Balandin of the Investigations Branch of the Gorky NKVD and is authorised by the new Gorky NKVD chief, Major Gubin.

Two months later, this changes. Another decree, issued by the very same people at the end of February

1941, declares that new circumstances had arisen in relation to Yasha's case which demanded investigation. For some reason, it had become 'imperative that Onikul be interrogated about the facts set out in his complaint'. The Gorky NKVD also wanted to question Yasha in relation to another matter before them. The decree concludes:

> *Onikul Y.G., is to be transferred from the Ivdel Lag camp of the NKVD to Gorky Prison and detained under guard at the Investigations Branch of the Gorky Regional NKVD.*

In May 1941, Yasha was back in the interrogation room at Gorky—with none other than Lieutenant Balandin of the Investigations Branch.

Judging by the three records in Yasha's file, the atmosphere at the Gorky NKVD was markedly different from that which prevailed during his earlier interrogation round in 1937. Two of the three records, dated 19 and 20 May, are typed and note the time each session started and finished. The interrogations took place in broad daylight between 13.00 and 16.00 hours. The third record, dated 27 May, is neatly handwritten. In all three, the questions follow a logical and orderly sequence and are sober in tone. Gone are the shrill polemic and accusations. There are no more 'White bandit', 'White guard' and 'fascist' accusations. Instead, the interrogator delves in detail into the Onikul family history, their life in Hailar and their move to the Soviet Union.

The answers Yasha gives bear out information I have read in previous records, though there are a few obfuscations.

In the first interrogation, Yasha says Manya went directly from Hailar to Moscow in 1934, omitting her sojourn in Shanghai and Vladivostok. But in the second interrogation, the investigator asks him what he knows of his sister's trip to Shanghai. Yasha explains that in 1933 or 1934, Manya worked for a short time as a dentist in a polyclinic before going to Vladivostok 'on the instruction of the Soviet consulate in Shanghai'. I notice too that Yasha now describes his three to four-hour 'detention' by the Japanese Gendarmerie at Harbin Station in 1935 as an 'arrest' which lasted for two days, complete with 'severe beatings'. Perhaps this reflects Yasha's experience in Gorky Prison.

The subject I have been waiting for—Yasha's connection with the Soviet secret service—comes towards the end of the first interrogation:

Question: *While in Hailar, which intelligence agencies did you have connections with?*

Answer: *While living in Hailar, I was a secret agent of Soviet intelligence.*

Question: *When were you recruited by the Soviet secret service?*

Answer: *I was recruited in 1930.*

I calculate that at the time, Yasha would have been sixteen years old. Details of how he was recruited and the 'tradecraft' he practised come in his second interrogation:

Question: *Who recruited you?*

Answer: *My brother Onikul, Abram Grigorievich, was the first to be recruited to work for the Soviet secret service by Popov [the Hailar representative of the Soviet consulate] . . . My brother Abram then pulled me into intelligence work also. After working for a short time with my brother, I went with him to see Popov, who, in my brother's presence, proposed that I take up active intelligence work.*

Question: *Did Popov get your signed agreement to working for the Soviet secret service?*

Answer: *Popov did not ask for any signature.*

Question: *When you passed information to Popov and other agents, what code name did you use to sign the documents.*

Answer: *I did not have a code name. When I had to write down information given to me by Soviet agents who were my contacts, I would pass them on to Popov or others without signature or my brother would sign them with his code name 'Rom'. At other times, I would pass information verbally.*

Yasha explains that, as well as Popov, he worked with Morov, head of the CER lands department, who was effectively the head of the Soviet secret service in Hailar at the time. When the Japanese occupied Hailar in 1932, Popov, Morov and Abram had all left for the USSR. Yasha says he was then passed over to another controller with whom he worked until 1935. For a short time before his departure for Gorky in 1936, Yasha says he worked with one of the officials of the Soviet consulate in the town of Manchuria.

Asked about the nature of his work, Yasha describes his main role as a sort of go-between, receiving information from other Soviet agents to pass on to his controllers and passing messages and instructions to the agents. Asked to name some of these agents, Yasha can only remember a Mongol who was employed by the Japanese secret police; and a couple of Tatar brothers who worked in a private company.

The very next day, 21 May 1941, Gorky NKVD sent the details Yasha gave about his alleged involvement with the Soviet secret service to the NKVD's Foreign Intelligence Bureau (INO) in Moscow, requesting urgent verification:

> As we are currently reviewing Onikul's case, we request that you urgently check your records and advise whether Onikul really was a secret agent of Soviet intelligence in Hailar and whether he had links with the people referred to above. At the same time, we ask that you establish through Popov, Morov and . . . whether Onikul was associated with Japanese intelligence agencies and obtain from them references about Onikul's work.

From the response that came back two weeks later, it is clear that there were several different Soviet intelligence agencies running agents in Manchuria in the 1920s and

1930s—with little coordination. On the information provided, the INO was unable to confirm that Yasha or most
of the other people he mentioned were working for the
Bureau in Manchuria. They suggest that Gorky make
further enquiries with the NKVD's regional directorates
in the Far East and eastern Siberia, as well as some other
agencies.

But the INO's advice does contain one big revelation.
It is about Manya.

> . . . *according to materials in our possession, the subject's*
> *sister, Onikul M.G., during her time in Hailar, was*
> *employed by the INO NKVD DVK.*

This, I work out, is the Foreign Intelligence Bureau of
the NKVD's Far Eastern Regional Directorate based in
Khabarovsk. I wonder just how Manya was 'employed'?

My aunt Ira Kogan has told me that Manya used a
room at her parents' house as a dental surgery and there
were always people coming and going. I guess a surgery
would have provided quite good cover for meetings.
Although Ira was a child at the time, when she thinks
back she remembers that Abram also used Manya's room
for meetings, including with people who she thinks were
Soviets. I search the rest of the documents in Yasha's file
for information about Manya, but there is nothing more.

At the end of Yasha's second interrogation, he is questioned about the people from Hailar mentioned in his indictment. First is Panfilov, the 'executed Japanese spy' on whose testimony Yasha, Manya and Girsh were all convicted. Yasha says he did not know him personally and cannot say whether he was involved with Japanese intelligence.

Next come Baksheev, Grigerman and Bendikov, the 'White émigré-fascists and Japanese collaborators', with whom Yasha is alleged to have associated. Yasha's response on the first two is brief: he denies any association with Baksheev, whom he describes as a 'personal enemy' because he worked for the Japanese Gendarmerie in Hailar. Though he was not a close friend of Grigerman, Yasha says he knew him as an employee of the Far Eastern Bank in Hailar who was 'loyal to the Soviet government'.

Yasha is more forthcoming about Bendikov. His description of how Bendikov suddenly abandoned his earlier anti-Soviet and White Guardist views in the mid-1930s and emigrated to the USSR is consistent with what I read in his record in 1937. At that time, Yasha denied any knowledge of whether Bendikov was a Japanese spy. Now he changes his line:

> *I cannot exclude the possibility that Bendikov was sent to the USSR by the Japanese secret service. In 1936, Bendikov was arrested by the NKVD in Gorky on the basis of my materials.*

Teenagers Ronia Onikul and Ira Kogan in 1935 when they were living with the Zaretskys in Harbin.

Jacob Onikul (left) and Tima Litvin (right) in their twenties. Both were later imprisoned by the Japanese in the 1940s.
Photo courtesy of Tima Litvin.

My grandmother Gita's cousins, Lyova Rayak and his brother Yakov, dressed in their best during my visit to Moscow in 1996.

Right: Olga and Bradley Wynne in Zagorsk during their Russian posting.

Left: Yasha Onikul and his wife, Galya Sviderskaya, in the late 1940s.

Above: Looking at the Onikul photographs and papers with Galya in 1992.

The 'Vorobyovka', headquarters of the FSB in Nizhny Novgorod, where the Onikuls were interrogated by the NKVD after their arrests.

The prison in Nizhny Novgorod in 1996. Somewhere in the central yard was the *Spets Korpus*, where the Onikuls were imprisoned.

Abram in the uniform of an NKVD *pogranichnik* (border guard). A photograph he sent to his parents in 1937.

Abram's prison shot taken in 1938 during his incarceration in the NKVD internal prison in Khabarovsk.

In 2000, the window of the underground cell of the former NKVD internal prison in Khabarovsk was just visible below the pipe on this wall.

My great grandmother Chesna Abramovna Onikul returned to Harbin for six months in 1956–57. She is pictured (*left*) with me in the city park and (*right*) with my parents, grandparents and me.

Late in 1957, Yasha Onikul transited through Harbin station on a tour of China. Friends and relatives waiting on the platform to greet him (*above*), and (*left*) my grandparents and I farewell him on his return journey to the USSR.

With my grandmother
Tonya in Harbin in 1959.

My father Alec (perched
on the chair right) with
his parents Muhamedjian
Mustafin and Tonya
Shelamanova and young
friend.

Happy days in Harbin for my parents in the 1950s. Inna and Alec
with friends (*above right*) sailing on the Sungari River and (*above*) at a
New Year's Eve celebration at the Soviet Club.

Some things never change. Pictured in front of the Flood Control Monument in Harbin in the 1950s and again in May 2000.

In May 1959, we arrived in Sydney, where I am pictured with my mother in front of the Harbour Bridge.

Left: With Efrosinia Andreyevna Nikiforova, a friend of my grandmother Tonya. In 2002, she is the last of the old Russians still alive.

Right: 'Our man in Khabarovsk', former KGB/FSB Colonel Sasha Lavrentsov, pictured with his favourite medal in May 2000.

In November 2000, Sasha and I mounted a plaque in memory of Abram on the remembrance wall at the Khabarovsk cemetery. It is the last one on the top row, to the right.

Is this true? If so, why didn't he say so in 1937? Or is this an embellishment to help his case? Even if Yasha did not know for sure that Bendikov had been executed as a Japanese spy, he may well have guessed. Perhaps he figured that he had nothing to lose in subsequently claiming responsibility for Bendikov's conviction?

In his third interrogation on 27 May 1941, Yasha is asked which relatives he still had in Gorky. Apart from his cousin Sanya Onikul, whose whereabouts Yasha says he does not know, he mentions his cousin Mark Tsirlin and his wife Fanya Klebanova. Although Yasha says he is not sure where in the GAZ they were working and that he had no contact with Mark, he says he corresponded with Fanya, who also helped him financially.

Asked where the Tsirlins came from and whether they had ever lived in Manchuria, Yasha explains that they had never lived anywhere outside the Soviet Union. He was obviously aware that in the prevailing climate, any hint of a foreign connection could incriminate them. He also stresses that the Onikuls only established contact with the Tsirlins before they came to Gorky.

From Yasha's answers, I deduce that Fanya was probably his source of information about Chesna. Maybe she had not told Yasha of Sanya and her husband's arrests.

Though the Tsirlins managed to escape any guilt by association with the Onikuls, sometime in the early 1940s, Mark was caught on another absurd charge. The story, according to Ira Kogan and Uncle Lyova, was that during a discussion in Mark's office, one of the three men present remarked on the youthfulness of the new local Party boss. The next day three of the four were arrested. Mark was accused of heading a subversive-espionage Trotskyist conspiracy and sentenced to eight years in the Gulag, then disenfranchised for another five years. After her husband's arrest, Fanya prepared herself for the worst. She sent her two children to the country-side with their nanny to spare them from an orphanage for children of 'enemies of the people'. Miraculously, she escaped arrest.

I find no more papers in Yasha's file to confirm whether or not he worked for Soviet intelligence in either Hailar or Gorky. Nor anything to indicate what happened to him after these three interrogations in Gorky. Did the requests for verification bear out his story? Was he freed after the review?

The next document in Yasha's file is an undated summary which indicates that the charges against him were still in force in 1948. After that, there are nine numbered pages missing from the file. But there is nothing to suggest that Yasha returned from Gorky to the Ivdel Lag labour camp. On the strength of that, I figure that his fate must have taken a new turn. The question is, in which direction?

I know from my discussions with Yasha's wife Galya in Riga that she first met Yasha in 1946. He had come to visit friends in Dnepropetrovsk in the Ukraine, with whom she happened to be boarding. Sometime later that year, Yasha invited her to visit him in Latvia, where he was working at a sanatorium near Riga and she ended up staying. From that time until his death in 1985, the two were together. But the five years of Yasha's life from June 1941, when his interrogations in Gorky ended, until 1946 remain a mystery.

As I try to piece together Yasha's story, I reflect on my two meetings with Galya in 1992 and 1996, searching for clues and insights.

At our first meeting in 1992, Galya told me she knew little about Yasha's life before they met. She was aware his family had been 'repressed' during Stalin's purges, but was under the impression that Yasha had been somewhere in Byelorussia studying medicine during those years.

In light of this, I remember being surprised to discover Yasha's certificate of rehabilitation among the papers Galya gave me, but assume she had not seen it. It was folded together with the rehabilitation certificates of the rest of the family among papers that once belonged to Yasha's mother, Chesna. There was no reason why Galya should have looked through them, I thought. After all, not everyone was as obsessed with old bits of paper as I was.

Still something made me uneasy. Was it really possible to live with someone for forty years and not know what happened to them at such a cataclysmic point in their life?

My suspicion was compounded when, shortly after my conversation with Galya, Uncle Lyova in Moscow told me that all the Onikuls, including Yasha, had been arrested as spies. How come he knew this and Galya didn't?

When I visited Galya again in October 1996 just before going to the archives in Nizhny Novgorod, I remember my ambivalence about telling her the information about the Onikuls I had received from the Nizhny Ministry of Security. How would it feel, I wondered, to hear after forty years that your husband had been arrested and sent to a prison camp as an alleged Japanese spy—and that he never told you? And how bizarre to hear it from a relative stranger?

That is, of course, if Galya really didn't know.

It certainly occurred to me at the time that perhaps Galya *did* know the truth and knew it all along. Perhaps she had promised Yasha she would never tell anyone? Or maybe she simply did not want to tell me. If this were the case, I would put her in an awkward position if I raised the issue. She might feel caught out or even hounded by this inquisitive relative from the other end of the world whom she barely knew. The fact that I was staying with Galya made it even more difficult for me to broach the subject. But I had already told her that I was on my way to the archive in Nizhny Novgorod to gather information on the Onikuls and she kept asking me how I had arranged it.

In the end, I decided in favour of the truth. On the day I was leaving, I showed her the Ministry of Security's summary.

Galya was visibly stunned to discover that Yasha, like the rest of his family, had been arrested as an alleged Japanese spy and sentenced to ten years in the Gulag. She insisted that he had never told her any of it. After musing for a while, she said it helped to explain why they had moved from place to place so often.

Having spent most of the previous night tracing Yasha's career path through the pile of *spravkas* Galya had given me to look at and making notes on my laptop computer, I understood what she meant. For fourteen years, they had moved from one side of the Soviet empire to the other, as Yasha alternated between assignments as medical administrator of various sanatoriums in the Baltic Republics and leprosariums in Soviet central Asia. In each place, he won high commendations for his work, including awards, financial bonuses and medals of excellence. It is clear to me in retrospect that Yasha was working to lose his *zek* (prisoner) identity and build a new one. Only in the late 1950s, after his rehabilitation, did he put down roots in Riga.

It dawns on me too that the fact that Yasha had been able to visit Dnepropetrovsk in 1946, a year before his ten-year sentence was up, suggests that his term may have been cut short. But I am still no wiser as to where he spent those unaccounted for five years.

I write to Uncle Lyova in Moscow with a string of questions, including this one, and ask his grandson Sasha to record the answers. When the tape comes back, it is clear that even the family encyclopaedist is unable to cast any light on the matter.

I think about approaching Galya again, but am reluctant to do so. I sense that I have probably upset her enough with my revelations. Besides, I don't want her to think that I doubt what she has told me.

There is still another reason for my reluctance. I find that I have mixed emotions about Yasha's story. My childhood—and enduring—image of Yasha is of a kind, clever and amusing man; a doctor and a hero who survived times I could not even imagine. When I was seven years old, he sent me a book about a girl searching for her father during the Second World War, which I still treasure. The inscription reads:

As a mark of our struggle for peace, so that the children of the world should never have to experience what the little girl in this book had to live through.

As a child, no adult had ever taken me that seriously.

But what if the story Yasha told the interrogators about working for Soviet intelligence in Hailar and Gorky is true? What if he *did* work as an NKVD agent in Hailar and at the GAZ in Gorky?

I find no difficulty reconciling myself to the idea that Yasha may have been a Soviet secret agent in Hailar. Yasha would have been sixteen in 1930 when he says his older brother Abram let him in on his secret work for the Soviets. Abram, by all descriptions, was outgoing, handsome and clever; a romantic figure whom Yasha probably admired. If, as it now seems, Manya was working for the Soviets also, then why not Yasha?

As Russians with Soviet citizenship living in the CER Zone, the Onikuls would have regarded it as an act of patriotism to support the new Soviet state against the forces of darkness—anti-Semitic Cossacks, White Guards, fascists and the Japanese. After the Japanese occupation of Manchuria in 1932, their work would have been even more significant and considerably more dangerous.

The possibility that Yasha may have worked for the NKVD in Gorky is much more distasteful to me. This would make Yasha an 'informer'. Eventually, I force myself to step into his shoes and think it through.

I imagine Yasha arriving in Gorky in 1936, relieved to have escaped the pressure of the Japanese. At the age of twenty-two, he is delighted with his prestigious new job as an English interpreter at the GAZ. He is quickly establishing a new circle of friends and enjoying his new life in the Soviet Union. Then he is summoned by the chief of the GAZ NKVD and his past suddenly catches up with him.

The chief probably opens the discussion with a reference to the latest public exposure of 'enemies' in senior Party ranks, throwing in the hypothesis that the Soviet Union is facing its greatest challenge since the 1917 revolution. Yasha nods in earnest agreement.

The chief then moves on to the situation at the GAZ. Is Yasha aware that enemies are being uncovered on a daily basis? Yasha nods but is paralysed with fear. Where is this conversation going? he wonders. Will he now be accused of being an enemy himself?

No accusation comes. Instead, the chief reels off the names of the latest senior officials arrested at the GAZ. Why is he telling me this? Yasha thinks, and momentarily loses his focus.

'. . . the utmost vigilance is required—vigilance to root out enemies and saboteurs,' the chief is saying. Again Yasha nods.

'We are aware of your work for our organs in the CER Zone in Harbin.' Hailar, thinks Yasha, but lets it ride.

'. . . an important effort in most trying circumstances. The White bandits are a pernicious enemy, especially now they are working openly with the Japanese and other counter-revolutionary forces.'

Yasha draws breath.

'I am sure it is no news to you that they have penetrated our country and are setting up spy networks inside,' the chief continues. 'Yes, even here in Gorky . . .'

Then the chief comes to the crux of the matter. 'In short, we need your help . . .'

Yasha winces. He thought he had left all that behind. But the chief picks up on Yasha's reticence. 'You must realise, of course, that you and your family are not beyond suspicion. Were you to decline . . .'

In a conversation along such lines, what choice did Yasha have but to say yes? He would have been working against the same targets he had in Manchuria—White Guards and Japanese spies. Only now he was harnessed to the same campaign against 'enemies of the people' that would eventually entrap him and his family.

If this scenario in Gorky were true, Yasha would have paid the price of a choice made at the age of sixteen in far-flung Manchuria. Abhorrent as it was, it was the price of his survival.

What would I have done in his place, I wonder? And if Yasha's story about working for the NKVD in Hailar and at the GAZ was an invention to get himself out of the Gulag, then perhaps his bluff paid off?

———✦———

Finally, in June 2001, I decide to take the risk and ask Galya again what she knows. I have already told her that I am writing a book which draws together the material from the Onikul NKVD files to tell the story of their fate during the purges. I send her a letter with an outline of my book which mentions some of the information I have uncovered and ask her help on a series of questions.

A month or so later, I receive her reply. It starts:

Dear Marochka
Your letter has perplexed and agitated me. I am very upset and regretful that I know so little about the questions you ask me, especially since I would very much like to help you . . .

. . . I do not know anything about why and when the Onikuls returned to the USSR or about their time in Gorky, Gorky Prison or the labour camp in Sverdlovsk.

Yasha never told me anything about any of it. On this

subject, Soviet people had a taboo. People were so terrorised that they felt the fewer people who knew, the safer it would be for both the teller and the listener. Clearly he did not want to entangle me in this.

I did not even know that Yasha was sentenced to ten years and was shaken when you told me of this in Riga in 1996. I recall saying at the time that this explained why we moved so often. I thought then that it was probably so he could not be easily found.

So I don't know in what year exactly Yasha arrived in the USSR, the exact term of his sentence and where he served it . . . Now it appears that it is I who have to ask you the answers to questions . . .

. . . Yasha never told me that he worked at any stage for the NKVD . . .

. . . with regard to Chesna Abramovna's life in Kazakhstan . . . her efforts to rehabilitate her family and how she discovered the fate of Abram, I regret I don't know.

Maybe Lyova Rayak may be able to help you in this regard. He always knew a lot about all the relatives and I dare say a lot was told there (unlike to me) . . .

I cannot sleep at night, thinking of ways I might give you some concrete help, but I cannot think how. I only know about my life with Yasha. That is all . . .

But Galya does help me. She writes me a detailed account of Yasha's work and their life together after 1946. She also sends me Yasha's two earliest postwar work references, dating back to 1946. I have seen them before and later find that I even copied them into my computer. But I did not read them very carefully. Now I discover that they cover the period from August 1941 to May 1946—Yasha's missing five years.

One of the documents is a copy of a *spravka* from the Department of Military Construction of the Moscow Region (MOVSU) which is a statement of Yasha's service. Later I learn that MOVSU's tasks included building military barracks, hospitals and stores during the war. The *spravka* is issued to 'Doctor Onikul Y.G. in place of an employment record book, at the end of his assignment'. It certifies that Yasha worked as head of the medical unit of Area 11 from August 1941 to May 1946 and commends his 'exemplary organisation of medical treatment of the soldiers and officers of Area 11 and the significant reduction of illness in all sites', noting that he received several awards for his efforts.

The document has been stamped and certified by a notary. As with all *zeks*, Yasha's employment book would have been confiscated when he was arrested in Gorky. This *spravka* would have been his main document of identity.

The second document, a personal reference from the military chief of Area 11, identifies its location as the town of Buy, which I find to be near the ancient Volga town of Kostroma.

All this explains what Yasha was doing after his second round of interrogations ended in Gorky in May 1941.

How did Yasha manage in three months to get from the interrogation room in Gorky to a first aid unit at a military construction base in Buy, some 385 kilometres north-east of Moscow? My guess is it had a lot to do with the desperate situation the Soviet Union faced after Hitler's armies invaded in June 1941—just as Stalin had been warned they would, but refused to believe.

By August, Minsk—the city from which Yasha's forebears came—was in Nazi hands, Leningrad was under siege and Kiev was about to fall. The Nazis were advancing on Moscow. In the massive mobilisation of conscripts and reservists, even prisoners from the Gulag were being redirected to the war front, though usually these prisoners were not 'politicals'.

Perhaps Yasha managed to persuade the NKVD that at the age of twenty-seven, he could better serve his country in the defence of Moscow than back in the Gulag? However it came about, Yasha seized the opportunity to build on his recently acquired skills as a medical orderly in the camp hospital. In the prevailing circumstances of war, no-one was checking qualifications. By the time the war ended, Yasha had earned his stripes as head of the medical unit for five difficult years. His testimonies praised him as an 'energetic, enterprising and thoughtful worker who had put considerable effort into the victory over the enemy'.

As the Soviet Government began the task of reconstrucing its war-ravaged country, Yasha joined the Ministry of Health's effort to develop the nationwide network of sanatoriums and to eradicate infectious diseases. For the next fourteen years he moved from sanatoriums in the Baltics to leprosariums in central

Asia, collecting glowing references for his work. These were important testaments for a man trying to lose his past and create a future.

Yasha was a survivor.

CHAPTER 11

OUR MAN IN KHABAROVSK

THE NKVD FILES I obtain from the archive in Nizhny Novgorod in 1996 give me a good idea of what happened to Manya, Yasha, their parents Girsh and Chesna, even their cousin, Sanya. But Abram's life remains an enigma. He is the missing link. All I have are a few photographs of a handsome, young, dark-haired man taken in exotic locations, and a few tantalising fragments of information —which only open up more questions.

Since my first discussion with Uncle Lyova in Moscow in 1992, I have known that on leaving Hailar in the early 1930s, Abram went to study in Vladivostok and joined the NKVD. Abram's intelligence connection was confirmed in the brief advice about his unwarranted arrest and rehabilitation which I received from the Russian government early the following year. Reading between the acronyms and clause numbers, I deduced that Abram had been an interpreter for the NKVD in the Far East, was arrested in October 1937 and sentenced by a military tribunal in Khabarovsk in 1939.

Abram's name comes up in passing in the early interrogation records of the Onikuls in Gorky when they were asked about their family composition. Not all the answers are the same. Manya and Sanya simply say Abram lives in Vladivostok. Chesna adds that he is studying at the Institute of Oriental Studies there. Girsh and Yasha, on the other hand, say Abram is working for the NKVD border guards—the *pogranichniki*—in Grodekovo, which I discover is a town fifteen kilometres east of the Chinese border, 150 kilometres from Vladivostok. Today it is the main border crossing point with China in the Russian Far East.

Abram gets a little more attention in Yasha's second interrogation round in May 1941. Most intriguing is Yasha's tale of how his brother pulled him in to work for the Soviet secret service in Hailar. If this is true, it suggests that Abram's career with Soviet intelligence began back in Manchuria and that he enmeshed other members of his family in this net.

Vladivostok, Khabarovsk, Grodekovo—I know the key to Abram's story lies somewhere in the Russian Far East. Since Abram was sentenced in Khabarovsk, there is a fair chance that his file might be there. But Khabarovsk's location in the far east of Russia, just north of the Chinese border, does not make it easily accessible. It is not somewhere I can simply drop into on one of my regular trips around south-east Asia. I consider writing a letter to the Khabarovsk archive and hoping for a response. It's a long shot, but what option do I have?

My friend Igor Savitsky comes to the rescue. Another of the many *Harbintsy* who emigrated to Australia in the 1950s, Igor is a successful entrepreneur specialising in trade with Russia. To my good fortune, he is visiting Moscow in November 1996 when I get back there from Nizhny with my treasures from the archives. In the grand old dining room of the Hotel National near the Kremlin, Igor toasts my success with Russian champagne and caviar.

'Give me the details and I'll talk to a good friend in Khabarovsk,' Igor says, when I tell him that my search for information on Abram is leading me to the Far East.

Outgoing, amiable and a consummate networker, Igor has 'good friends' all over Russia, but especially in the Far East, which is the focus of his business activities. On this occasion, his 'good friend' turns out to be a colonel from the Khabarovsk FSB (former KGB) named Lavrentsov, who earlier helped Igor track down material on his own family.

Within two months, the information on Abram arrives. The story it tells is staggering.

In Gorky, Girsh and Manya's lives ended quickly and brutally: the supreme measure of punishment—nine grams in the back of the head. When I read the words 'to be shot', 'shot 14.01.38 in Gorky' in their files, I thought nothing could match them on the scale of brutality. I was wrong. What I read about Abram's death in the letter from Khabarovsk is spine-chilling.

Written as a personal letter to me on plain paper

without letterhead, the document from Lavrentsov starts with background about the Onikul family which I already know, then goes on to trace Abram's work history in Manchuria. It paints him as an enterprising young lad, who at the age of fourteen was already working as a wool washer. Later, he was a bookkeeper, then a contractor for a string of companies with foreign names.

The letter says Abram arrived in Khabarovsk in 1933, where he joined the NKVD's predecessor, the OGPU, and was sent to study at the Far Eastern State University in Vladivostok. While studying, he also worked as a Chinese interpreter. The timing described certainly fits the timing of Abram's sudden departure from Hailar when Japanese troops arrived in December 1932.

Then come a couple of paragraphs about the purges:

The repressions of the 1930s did not bypass Abram Grigorievich. In 1937, the so-called purges were sweeping the whole country. His previous life in Manchuria became the reason for his unwarranted arrest on 17 October 1937.

He was under investigation for almost two years. On 4 October 1939, he was sentenced by the Military Tribunal of the NKVD Forces under Article 58.1a (treason against the Motherland) and Article 58.11 (organised anti-Soviet activities) to ten years imprisonment.

At first I find the letter's tone of polite equanimity distinctly irritating. What is this— 'Stalin's Purges for Beginners'? But I quickly realise that my correspondent is actually being helpful—demystifying the usual Soviet-speak into polite Russian and giving explanatory information:

> *He was sent to serve his sentence in Sevvostoklag. This is now in the territory of Magadan. The camp was at the Shturmovoy goldmine of the Yagodinsky district, several hundred kilometres from Magadan.*

In Russian, *sevvostok* is an abbreviation for 'north-east' and *lag* is short for 'camp'. I know that Magadan was the gateway to the Arctic death camps of Kolyma. I have read how millions of prisoners were sent to this remote region in the far north-east of Siberia to dig for gold in the frozen ground. To dig and to die. Now I discover that Abram was one of them.

Dressed in flimsy boots and wadding coats which offered no protection against the extreme sub-zero cold in which they toiled, Kolyma prisoners were set impossible work quotas which determined their food rations. Each time a prisoner failed to meet the quota, his meagre ration of bread and gruel was reduced. Most died of hunger, cold and exhaustion—a death of prolonged agony.

Lavrentsov's letter puts it more clinically:

> *. . . Minus forty degree frosts and malnutrition took their toll. He fell ill at the beginning of February 1941 and died on 11 February. The causes of death were lobar pneumonia, enteritis, thrombosis of the pulmonary artery and hypersplenism.*

My cousin, a doctor, confirms that these medical descriptors amount to being frozen and starved to death. Abram was thirty-three. The letter says he was 'buried at the camp cemetery in Shturmovoy'. I figure that probably translates to a mass grave in the permafrost.

The letter restates the details of Abram's 'posthumous rehabilitation' in 1957 and says more material on his case might still be forthcoming. The last sentence notes that a photograph of Abram, taken in Khabarovsk prison during his investigation in 1938, has been kept in his file in Magadan and a photocopy is attached.

What I see on turning the page leaves me speechless. What did they do to transform the carefree young man with film star looks into this hollow ghost with tortured eyes? And that is even before they sent him to Kolyma!

Whatever it was Abram had to endure, I owe it to him to find out.

My friend Igor makes several attempts to get me more information from Khabarovsk, but they are unsuccessful. It is clear that the only way I might find out something more is if I actually go there.

Just as Manya's mysterious image in the trenchcoat drew me to Nizhny Novgorod, Abram's haunted eyes now drive me to Khabarovsk.

———⁕———

I get there in May 2000.

As with my visit to Nizhny Novgorod four years

earlier, my trip is arranged on the spur of the moment. While booking airline tickets for a trip to Harbin with my parents, I suddenly remember how close Harbin is to the Russian Far East. Here is my opportunity to visit Khabarovsk and Vladivostok, to try to track down more information on Abram and see the places in which he once lived.

My friend Igor has also told me that some of the files the Soviet Red Army took out of Harbin after the Japanese defeat in 1945 are now in the Khabarovsk state archive. That was where his 'KGB friend' found files on Igor's family in Harbin. Who knows what family secrets I might find there?

I book six days in Khabarovsk, then an overnight trip on the Trans-Siberian to Vladivostok for two days. Surprisingly, my parents decide to join me on this leg of the journey. Born in Harbin, they have never set foot on Russian soil. Though they have travelled to the Mediterranean, to America and Asia, Russia has never been top of their agenda.

But I have no sense of how momentous the journey to Khabarovsk is for my parents until I notice on the flight from Harbin that my mother is looking nervous.

'You're not scared of flying are you?' I ask her.

'No,' she replies, 'just apprehensive about landing—in Russia.'

Almost a decade after the collapse of the Soviet Union, my parents still see Russia through a Soviet prism, deeply coloured by their former experiences in Harbin.

Russia is the place where friends and family went,

later to die or disappear. Such was the fate of the Onikuls who went of their own volition in the 1930s. A similar fate befell many of those deported by the Red Army in 1945. Even my father's mother, who returned voluntarily in the 1960s, met an early death there. Rationally, my parents know the Soviet Union is dead. Yet emotionally, they cannot believe that 'the system' died with it. When we land at Khabarovsk airport, they half expect to be met with cold officiousness, red tape and to be treated like émigré traitors to the Motherland.

What happens is quite the opposite. The airport officials are friendly and polite, apologising discreetly for the absurdly detailed customs declarations as 'a hangover from Soviet days'. Khabarovsk is a picturesque nineteenth-century Russian town, with wide boulevards and finely restored art deco buildings. It immediately reminds my parents of their old Harbin.

Far from treating us as traitors, most people we meet in Khabarovsk are warm and keen to talk. As Far Easterners, they feel a common bond with *Harbintsy* as fellow Russians from the edge of empire. Some of them joke that the Russian we speak is 'purer' than their own, untainted as it is by Soviet jargon. All are full of questions about what life is like for Russians in Australia and the prospects of sending their children there to study.

Within an hour of our arrival, we are eating shashlik and drinking Georgian wine in an excellent Armenian restaurant, with the unlikely name 'California'. At half past three, I head for my 'assignation with the KGB'— Igor's friend, Aleksandr Pavlovich Lavrentsov. My parents stay on at the restaurant chatting happily about old friends from Harbin who live in Khabarovsk. They have already made arrangements to meet a former sailing friend of my father's, now a professor of sport at Khabarovsk University. Though my mother cannot resist telling me to 'be careful', I can see that her fears about Russia are dissipating.

———•••———

Before leaving Sydney, I had made contact with Lavrentsov to tell him I was planning to visit Khabarovsk. Thanking him for the material he sent me on Abram through Igor four years earlier, I asked if any more information might be available. I mentioned that I was also interested to see whatever material there might be on my family among the files brought out of Harbin by the Red Army, which I understood was now in the Khabarovsk state archive.

Lavrentsov was predictably dismayed at my lack of forward planning and the brevity of my stay, but said there would be 'no problem'. Although he had retired from the FSB and was now working as an adviser to the director of the Far Eastern Railway, Lavrentsov told me he would 'arrange everything'. All I had to do was fax him a list of the names of the relatives in whose files I was interested. He offered to help me with hotel bookings and any other arrangements, but everything had already been taken care of. 'So I look forward to meeting you when you arrive. Please telephone me when you get to Khabarovsk.'

I call Lavrentsov from the Intourist Hotel where we are staying as soon as we arrive.

'Welcome to Khabarovsk,' he says, 'I have already been informed of your arrival. I believe your rooms are on the twelfth floor. I will call to see you there at four o'clock.'

Am I supposed to be impressed? I had noticed the two apparatchiks sitting at a desk in the lobby of the hotel when we first arrived and mentally tagged them as 'security'. Lavrentsov obviously knows them. In spite of privatisation, the hotel has retained the style and trappings of Soviet times. Female 'duty managers' still sit on each floor, controlling keys, hot water, laundry and information. The security apparatchiks sit in the lobby, registering passports and identity cards and simply watching. One difference, I later learn, is that the apparatchiks are now there to keep an eye on the Russian mafia, rather than on foreign tourists.

At five o'clock—one hour late—Lavrentsov is knocking on my hotel door.

'Welcome to Khabarovsk. I'm Lavrentsov—Aleksandr Pavlovich', says the dark-haired man as he thrusts three red carnations into my hand and barges into my cramped hotel room. Athletic and ruggedly handsome, he looks to be no more than fifty. His European-style velour jacket suggests he cares about his appearance. Or someone does.

'Thank you. I'm Mara,' I reply, wondering why he did not call from reception.

'And what's your patronymic?' he asks.

'I don't have one. Most Russians in Australia are not that formal. Patronymics are for old people. Besides, my father is half Tatar and his full name is Alimjan. "Marianna Alimjanovna" just doesn't have the right ring about it. Please just call me Mara.'

'Okey,' Lavrentsov says in pronounced English. Clearly I have won that point. It takes a few more hours and a vodka shot before he reciprocates by suggesting that I should abandon formality and 'just call him Sasha'. 'Well, you're not exactly as I imagined you from our conversation,' he continues. 'I thought you would be . . . well, lighter in colouring.'

I wonder what possible impression of my colouring could he have from two conversations on a crackly line across the Pacific? Lavrentsov is at once intrusive and formal. Well, I think to myself, you're younger and better-looking than I imagined, but I let the exchange pass with an, 'Oh really . . .'

'So let's talk about your program in Khabarovsk,' he says. 'This evening I will take you for a walk around the town. That way, I can point out some of the key places and help you get your bearings. Tomorrow— Friday—I'll meet you at 8.30 outside my office and take you to the state archive. There you can look at some of the files the Red Army brought from Harbin in 1945. I have already passed on to them the names of the people you listed in your fax. They also have a good collection of Harbin newspapers and other material. On Monday, I will take you to the FSB, where you can see the file of your great-uncle, Abram Grigorievich.

The rest we can work out later. How does that sound—Okey?'

He did tell me he would 'arrange everything' and he has. 'Thank you for being so helpful,' I respond. 'I'm just worried about leaving the FSB until Monday. Are you sure I'll have enough time to go through all the material?' I am concerned that we have to leave for Vladivostok the following Wednesday and would rather sacrifice the archive than run out of time with Abram's file. 'Couldn't I start at the FSB tomorrow and leave the other archive till next week?'

'Don't worry,' Lavrentsov retorts, 'you'll manage. Besides, it's already fixed.'

By this time we are walking down the main street of Khabarovsk, which runs from the old part of town near the Amur River to the administrative district and beyond. Known as Karl Marx Street during Soviet times, the old part of the street has now reverted to its original name of Muravyev-Amursky, in honour of the first governor-general of eastern Siberia.

The facades of the buildings in the old part of town have been restored with great care. Lavrentsov gives a running commentary: 'In this square once stood a cathedral. It was torn down by the Bolsheviks in 1925. This was the house of a rich merchant—it is now our library. This pink and white building with the cupola was the Japanese consulate until 1930.'

As we approach the centre of town, I notice the NKVD creeping into the commentary and much more focus on what happened in the various buildings during the purges. Ironically, we are passing a street named after Feliks Dzerzhinsky, the grandfather of the KGB.

'This big yellow building on the left was called the Commune House,' Lavrentsov says, 'and that is what it was. Many officials lived there in the 1930s, including some from the NKVD. In 1937, the head of each family was arrested and shot. Now it houses communal apartments for retired government workers . . .'

A block later, again: 'About a hundred NKVD officers lived in that building, down this street—all of them were arrested between August and October 1937 and shot . . .' It is Volochayevskaya Street. As we turn into it, Lavrentsov points out a couple of buildings which now belong to the Department of Security. In the 1930s, they belonged to the NKVD.

'When your great uncle, Abram Grigorievich, was arrested, the police van, known as a 'black raven', drove him in through that gate. Behind it was the NKVD internal prison, where he sat for two years. The military tribunal where he was tried was on the second floor of that reddish brown building. You can see the windows. Prisoners were shot in that yard. The guards would rev up tractors to conceal the sound.'

Further down the street is the huge monolith that is now FSB headquarters, then more buildings bristling with roof-top antennae.

'So this was the NKVD part of town,' I say. 'I'd like to take a look around.' But the light is fading fast.

'You should come back in daylight,' Lavrentsov suggests.

On the way back to the hotel, we stop at a bar for a snack. We have been walking for several hours and the cafes and bars are filling up with evening customers.

'Do you drink vodka?' Lavrentsov asks, 'or would you prefer something else?'

'What sort of Russian would I be if I didn't?' I answer. We order a half-litre carafe, together with a local specialty, calamari salad and wonderful Russian black bread.

There is nothing like black bread, icy cold vodka and a dill cucumber to break the ice in any Russian social interaction. Naturally, our first toast is to our meeting. As it is customary to make a toast with every shot, it is the first of many. Like my companion, I empty my shot glass in one hit. From this point onwards, we are friends, both on first name terms with no more patronymics.

'This vodka is from Moscow,' Sasha screws up his face. 'Ours is much better. Anyway, it's probably just as well that I don't drink too much. I had a lot last night.'

As we eat, Sasha explains that in his last assignment at the FSB, he led the review of thousands of cases of victims of Stalin's purges and their rehabilitation. This work started in 1988, in Gorbachev's days of *glasnost* and *perestroika* and gained real momentum after the decree on Rehabilitation of the Victims of Political Repression was enacted as law in October 1991. They also had to find the mass graves where the victims were buried. He offers to take me and my parents to Khabarovsk cemetery on the weekend to see the memorial to the victims of the purges.

It becomes clear to me over the next couple of days that Sasha's drive to uncover the truth about the purges and remember its victims was never just a job but a matter of personal conviction. A founding member of the local Memorial organisation, he remains the driving force behind the publication of 'books of memory', which contain the names and biographies of local victims of the purges as well as articles revealing the truth of what happened in the Far East in all its unexpurgated horror.

But purges and mass graves are not our only topic of conversation. Between toasts to each other's health and mouthfuls of calamari salad, we exchange views on everything from Russian politics and the mafia to Sasha's obsession with soccer and swimming, and his aspirations for his three sons.

Sasha does not hide his disgust with the gains the 'new Russians' have been able to make at the expense of ordinary people. But he is pleased with the recent election of Vladimir Putin as president and is optimistic about the country's future.

'Things will get better. You will see. After all, he's one of us—a *chekist*,' he laughs. Like many security insiders, Sasha still uses the name of the original Soviet security police. I am tempted to remind him where *chekists* have taken Russia in the past, but refrain. Sasha raises his glass in another toast: 'To Russia!'

'And Khabarovsk!' I respond.

Sasha is a patriot but also a regionalist, intensely loyal to the Russian Far East. He tells me his grandparents had been deported here as *kulaks* (prosperous peasants), after being stripped of their land and possessions in 1929 during Stalin's collectivisation. Sasha speaks proudly of the Far Easterners who came from diverse ethnic and socio-political origins and built new lives on the edge of the empire.

'We have always been self-sufficient and independent—we've had to be!' But it was these same characteristics that aroused the mistrust of central authorities, Tsarist and Soviet alike, and the Far Easterners paid dearly during Stalin's paranoid 1930s.

Sasha explains how at the height of the purges, a 'Far Eastern conspiracy' was uncovered involving the top levels of the regional party, army and security apparatus. Hundreds of senior military, party and NKVD officials were arrested. The confessions beaten out of them led to arrests and executions throughout their ranks.

'Is that what happened to Abram?' I ask.

'A variation on a theme,' he replies. 'He was, in any case, caught by Yezhov's Harbin order. But it's a long time since I looked at his file, so I don't remember the details. When you read the file, you will see. But remember, you can't believe everything written in the records. Many of them were falsified. It will be a matter of judgment.'

From my experience with the NKVD file from Gorky, this much I have already learned.

I find no material on the Onikuls among the files of the Bureau of Russian Émigré Affairs in Manchukuo (BREM) which are waiting for me at the Khabarovsk state archive the following day. This is not surprising. Registration with BREM, the organisation established by the Japanese in 1934 to administer the Russian population, was compulsory for émigrés. But Russians with Soviet citizenship registered with the Soviet consulate instead.

There are, however, files on my father Alec and his parents, which the archivist has pulled out for me according to the names I faxed Sasha from Sydney. Later, she finds other files for my father's grandmother and other relatives, whose names I did not know or think to ask for.

Dating from 1936, each file contains an extensive biographical questionnaire completed on registration, as well as other assorted correspondence. Among the answers to seventy-seven questions are details of each person's origins in Russia, their escape to Harbin during the Russian Civil War and a year-by-year account of their life in Harbin. I can barely contain my excitement. Since my paternal grandparents died when I was young, I know only scant details about their early lives from my father. What a mine of information these files contain! I'm sure even Alec doesn't know some of it.

Having marked up these files for photocopying, I turn to the next couple. To my surprise, they belong to my grandfather Motya Zaretsky and his brother Ruvim. Why do they have files if they were Soviet citizens? I wonder. When I examine them carefully, I notice they are quite different from the others. They contain no biographical questionnaires, just a couple of typed reports about the Zaretskys' business activities in Manchuria, a couple of press clippings that mention their names and some curious snippets of paper.

One snippet in my grandfather's file is headed with his name, address, the name of his dependants and their citizenship—'USSR'. Below are the names and addresses of two people from neighbouring apartments, with the words 'émigré' beside them. Below this is a heading 'Intelligence for 1/6/43'. The rest of the page has been cut off.

Puzzled by what I am looking at, I consult the archivist. She confirms my interpretation that Soviet citizens did not register with BREM.

'So what are the reports and cuttings of paper in these files?' I ask, showing her the file.

'Informers' reports—or at least pieces of them,' she answers. 'The rest of the reports were cut off by the KGB before they handed them over to us,' she shrugs.

I shudder. I have heard of neighbours having to inform on each other in Stalin's USSR and Nazi Germany, but never really thought about it happening in Harbin. From what I know, my grandparents had always been friends with their neighbours. Apart from anything else, their neighbours were their tenants.

Sasha tells me later that when the Soviets captured the BREM archive in August 1945 after the Japanese capitulation, agents of Soviet military counter-intelligence, known as Smersh—a Russian abbreviation for 'Death to Spies!'—used it to track down 'enemies' and 'Japanese collaborators'.

'Many of the thousands of people arrested and deported to the USSR were innocent,' he adds. 'But they were sent to serve long sentences in the Gulag or confined to special settlements in Siberia.'

This is not the first time I have heard this story. Among our friends and relatives are several families torn apart by these deportations. Still, it is weird hearing this admission from an officer of the former KGB.

———————

'The bodies of the executed prisoners were brought here in the dead of night and dumped into a pit—right here, underneath these graves,' Sasha says as my parents and I stand near the entrance to the Khabarovsk cemetery. 'They used two trucks—that's all the NKVD had in those days.'

This is the first mass gravesite located in Khabarovsk. Sasha tells us how, in 1989, a former NKVD worker whom they had tracked down in the Ukraine led his KGB team to this site. Twelve graves were located at the cemetery, in which some 12,000 people were buried at the height of the purges.

This is a fate Manya and her father shared in Gorky, I think to myself, as did Abram in the ice of Magadan.

Adjacent to the site of the mass grave is a small chapel which the Memorial organisation erected to commemorate the victims of the purges. Built in three months as a community effort, Sasha says its opening on 30 October 1990 coincided with the unveiling of the stone from Solovki in Lubyanka Square in Moscow.

To the right of the chapel stands a remembrance wall with an extract from the poem 'Requiem' by Anna Akhmatova, written prominently on a granite slab across the bottom:

> *I would have liked to name each one in turn,*
> *But they've taken away the list and there's nowhere to learn.*

The wall is covered with small, white oval plaques, each bearing a name, the year of birth and year of death— mostly 1937 or 1938—and one word: 'executed'. A few plaques also bear the word 'rehabilitated' and the appropriate year. I later learn that the construction of this wall was largely Sasha's idea.

'We are about to extend the wall,' Sasha tells me, as I am reading the names. 'Why don't you have a plaque made for your great-uncle, Abram Grigorievich?'

'But he died in Magadan, not Khabarovsk,' I protest.

'And when do you think you might get there?' he asks rhetorically. 'Besides, his tragedy started in Khabarovsk. It would be quite fitting to hang his plaque here.'

While Sasha goes to visit his mother's grave, my parents and I discuss his suggestion and agree it is a good one. Khabarovsk is the place where Abram started his new life in the Soviet Union in the 1930s and then spent two years in a prison cell. It is probably more appropriate that he be remembered here than in the anonymous ice of Magadan. What's more, the cemetery with its silver birch trees has a good feel about it, as does the city itself. Sasha undertakes to have a plaque made to be mounted when the additional wall is built.

Back in town, Sasha makes a detour to show my parents the former headquarters of the NKVD and the back of the prison where Abram was held. Sasha points to a pipe at ground level along the mouldy, grey wall.

'If you look carefully below that pipe, you can just see the bars on the windows. Those were the underground cells where Abram Grigorievich was held for two years.' Ironically, the apartment block where Sasha lives is directly across the road.

To relieve the emotional darkness of the morning, we collect Sasha's wife, Lyudmila, and youngest son, Nikita, and head for lunch *en famille*. Lyudmila, an elegant blonde who works at the university, is somewhat reserved at first. But once she relaxes, she reveals a feisty spirit which keeps Sasha on his toes. Eleven-year-old Nikita is delightful. An unusually reflective but amusing child, he has inherited his father's looks and temperament.

I had asked Sasha to find a restaurant with 'real' Russian food where the Moustafines could offer his family some true Russian hospitality. He chooses one named Old Russia. First we drink a toast to Abram with the best Khabarovsk vodka. And follow with countless more.

The restaurant is aptly named. Sitting around a table laden with Russian delicacies, we are only too aware that ordinary people in the 'new Russia' cannot afford to eat like this. No more than they could in the old Soviet Union. For foreigners with US dollars, it is a different matter.

After lunch we join other Sunday afternoon strollers in a promenade along the embankment of the River Amur. Watching the passenger boats plying their way up the river and the children playing on the beach, I wonder if Abram ever had the chance to enjoy this timeless scene sometime in the summer of 1936 or 1937. I certainly hope he experienced some of the lighter side of Khabarovsk before he descended into darkness at the NKVD end of town.

As I enter the cavernous two-level reception hall of FSB headquarters in Volochayevskaya Street early the next morning, I look up to see the familiar bust of Feliks Dzerzhinsky, patron saint of the Soviet secret police, looking down from the top of the central staircase. It is sculpted in the same neo-classic style as the one I saw in the FSB in Moscow in 1992, shortly after the collapse of the Soviet Union. Now in 2000, Feliks is still overseeing proceedings. It seems some things never change.

While Sasha calls his contact on an internal telephone, I sit down on the bench in the lower reception area to watch the passing parade. Young FSB officers walk briskly in and out of the massive swinging doors one after another. Smartly dressed in civilian clothes, they flash their passes at the two fresh-faced guards in uniform. The army crewcuts of the two lads remind me of Vladimir back at the Lubyanka in 1992. I wonder if he would believe how far I have travelled since I began the journey that day at the Moscow FSB. I barely believe it myself.

My daydream is interrupted by a thin, blonde woman in a mulberry-coloured suit descending the stairs towards us. Sasha introduces her as a former colleague whom he has asked to look after me. Reserved and serious, she ushers us into one of the two reception rooms on the lower level and goes to collect Abram's file. The room is bare except for a desk with a chair on either side. While she is out, Sasha explains that he will leave me here to examine the material. I feel uneasy. The reading room at the archive in Nizhny was much friendlier.

'Will I be able to make copies?' I whisper.

'Yes, but they don't have much paper,' Sasha replies. 'You might have to buy some.'

Abram's file arrives and it is enormous. The hand-written index at the front shows there are 252 pages. Some are typed, others handwritten. Some pages have been sealed up, but not that many. Unfortunately, it has been bound tightly in the middle, making it difficult to read the words at the inner edge. How on earth am I going to get through it all? I wonder. I figure I have two days and will just have to be systematic in my approach.

The first document in the file is an NKVD decree dated 17 October 1937. It says that evidence has been found to show that 'while working for the NKVD, [Abram] was engaged in espionage activities in the interest of the Japanese'—under the familiar Article 58.6-11 of the Criminal Code. I notice that this is not the same article on which Abram was finally convicted.

The decree notes that Abram was in Khabarovsk at that time and orders his arrest and detention in the NKVD prison. Abram was arrested the same day, though the warrant for his search and arrest is dated three days later. It gives his address as the Commune House hostel on Karl Marx Street. This is the large yellow building Sasha pointed out to me on our first walk down the main street.

Receipts in the file indicate that personal items confiscated at the time of Abram's arrest include his revolver and bullets, a watch, a knife, leather belt, cloth cap and keys. A few pages later I find a list of the entire contents of Abram's home in Grodekovo, where he was stationed near the Chinese border—104 items in total. These were apparently removed to an NKVD warehouse for safekeeping.

A few items leap out at me as I glance quickly down the pages—a gas mask, a billiard table, a *mah jong* set, a

Browning pistol, one box of contraceptives, half a bottle of eau de Cologne, a gramophone, a silk Japanese dressing gown, a brown leather jacket, and a bank book from Vladivostok which shows Abram had 1,056 roubles 53 kopeks. This item has been underscored and sidelined with a question mark; I guess it must have been a lot of money in those days.

Another page lists by name in English and Russian the contents of Abram's record collection. It shows a strong leaning towards opera, ranging from Bizet's *Carmen* to Mozart's *Magic Flute*, with *My Yiddishe Momme* and a few popular Russian romances like *Dark Eyes* thrown into the mix. I find it curious that the NKVD should bother noting the name of each record, while simply noting by number sixty Russian, twenty English and forty-four Chinese books.

My guardian returns to ask me how I am going.

'Slowly,' I reply. 'The handwriting is hard to read and my Russian is not that good,' I lie.

'How much longer will you be?' she says impatiently. 'There are others waiting to use the reception room.'

'What?' I exclaim. 'I thought I could work here all day. That's certainly what Aleksandr Pavlovich told me.'

'Aleksandr Pavlovich doesn't work here any more,' the woman responds, with a polite smile.

'Yes, of course,' I say. 'So what shall I do?' It is time to raise the photocopying option. 'Would it be possible to have the file photocopied?'

'Yes. How many pages?'

I look at her plaintively, 'All of it? Please? The information is so valuable and I've come so far. If I lived here, I could look at it a little at a time; unfortunately I don't have that luxury.'

The woman looks at me in disbelief and smiles.

'I'm happy to pay for the copies, as I do at the archive,' I say.

'But we don't charge,' she replies.

'You should,' I say. 'It's normal practice in all archives. Well, at least let me pay for the paper.' I slide a US $100 bill onto the table.

'We do not take money,' the woman responds like a shot.

'All right, please tell me where I can go to buy some paper and I will bring it back.'

The deal is done. Directions in hand, I walk six blocks in the rain to the stationery shop and return with two reams of the finest quality paper and a box of chocolates. Next day, my copies are done.

'Can I take a photograph of your Dzerzhinsky sculpture, please,' I ask the woman when I return to collect my papers.

'I'm sorry but photography in this building is forbidden,' comes the reply.

'What a pity,' I smile. 'It's such a fine bust and he's so rarely seen in public these days.'

'I have a present for you,' Sasha announces, handing me a document when he arrives at my hotel room on my last evening in Khabarovsk. Headed:

Personal Particulars
Special appointment of NKVD employee

it has been filled in with an ink pen in Abram's flamboyant handwriting. Sasha explains that it is a copy of the form Abram completed in July 1936 when he became a full-time officer of the NKVD— 'came in from the cold', so to speak. Fifteen pages of biographical information about him and the whole Onikul family. What a treasure!

A passionate historian himself, Sasha understands my obsession with old family documents. He also gives me the original archival note from the Magadan Ministry of Security in 1996, which sets out the gruesome details of Abram's death. These are the two documents he drew on when he wrote me the original letter about Abram's fate. Before we head off to his house for dinner, Sasha gives me a crash-course on the purges in the Far East which I record on tape. It later proves invaluable background in my effort to understand Abram's story.

Sasha, his family and a huge Alsatian live at the 'NKVD end of town' in a block which was especially built for senior employees of the KGB. His comfortable three-bedroom apartment, which he designed himself, is full of books and memorabilia. Later in the evening, I persuade Sasha to show me the medals from his distinguished KGB career. Most display the hammer and sickle but Sasha's favourite is one he received in post-Soviet times, bearing the double-headed eagle, last seen officially as the crest of the Tsar.

Dinner is a jolly occasion. Meeting for the second time and on home ground, Sasha's wife Lyudmila is relaxed and informal. She has cooked a sumptuous meal, including my favourite Russian *solyanka*, a spicy stew of vegetables and meat. Young Nikita uses the occasion to practise his English. As usual, we drink too many toasts to health and eternal friendship. I pass on best wishes from my parents who are dining with old friends.

'For someone who has grown up in a foreign culture at the other end of the earth, you are remarkably Russian,' Sasha says at one point during the dinner. 'You almost have a Russian soul.' This is a high compliment and leads to a lively debate as to what this soul constitutes.

After dinner, Sasha lets me in on his pet historical subject—the puppet emperor of Manchukuo, Henry Pu Yi. After the Japanese defeat in 1945, Pu Yi, together with some of his generals, ministers and officials, spent five years in detention in Khabarovsk. Sasha shows me the remarkable album of photographs he has put together of the detainees, as well as a number of articles he has published in Russia and Japan.

As it is almost midnight, I get up to leave. The following morning, I am bound for Vladivostok on the Trans-Siberian. Sasha insists on walking me back to my hotel. Crossing the road from Sasha's apartment, I glance momentarily at the wall of Abram's former prison,

269

ghostly white in the moonlight. As we turn into the main street of Khabarovsk, I reflect on how much has transpired in the week since my first walk with this remarkable 'KGB man'.

Having arrived knowing next to nothing about Abram's life, I have now retraced the steps of his last fateful days in this city and learned much about the prevailing environment in which he lived. I now have a copy of his hefty file full of information, plus the BREM files on my father's family and on my grandfather Zaretsky. On top of all that, I have made friends with some extraordinary people who have changed my preconceptions on many things.

'So what happened in this building?' my friend Sasha interrupts my reverie. 'NKVD officials lived there,' I answer. 'In 1937, most of them were shot.'

'How many?' It appears the spymaster is subjecting me to an interrogation.

'I don't remember.'

'One hundred. And what about this yellow one on the right? What was it called?'

'In the 1930s, it was known as the Commune House. Soviet officials and NKVD people lived there—including, for a while, my great-uncle.'

'And what happened to them?'

'In 1937, many were arrested. Some were shot. Others were more privileged. First they were tortured, then sent to dig for Stalin's gold and freeze in Kolyma. I'm not sure which fate was worse.'

'I did not tell you that,' says Sasha sternly. 'You know too much. For that I must kill you.'

Our man in Khabarovsk has retained his KGB sense of humour.

CHAPTER 12

SPIES IN THE FAR EAST

As I PACK my bags in Khabarovsk for my journey to Vladivostok, I stow Abram's NKVD file safely at the bottom of my suitcase. I know this hefty tome is not going to make light and easy reading—certainly not something for an overnight trip on the Trans-Siberian Express. Besides, I am looking forward to a few hours in the dining car, swapping stories with my parents over vodka and *zakuski* (appetisers). Although I know that the present day express train is as utilitarian as any other, merely the name 'Trans-Siberian' conjures up images of past elegance and romance that I yearn to indulge.

Still, the purpose of going to Vladivostok is to get some sense of the city in which Abram lived. The train trip gives me a chance to form a clearer picture of this man and get some clues about places of significance in his life which I should visit. I pull out a couple of Abram's inter-rogation records which contain biographical information and the priceless NKVD personal particulars form I received from Sasha. I put these documents in my hand luggage together with my *Lonely Planet* guide to Russia.

Tedious as it must have been for people living under Soviet rule to constantly write and recite their biographies in minute detail, I am grateful for it. The eighteen-page questionnaire Abram completed when he officially joined the NKVD in July 1936 is full of information about his life in Manchuria and his early years in Vladivostok— what he did, whom he knew. Some of the answers he gave the NKVD during interrogations in 1939 fill out the picture. It seems that my impression of Abram from the photographs in Chesna's photo album is accurate. He was clearly a young man with initiative and a taste for adventure.

In 1921, at age fourteen Abram had already started doing seasonal work for a couple of foreign wool companies in Hailar. At sixteen, he joined the Soviet-inspired Otmol youth association of the railway workers' union in Hailar, and with other students went to study at the Technical College in Chita, across the border in Siberia. He stayed for only one year because of what he described as 'economic conditions'. This could mean being expelled for inappropriate social origins as my grandmother suggested, as much as leaving due to financial hardship.

While in Chita, Abram joined the Komsomol and on return to Hailar, set up a Pioneers group for younger children; no doubt the same one that his younger brother Yasha joined. By 1925, Abram was in Harbin working for a meat and livestock agent at the abattoir. The following year, he went to Mongolia and worked as an accountant for a British fur company, Biderman and Co., in Ulan Bator and Ulia Sutay. These were the exotic place names I had seen on the back of some of Abram's photographs.

He returned to Manchuria at the end of 1927 and continued to work for Biderman and Co., buying up skins and furs from Chinese and Mongol traders; first in Hailar, then in a couple of other towns. In 1929, when the Chinese seized the Chinese Eastern Railway (CER) and started arresting Soviet CER workers in Hailar along with union and Komsomol activists, Abram went to Mukden, where he stayed until the Sino-Soviet conflict was over. From there, his career took a different tack. The last entry in the employment section of Abram's questionnaire reads:

> From 1930, while on secret work, I was a trading agent of Biderman and Co. and was engaged in other matters.

From his record of interrogation, I learn that this 'secret work' was for the NKVD's Foreign Intelligence Bureau—the INO—the same organisation Manya apparently worked for. Did Abram tell his management of his double life? Somehow, I doubt it.

The INO's main targets in Manchuria at the time were the émigré White Guards who continued to plot the overthrow of the Bolshevik regime. Abram's job as a trading agent for Biderman and Co. would have given him natural cover for gathering information on operations White Guard units were planning to launch across the Soviet border.

There were many old warriors from the Civil War who lived in towns and settlements around northern Manchuria. Some among them still dreamed of driving the Bolsheviks out of power, plotting acts of sabotage in collusion with the Japanese military and Chinese bandits. Most others had resigned themselves to the fact that the Soviet Union was there to stay and wanted to make their peace. It was some of these people, as well as Mongol livestock traders and Chinese smugglers, that Abram appears to have recruited as informers.

Reading and rereading Abram's background, I am puzzled by why he chose to join the secret service. Why hadn't he just remained a trader, like his friends in Hailar? It strikes me that with his experience in Mongolia and Manchuria, Abram would have been a natural business partner for my grandfather Zaretsky. Didn't it occur to them? If the horizons in Hailar were too narrow for him, why didn't he go to Harbin or Shanghai? What made him choose instead the path into the secret world, which led him to the Soviet Union and sealed the fate of the family who followed?

This is an issue neither the questionnaire nor the inter-rogation records directly addresses.

Reflecting on the political machinations occurring in Manchuria at the time, the picture I am building of Abram and the timing of his recruitment, my hypothesis is that Abram was driven by patriotism.

I figure that if, as he says, Abram joined the INO in 1930, his recruitment was somehow linked with the Sino-Soviet conflict in mid-1929. I imagine Abram would have been outraged at the Chinese seizure of the CER and the arbitrary arrests of Soviet citizens that followed. Perhaps his own involvement with pro-Soviet youth organisations like the Komsomol in Hailar made him personally vulnerable. It could explain why he stayed in Mukden until the end of the year when the Soviet army restored order.

Abram would presumably have also taken a dim view of White Guard collaboration with the Chinese and their continued acts of sabotage against the Soviet Union. This may have been the moment when some skilful recruiter chose to enlist Abram's help in defence of the Motherland.

Abram's secret work would have become even more significant as the Japanese rolled out their occupation of Manchuria after the Mukden incident in September 1931. While Harbin was taken in February 1932, Hailar and the area west of the Soviet border only fell at the end of that year. That still gave Soviet agents, Abram included, room to manoeuvre in their efforts to gather information about Japanese intentions and the anti-Soviet machinations of White Guard units now operating openly under Japanese patronage.

Much later—in fact, several years after I first read his file—I discover that Abram's recruitment may not have happened at all as I had initially envisaged.

From what Abram told the NKVD Military Tribunal in March 1939, it seems it may have been his father Girsh who first got involved with the Soviet secret service.

The reason I had failed to pick up immediately on such a critical fact is that it was buried in the midst of a handwritten transcript, which was hard to decipher. Unlike interrogation records, which clearly identify questions and answers, the transcript reads as a continuous record of Abram's responses. To make matters worse, the words along its inner edge were missed in photocopying the original file, whose pages were tightly sewn together.

It emerges from this transcript that at the request of an employee of the Soviet consulate, Girsh had been trying to recruit a former Cossack, who was prominent in the Hailar émigré community. When Chesna noticed Girsh's frequent meetings with the man and discovered what was going on, she put a stop to the visits. Abram took over:

One day I found out that Popov, who worked for the NKVD's INO, had proposed to my father that he work for the Soviet secret service. After that I told Popov that my father should not be involved in such work as he would not be able to carry it out. I took on the work proposed to my father myself.

Abram says he soon discovered that the Cossack was a 'provocateur'. For a moment, the vision of my naïve but well-intentioned great-grandfather trying to recruit a hardened Cossack as an informer for the Soviet cause strikes me as exceedingly funny. Especially when he was discovered by his astute and all-suffering wife. But then I am overwhelmed by the absolute wretchedness of the situation and its tragic consequences.

Girsh's time as a secret agent was so short-lived that Abram makes no mention of him in his questionnaire when asked to identify who else in his family was involved with Soviet intelligence. He answers that his sister Manya 'was involved in secret work in Hailar and Shanghai' and that his brother Yasha 'worked a little in Hailar'. Yasha's assertion that the entire family had been engaged in 'secret work' in Hailar was clearly an exaggeration, though he may have heard of Girsh's brush with fame.

It is not clear whether 'the work' Abram took on in lieu of his father was work with the INO in general or simply the case of the Cossack. Either way, it seems that once Abram started working for the INO, there was no way out.

In the same tribunal transcript, Abram is recorded as saying:

After the uprising in Hailar, I asked to be released from this work. But Morov [the NKVD station chief in Hailar] told me that, in the face of the approaching Japanese army, our operation was at serious risk and I could not stay in Hailar. He proposed that I leave for the USSR.

This was exactly the same proposition the unknown Skuratov put to Manya a year later, when he warned that she might be arrested if she stayed in Hailar. Perhaps Skuratov was also from the INO. But Manya initially went to Shanghai. Why didn't Abram do the same? Then Manya would not have followed him in 1934 and nor would the others.

But by the eve of the Japanese arrival in Hailar on 4 December 1932, Abram had left his departure too late to go anywhere except across the Soviet border.

According to his interrogation record which I read on the train to Vladivostok, Abram left Hailar together with his station chief Morov and another Soviet operative. They went to Khabarovsk, which was then the NKVD's Far Eastern headquarters. Abram says he had no correspondence with his family while they remained in Hailar. As family and friends living there at the time remember it, Abram simply disappeared, though they did somehow hear that he was in Vladivostok.

At the beginning of 1933, Abram was sent by the NKVD to study at the Far Eastern State University in Vladivostok. Not surprisingly, he joined the Oriental faculty and majored in Chinese. Perhaps the promise of higher education was the incentive used by his controllers to lure Abram to the USSR or the prize he extracted for services rendered. My understanding from the letter

Sasha sent me in 1996 is that Abram worked for the NKVD as a Chinese interpreter while he was studying.

At the time he filled in his personal particulars form as a fully fledged NKVD officer in July 1936, Abram would have been about to start his final year of Chinese. From the form, I learn that Abram also knew English and a little German and Yiddish. He had completed military training, attaining the rank of lieutenant. Though not yet a member of the Communist Party, Abram had been a member of the 'sympathisers' group since the end of 1934. None of this is surprising.

But from a comment Abram volunteers at the very end of his NKVD form, it appears there was a little more to his part-time work for the NKVD than mere interpreting:

From the time I arrived in Vladivostok, I have been head of the Chinese Group in the OO [Special Section].

I subsequently learn that the NKVD's Special Sections were responsible for military counter-intelligence. With spies, infiltrators and smugglers of various nationalities and persuasions moving in both directions across the porous Far Eastern border at the time, it is easy to see why the NKVD would have wanted to put both Abram's linguistic and information trading skills to good use.

Apart from the university where he studied, Abram's documents give me no clues to the landmarks of his life in Vladivostok. Though the university is not marked on the *Lonely Planet* map, I figure it will be easy enough to find. Given Abram's double life, I doubt that he would have lived in a university dormitory, but he might have found a room nearby. But with only two days in Vladivostok, I will probably just have time to find the university and wander the streets of the old city, trying to imagine how it would have been in the 1930s.

———

After the easy old-world charm of Khabarovsk, Vladivostok immediately strikes me as a city on edge— though on the edge of what is not easy to define.

Visually, it is spectacular: the city is set on a series of terraces that cascade down to the harbour on Golden Horn Bay. From its cosmopolitan roots at the turn of the century, Vladivostok might have grown into a bustling port city to rival Hong Kong. Instead, it was closed to the world and became the base of the Soviet Pacific Fleet, remembered only because its warships were a constant factor in Western calculations of Soviet military power. Looking at the rusting hulls on the harbour front in May 2000, it occurs to me that the truth the Soviets may have been trying to hide was that the threat was hollow at the core.

Driving in the drizzling rain from the station to the Hotel Vladivostok, the city looks grey and shabby, the people on the streets preoccupied. Ten years after it opened up, Vladivostok is still in the grip of post-Soviet stress. Power struggles have paralysed local administration, government workers have been unpaid for months, power blackouts are frequent and residents are bracing themselves for another winter without heating.

Here it is easy to understand the despair of older people when they ask what all the struggle and hard work through the Soviet years have brought them. Yet there are others who, through it all, maintain a stoic dignity. Some work two or three jobs to enable their children to study English or Japanese to secure their future.

Wandering through the streets of old Vladivostok, it is gratifying to see the splendid buildings of the city's cosmopolitan past still standing; some already restored to an earlier splendour. If I shut out the advertising billboards and the Japanese cars, I can easily imagine what it may have been like in Abram's day. The grand old railway station with its Gothic turrets would have looked much the same. So would the statue of Lenin in the square across the road, though his raised hand would have been pointing to a radiant future beyond the Samsung sign.

By the mid-1930s, most of the buildings which had previously belonged to rich merchants, like the grandfather of actor Yul Brynner, had been taken over by various Party and government institutions. Now, many were again reverting to private hands. Some, like the old post office and the GUM general department store, still functioned in their 1930s incarnations.

Locating the Oriental faculty of the Far Eastern State University where Abram studied turns out to be a more complicated matter. It is not at the university's current location; as a postwar development, it is in the new part of the city. Nor does it turn out to be in the red brick building—guarded in traditional Chinese style by two stone lions—which had been the home of the original Oriental Studies Institute.

In fact, it has moved just a few streets up the hill to a distinctive art nouveau-style building on Sukhanov Street. But it takes me the rest of the day, a bus trip to the new campus and a miraculous meeting with three professors of the history department to discover this—no mean feat for a Friday afternoon. Through these connections I also learn some of the university's tragic history.

In the face of the Japanese threat to the USSR's eastern border in the mid-1930s, graduates from the Oriental faculty, like Abram, were in great demand. Especially keen to recruit them were government institutions like the army and the NKVD. But as paranoia about spies grew, so did suspicion about those with a knowledge of Asia. Amid the hysteria about a Japanese 'fifth column' in the Russian Far East, the staff of the Oriental faculty were all arrested as Japanese spies. In September 1939, the university was closed altogether. Ironically, the building was taken over by the NKVD.

According to his record of interrogation, at the time of his arrest in October 1937, Abram was working as a

Chinese interpreter at an NKVD operational point at Grodekovo. Grodekovo, as I have already learned, was then a small town fifteen kilometres from the Manchurian border and 150 kilometres from Vladivostok. Named in honour of a regional governor-general, it had been a Cossack stronghold during the Russian Civil War.

What puzzles me is how and why Abram ended up there. I understand why a restless young man might move from provincial Hailar to bustling Vladivostok, particularly when a higher education came as part of the bargain. But from Vladivostok to a border post in the Soviet Far East? Why?

I know that the answers to these and many more questions are buried somewhere in the 250 pages I have copied from Abram's NKVD file in Khabarovsk. But unravelling the story is a daunting task.

Much of the material is handwritten, some of it barely legible and not in date order, not to mention cut off in the process of photocopying. Though the Onikul files I brought from Nizhny have given me much practice, I still find illegible Russian much harder to decipher than English. Many pages of interrogation records belong to complete strangers and mention Abram only in passing.

For a long time, inertia gets the better of me. I do nothing. Finally, I decide to wrestle with the material. By this time my quest to unravel the mystery of the Onikuls and the story of the *Harbintsy* has taken hold of me.

I realise that the only way through Abram's enormous file is to be systematic. I draw up a table, sorting the documents by date and summarising key points of information relevant to Abram's case. I find the key in two petitions Abram wrote to the NKVD military tribunal in 1939 and a protest to NKVD chief Beria in 1940.

The second petition, which Abram wrote in the course of reviewing the material in his file at the end of his investigation, is especially useful. In it, Abram gives a detailed commentary on the conduct of his investigation, specifying dates and names of interrogators. These letters, together with the records of Abram's tribunal hearings, help me contextualise the rest of the material in his file.

And what a story it turns out to be.

———————

In 1936, while still in Vladivostok, Abram was head-hunted by Leonid Popov from the NKVD's International Department (no relation to the one in Hailar), as one of the students who should be recruited as an interpreter and Eastern specialist. Abram says that at the time, Popov offered many students work in the NKVD, which some did not accept for financial considerations. Abram apparently felt a sense of obligation since his education 'had been provided by the Soviet state'.

In testimony about Abram which I find in the file, Popov says he advised NKVD regional headquarters in Khabarovsk that Abram, who was already working under cover as head of the Chinese group, was regarded by the university board as 'the best student' in Chinese and that there were 'no compromising materials on him'. Abram says Popov took him to Khabarovsk for discussions in July 1936, where he agreed to join the NKVD. This must have been when he completed his personal particulars form.

Abram says he was immediately offered an assignment as head of a new intelligence unit in a border guard detachment not far from Khabarovsk. In one of his petitions to the military tribunal, Abram explains why he declined and ended up in Grodekovo:

> I did not have the audacity to go as the chief when I had never even worked in the border guard system . . . I was then offered the position in Grodekovo as assistant to Morov [then NKVD operations chief there]. I accepted because I knew [from working with him in Hailar] that Morov was not a stupid man and I could learn from him . . . In fact, I had always planned to go to work in the centre but I was forcibly pulled into this work as a China specialist and nothing more . . .

The Soviet Union's extensive and exposed borders made the work of the NKVD border guards—the *pogranichniki* —critical for its security. In Soviet propaganda of the mid-1930s, border guards were placed alongside aviators and polar explorers as the exalted heroes of Soviet youth. Soviet children sang songs and recited poems about courageous *pogranichniki*—on alert at the border 'through snowstorm and blizzard', defending the nation against spies and infiltrators.

Abram started working with Morov in Grodekovo in September 1936, returning to Vladivostok four months later to prepare and sit for his final university exams. By the time he came back to work in Grodekovo in July 1937, Morov had moved on. From what I could piece together, Abram's unit ran operations across the border in Manchukuo—planting and recruiting agents, collecting information on Japanese plans and White Guard activities in the border area and thwarting counter-intelligence efforts against the Soviet Union.

From Abram's petitions, it is evident that he took his work very seriously. His concern about 'abnormal' operational practices at his post and the 'negligent attitude towards matters of national importance' on the part of the NKVD hierarchy in Khabarovsk is a constant theme. In late September and early October 1937, Abram had tried to get a response from his superiors in Khabarovsk on a number of operational issues—to no avail. He had been particularly concerned that a sensitive cross-border operation which he had planned had been countermanded by the new NKVD deputy, Osinin:

I refused to implement Osinin's instruction to send a 'shock' team over the border because their unsuccessful deployment could create political difficulties. The military operations chief in Grodekovo ... was in total agreement with my plan and did not take it upon himself to carry out Osinin's order without me ... In my view, Osinin, a recent appointee, was not giving sufficient consideration to the peculiarities of local circumstances. That was why I wanted to explain my plan to him face to face ... I also wanted to report to him a number of other important issues of which he was not aware ...

In a telephone conversation with headquarters in early October, Abram invited himself to Khabarovsk for discussions with Osinin and his colleagues. His plan was to stay for just one day. But ten days later, he was still there waiting for a meeting.

Abram says that at around midnight on 17 October, there was a knock at the door of the room where he was staying at the big yellow Commune House on Karl Marx Street. It was Malkevich, head of the NKVD's International Department in the Far East and one of Abram's superiors. But Malkevich had not come to discuss operational matters and was not alone. He was there to arrest Abram. Though no arrest order was produced, Abram later learned that his arrest had been authorised by the same Osinin whom he had been trying to see for the past ten days.

———

Confronting a new deputy in the NKVD would have been a career-limiting move at the best of times—even if the matter was of a purely operational nature. In 1937, telling a chief newly arrived from the centre that he did not sufficiently appreciate the special circumstances in the Far East was potentially suicidal. Stalin had long been suspicious of the autonomous tendencies of the Far Eastern Party and military establishments. Yet efforts to bring them under control had invariably failed, in spite of the linkages drawn with all the major conspiracies uncovered at the centre.

In 1937, Stalin and his NKVD chief Yezhov moved to crush a 'Far Eastern parallel rightist-Trotskyist centre'. In July, they sent a new regional NKVD chief, Lyushkov, to Khabarovsk with express instructions to cleanse the Far East of enemies, spies and traitors. As his deputy, Lyushkov brought Osinin, who, it emerges, was his long-time trusted associate. Moscow visited its revenge on the Far East through extremely high quotas for arrests and executions in its key establishments—the Party, the army and the NKVD.

Whether Abram's actions and arrival in Khabarovsk heightened his chances of arrest is difficult to know. The special operation to 'arrest all *Harbintsy*' under Yezhov's Operational Order No 000593 of 20 September 1937 had already commenced by the time Abram got to Khabarovsk. Employees of the NKVD with any connections to Manchuria were targeted for the first round of arrests. Like his family in Gorky, Abram was arrested under Article 58.6—espionage activities in the interests of Japan. But his charge had the aggravating factor of Article 58.11—that he had engaged in these criminal activities as part of 'an organisation'.

As in Gorky, the NKVD investigators were not interested in truth, only confessions. In his petition to the military tribunal, Abram writes how the head of the International Department, Malkevich, summoned him for interrogation on 9 November 1937 and demanded that he 'confess to being a member of a right-Trotskyist fascist subversive espionage organisation'. In spite of two sessions on the 'conveyor'—continuous questioning without sleep or respite—Abram refused to confess.

By the end of January 1938, the investigators found three others who did. All three had at one time worked in Manchuria and at the Grodekovo border post. Abram's former boss, Morov; a radio operator at Grodekovo named Markin; and another NKVD operative named Novoselov all confessed to a 'conspiracy' to supply secret intelligence material to the Japanese. In their lengthy interrogation records which I find in Abram's file, each mentions Abram as a collaborator. Most significant is the 'evidence' of Markin, who claims that Abram worked with him to collect secret material which Markin transmitted by radio to the Japanese Military Mission in Harbin.

On 2 February 1938, Abram was confronted with the charge of spying for Japan for the first time, then with Markin's 'evidence'. According to the record of interrogation, he rejected both outright:

I was never involved in espionage for Japan and was never recruited by anyone for this purpose . . . I reject what Markin says. I was not a spy.

Writing about it in his petition to the military tribunal,

foremost in Abram's memory of the encounter are the comments of both the interrogator and Malkevich: that Abram would 'lose his head before the month was out'. About an hour after this interrogation, Abram was brought back for a face to face 'confrontation' with Markin in the presence of three investigators, including Malkevich. In Abram's words:

Markin was barely alive, with a huge scar on his hand, and did not look me in the eye once during the confrontation.

According to the record of the confrontation in Abram's file, Markin claims that he and Abram struck up a friend ship shortly after Abram arrived in Grodekovo at the end of 1936. Discovering that they were both Japanese agents, they decided to work together. Among the secret material they transmitted to the Japanese in Harbin was information on the size and composition of the Grodekovo border detachment, details about the nearby Zharikov airport and the defence of the surrounding district.

Abram tells the military tribunal that he disputes whether or not Markin actually gave this evidence as Malkevich had sent Abram out of the room at the time and did not allow him to subsequently question Markin. When Abram was brought back, Malkevich forced him to sign the record without giving Abram a chance to read it.

In the whole confrontation I said only one word— 'No'— but my answers were recorded in my absence and not from my words.

Why then did Abram sign the record?

> *Because I did not want to go through the tortures I had been subjected to in previous days. Besides, the hysterical cries and groans of men and women and the foul language of the investigators on the fifth floor during the first half of 1938 did not give grounds to expect anything better, let alone objectivity.*

Abram describes in gruesome detail the beatings to which he had been subjected a week earlier, giving dates and names of his investigators and violators:

> *On 22 January 1938, soon after wake-up, I was summoned for interrogation by I. [my abbeviations], assistant to the chief of the 7th [International] department and was returned to my cell only on 25 January 1938, having spent three and a half days in the interrogation room without food or drink, being beaten mercilessly by [I., P. and V.]. The latter did not even let me out to the toilet. At the end, I barely made it back to my cell. But I confessed to nothing as I had enough strength to fight the provocations of the interrogators. Malkevich and [another senior NKVD officer] R. came in to the interrogation, but they did not beat me. V. handcuffed me in front of R. during the day on 23 Jan 1938. I was handcuffed by P. during the night from 23rd to the 24th I was handcuffed by P. and by V. and P. on the night of 25 January until I was returned to my cell. I. did not handcuff me. For the main part, they beat me about the head and on my back, after which I pissed blood.*

In his letters and testimony before the military tribunal, Abram refutes the 'evidence' of his three alleged co-conspirators in minute detail. In the case of Markin, Abram says he had not even met him at the time of their alleged friendship and only worked with him at Grodekovo in the last month and a half before his arrest. Abram notes that the 'evidence' of all three was obtained three and a half months after his arrest. He expresses surprise that the full records of their interrogations were put in his file when each contains no more than a few lines about him. Abram's guess, based on his own experience, is that their 'evidence' was beaten out of them:

> *Maybe the evidence of Morov, Markin and Novoselov is the slander of enemies. But I cannot rule out that this evidence was beaten out of them, just as the day before, I was beaten to give evidence against Morov and even against the [NKVD] station chief at Blagoveshchensk, . . . whom I had never seen in my life and against his sister, of whom I had never even heard.*

Throughout 1938, the NKVD interrogators continued their efforts to extract a confession from Abram through intimidation and torture—all of which he describes in his petition to the military tribunal. He writes that the investigators rebuffed his repeated complaints about the confrontation with Markin being conducted 'improperly'. They rejected his demand for a new confrontation with Markin, as well as one with Morov, saying he could have a confrontation with both of them 'in the basement before his execution'. Abram says that at the end of September 1938, he was forced to write a confession that he had been a member of a fascist organisation in Hailar:

> ... *After they tortured me, I wrote the same confession over and over again. But this confession was not put in my file. Apparently even the investigators realised its absurdity—that as a Jew, I could not be a fascist. Besides, up until the time I left Hailar, there had been no fascist organisation there ...*

Abram describes his beatings in forensic detail:

> *On 23 September 1938, I was summoned by Lieutenant S. and here began my next series of tortures, which ended in mid-October. There were no conveyors, but sometimes they beat me from 9 pm at night till 5 am in the morning without stop. I would then crawl back to my room. Sometimes I would be beaten by S alone, at other times by two, three and up to five people. His assistants in execution were ... [6 names]; instruments of interrogation: belts of different calibres—staff sergeant's, Red Army and bag straps. They hit me with the buckles, fists, feet and stuffed a gag into my mouth. They disfigured my head. In July this year I had a fit. I thought I was going mad. I gave no peace all night to the nurse or the duty officers. On my back I still have the scars of skin chopped to pieces by buckles ...*

Abram appeals to the tribunal to let him go before a medical commission to verify the truth of his words. He gives the names and designations of his cellmates, who could confirm the condition in which he returned from the beatings, among them some middle-ranking party and army figures.

This is how they got evidence from us—they beat evidence out of innocent people about other innocent people—just like molesting naïve infants.

———

At the end of 1938, the beatings suddenly stopped. New investigators took over Abram's case and a flurry of paperwork began, addressing formalities that had been overlooked from the start of his investigation. In December 1938, Abram was formally presented with the charges against him—Articles 58.6 and 58.11—and asked to sign the document which had been issued in February 1938 on the authority of NKVD officials who were no longer around. Early in January 1939, he was taken through the biographical questionnaire that should have been part of his very first interrogation.

Then at the end of January 1939, he was advised that his case had been reviewed and the charges against him had changed. The charge of 'espionage'—Article 58.6— had been replaced with Article 58.1(b)—'treason against the Motherland'. The (b) meant it was punishable by execution. Abram says he rejected these charges, just as he had the earlier ones.

The NKVD's sudden effort to put Abram's case in order and to conduct his investigation by the rules was clearly a reaction to the major crackdown on the NKVD after the Politburo decision in November 1938 to bring the repression under control. Laying the blame for the excesses of the purges squarely at the feet of the NKVD, the decision ordered that arrests and investigations be conducted in strict observance of the laws and procedures and warned that any violations would lead to 'severe judicial penalties'.

By the end of the month, NKVD chief Yezhov had resigned and the removal and arrest of his close associates, including many of Abram's tormentors, was underway. Now it was the turn of Osinin, Malkevich and the others to be arrested as enemies of the people. In fact, Osinin had been arrested in the middle of the year after his boss, Lyushkov, the NKVD chief of the whole Far Eastern region, had walked across the border into Manchukuo and defected to the Japanese. According to an article by an NKVD veteran I find in one of the Khabarovsk 'books of memory', it was Osinin who had tipped off Lyushkov that a new purge of the NKVD leadership in the Far East was on its way.

As Abram's investigation had dragged on for well over a year, the NKVD investigators were under pressure to bring it to a conclusion. In early February 1939, Abram was advised that his case was being referred for hearing to the NKVD Military Tribunal of the Far Eastern Region. It would be heard 'in closed judicial session, without prosecution and defence and without witnesses being called'.

Abram responded with a cleverly written petition to the tribunal, setting out eleven demands which, in passing, set out the illegalities perpetrated during his investigation.

Abram's demands include full access to his investigation file and confrontations in which he would have the opportunity to cross-examine his alleged co-conspirators, Markin and Morov, whose 'slanderous evidence' had been used against him. He also asks that the tribunal obtain various reports from his work files to refute bogus allegations, as well as references from his superiors in the Vladivostok NKVD and Party Committee, which would vouch for his good character and standing. He questions the credibility of the case against him, pointing out that the people who started it, including Osinin and Malkevich, 'have themselves turned out to be conspirators and enemies of the people'.

Abram was still deeply riled by the failure of the NKVD hierarchy to treat seriously the concerns about border operations which had brought him to Khabarovsk that fateful October in 1937. The issue takes up a page and a half of his petition and is also the subject of a separate letter to the new NKVD chief for the Far East:

From the first day of my arrest ... I tried every day to get a meeting with someone in authority so I could inform them of a range of operational issues of national importance ... Nothing has been done about many of these matters, which remain relevant to this day. But the investigators would only give me access to the authorities if I confessed first ...

Abram claims that his information 'has not lost its value' and his proposals 'could still be used successfully in the interest of the Soviet Union'. The letter requests a meeting with the chief and ends on a note of melodrama:

> *I cannot find a place for myself in my cell, knowing that I have not shared the information with anyone—though not for want of trying on my part.*

Could Abram have so quickly forgotten what it was like to crawl back to his cell after his beatings? Was Abram's tale about information of 'national importance' real or just a yarn he was spinning to get himself out of prison? There are no more details in his letters to indicate the nature of the information.

In mid-March 1939, Abram's judicial process before the military tribunal got underway. The tribunal comprised four men—two military jurists and two NKVD state security officers. The first hearing lasted only twenty minutes because Abram identified one of the NKVD men as someone who had been present at one of his interrogations—and as he later mentions in a petition, someone who had beaten him. The tribunal was reconvened with four new members the following day. This time the hearing went for three hours.

Although the transcript of the hearing records Abram's answers without the questions, it still gives a sense of the proceedings. Abram speaks at length about his work for the NKVD, both in Manchuria and the Soviet Union, clarifying his relationships—or lack of them—with his alleged co-conspirators. He responds in detail to the allegations against him taken from the 'evidence' of others, pointing out the illegalities perpetrated in his investigation, including efforts to force confessions out of him by physical means.

At the end of the hearing, Abram complains that his investigators never bothered to check out his work record:

In Hailar...my network and I worked honestly for Soviet intelligence. Not everyone on the Manchurian side of the border were spies...During my four years in Vladivostok, I was involved in secret work and worked with many people who honestly fulfilled their responsibilities. I asked that all my work be checked, but that was not done. While in Vladivostok, I exposed a range of people who were working against Soviet interests and uncovered a series of abnormalities in the work of the border detachment. But none of my investigators were interested in this. They just tried to make a spy out of me. I request that my case be reinvestigated as the materials in it are false.

The tribunal agreed. Abram's case was returned to the NKVD for 'further investigation', together with a list of questions for follow-up. Apart from verifying dates when Abram and other key players worked in particular places, the NKVD were instructed to check on Abram's work in Manchuria and the circumstances of his departure for the Soviet Union; and whether he really did undertake secret work for the NKVD in Vladivostok.

There is also an instruction to interrogate Abram's relatives in Gorky about their life in Manchuria after Abram left Hailar and to check whether the NKVD had any compromising materials on them. Clearly, the NKVD in the Far East was not aware that Abram's father Girsh and sister Manya had been sentenced to capital punishment.

Judging by the clutter of stamped *spravkas* which found their way into Abram's file, information started to flow back in May and June 1939. Among them are three *spravkas* showing that Abram's alleged co-conspirators were sentenced in January 1939 to 'VMN'—the Russian acronym for 'supreme order of punishment'. Another *spravka* says information on Abram's work in Manchuria could not be provided as no archival materials existed in the International Department and none of his former colleagues was in Khabarovsk. A typed copy of his mother Chesna's record of interrogation from Gorky also found its way into his file.

But positive references had been obtained from Abram's superiors in Vladivostok. One, from Popov, the NKVD head-hunter who recruited him, says Abram had been the top student in Chinese in his year, with an unblemished personal record. The other, from Abram's superior in Vladivostok for three years, describes him as 'conscientious, precise and active' in his secret work, for which he had received financial bonuses from the head of the bureau. By the time they wrote these references, both men were also in prison in Khabarovsk.

But the reinvestigation did not help Abram. On 20 June 1939, he was told that his case had been concluded and the charges against him—Articles 58.1 (b) and 58.11 —stood. Abram was given the opportunity to review his file as specified in Article 206 of the Code of Criminal Procedure. Abram again refuted the charges. He offered a number of clarifications and requested confrontations with Morov and Markin, whose 'evidence' formed the basis of the case against him. Not surprisingly, his requests were refused—Morov and Markin were long dead. On 26 June 1939, Abram signed in a shaky hand that he had read ninety-three pages.

Abram's indictment, drawn up on 10 August 1939, is predictable. Based on the 'evidence' of Morov, Markin and Novoselov, it alleges that Abram had been recruited by Japanese intelligence back in Manchuria, was sent to the USSR in 1932 and worked with them to collect and pass secret information to the Japanese, including details about the Zharikov airport and the strength of the border detachment. Abram was charged with 'engaging in espionage activities in the interest of Japan'.

Interestingly, the charge was changed from Articles 58.1 (b)—punishable by execution—to 58.1 (a)—punishable by ten years imprisonment. Article 58.11 stood. The indictment mentions in passing that Abram's father and sister had been sentenced to 'VMN' as Japanese spies. It also names as Japanese agents several of Abram's NKVD colleagues from Hailar; and Popov, the man who recruited him in Vladivostok, as an 'enemy of the people'.

A week later, Abram was asked to sign a receipt to say he had read the indictment and had been advised that his case was again being set for hearing by the military tribunal. It was at this point that he handed over the six-page petition to the tribunal which helped me understand his story. It directly attacks the NKVD's conduct of his investigation over twenty-two months—both before and after his last hearing—arguing that over the twenty-two months of his detention, there had been 'no proper investigation' of his case.

In the five months since the re-investigation commenced, I have been summoned for interrogation no less than ten times, but there has only been one record added to my file with just one question: 'Do you admit your guilt?' I have pleaded with the investigators that they should take a detailed record from me on the substance of the slanderous evidence which has been placed in my file. I have asked them to unearth documents and interrogate people that will refute all the lies and dirt poured on me by the investigation. But I got the same response: 'Everything is clear to the investigation and nothing more is necessary'. This answer is understandable because the people who tortured me during my investigation are not all behind bars and some of them were even present at my most recent interrogations at the end of June 1939. They threatened me with the isolation cell and beatings—

though this time they just threatened. Nevertheless, they did not bring any clarity to my case. In fact they deliberately confused it.

Abram notes that his faith in the procuracy had also been misplaced. The procurator, with whom he managed to get a meeting in April 1939 by resorting to a hunger strike, had promised that he would get all the documents Abram had referred to and be present at all his interrogations. Nothing had come of these promises. Abram prepared a detailed statement of 'the methods of interrogation' used against him. But his investigators had refused to take it into account, saying they would not allow 'slander' against the NKVD.

Now all my hope is on the people's court, which abides by revolutionary legality, punishes the guilty and clears the innocent. I wait only for my freedom and the punishment of my tormentors.

Abram obviously considered the petition to the military tribunal to be his last means of defence. In it he itemises the tortures to which he had been subjected, as well as his responses to all the 'evidence' that had been placed in his file. He again sets out a list of requests which would 'help the court reach an impartial understanding' of his case.

From his file Abram discovered that his arrest was based on just one report—by another former student of the Oriental faculty also working for the NKVD. From the index at the front of the file, I identify this as one of the reports to which I had been denied access—perhaps because it is the report of an NKVD informer. From Abram's comments, it appears that the author alleged that Abram lived in Millyonka, the Chinese district of Vladivostok, and was involved in 'shady deals with Chinese'. Abram dismisses the report as 'slanderous and provocative', saying he did not know its author either personally or socially. They had studied different subjects several years apart.

In his petition, Abram also refutes the substance of a report from a former interpreter at Grodekovo, which I was also unable to see. The gist of these allegations seems to be that Abram had forged two receipts for twenty Japanese yen each for his boss Morov from the border post's account and that he had been dealing in leather obtained from cross-border agents. Abram denies these charges unreservedly. He points out that his accuser's signature was required for all transactions and that the incident involving illegal import of leather had predated Abram's arrival at Grodekovo. He also mentions that he reported a range of improprieties in the border detachment, including personnel offering him Japanese yen to get them foreign goods from across the border. No action was ever taken to stop such practices.

Another issue Abram raises is the fate of his family. He seizes on the comment in his mother's record of interrogation, that she and the whole family had been Chinese citizens in Manchuria, branding it 'an invention and a slander by her investigator'. Abram insists that no-one in his family ever had Chinese citizenship. All had been registered Soviets long before he left Hailar in 1932.

Curiously, Abram also learned that Chesna had been sentenced by a troika to exile in Alma Ata, but that the sentence was subsequently revoked. Aware from his indictment that his father and sister had been executed, Abram asks the tribunal to obtain and review their cases as he knew them to be honest citizens, loyal to the Soviet Union.

> *Maybe they were sentenced by a troika as Chinese citizens at the time—which is not true. Many investigators at the time . . . turned out to be enemies of the people themselves and often created enemies out of innocent people. I ask again that their cases be obtained and reviewed, lest this be a black mark against me . . .*

On this point, at least, Abram's petition had the desired effect. On 3 September the military tribunal delayed its hearing while they requested the files of the other Onikuls from Moscow. Whether or not the material arrived is unclear from Abram's file, though a follow-up request was sent to Moscow on 19 September.

On 4 October 1939, the military tribunal reconvened. The record of the hearing covers familiar ground, including Abram's operational relationships in Hailar and the Soviet Union and the sequence of his family's departures from Manchuria. Abram mentions that Manya stayed with him in Vladivostok for about twenty days on her way from Shanghai to Moscow. He says he heard of her arrival from Shanghai from another NKVD operative in Vladivostok, though he had no idea why that man knew of it. This implies that Manya may still have had a link with the NKVD in Shanghai.

Abram also refers to people like Bendikov, Baksheev and Panfilov, who were central to the cases of the Onikuls in Gorky. This suggests that the tribunal did obtain information on the cases of the others. Abram says he has no idea whether Bendikov had been a member of a White Guard organisation in Hailar, but when Manya had written to tell him that Bendikov had turned up in the USSR under a false name, he had advised her to report this.

On the allegations that he passed materials about the airport and the strength of the border detachment to the Japanese, Abram says he knew nothing about the airport and had no links whatsoever with the military hierarchy. Given the last word at the conclusion of the hearing, Abram denies ever having been involved in espionage and says he has always worked loyally for Soviet intelligence. He asks the tribunal to clear him of slander.

After thirty-five minutes deliberation, the tribunal announced its verdict. Abram was found guilty of the charges and sentenced to ten years imprisonment in a corrective labour camp, with confiscation of all personal property and loss of political rights for five years. Pending his removal to the camp, Abram was to be transferred from the NKVD internal prison to the main Khabarovsk prison. He was given three days to appeal.

The papers in his file indicate that Abram did so the next day, though the text of his appeal is missing. In any case, the Military Collegium of the Supreme Court of the USSR dismissed it on 17 November 1939 and confirmed his sentence.

After that a flurry of secret *spravkas* flew in all directions—advising Abram's sentence, instructing that his passport be destroyed, his personal effects be sold and proceeds directed to internal revenue. Suddenly Abram's bank account in Vladivostok yielded 1,056 roubles into government coffers, a substantial amount of money in those times. For some reason, his investigators had been unable to find this money earlier when Abram had needed it to buy medicine to treat his scurvy, sciatica and lung disease. The sale of his belongings in Grodekovo produced 1,722 roubles more.

But Abram refused to disappear quietly. Locked in the bowels of the NKVD prison in Khabarovsk for two and a half years, he still managed to stay abreast of key political developments. He knew of the major convulsion which seized the NKVD in 1939 and who had been caught by it. He knew about the defection of Lyushkov. He knew the contentious issues to raise and the right language to use.

From his 'transit prison' in Khabarovsk at the end of March 1940, Abram wrote a lengthy appeal to NKVD chief Lavrenty Beria. In six closely written pages, he lays out his complaints about the perversions of socialist justice perpetrated by the NKVD during his investigation. He refers explicitly to the tortures through which the investigators had attempted to extract confessions and their refusals to collect objective evidence.

In language reminiscent of the March 1939 Party Congress, Abram invokes Stalin's sentiments about enemies of the people using the Soviet security organs and Soviet laws to 'torment honest hardworking Soviet cadres'. He writes that in the Far East, this has been played out in the 'Lyushkov saga' of which he regards himself a victim. Abram appeals to Beria to intervene in his fate:

> . . . the fate of a Soviet person, a devoted son and patriot of his socialist Motherland, who is young and could still be a useful member of its socialist society.

Very cleverly, Abram attaches a brief covering note, in which he repeats one of the final paragraphs of his appeal which would be sure to get attention:

> I ask you to summon me to Moscow to give evidence on issues of national importance. I ask you to believe that this request is not the result of a rash action and is not of a personal nature. I ask you only to keep in mind the conspiratorial nature of this evidence and its special state significance.

The route by which Abram's appeal reached Beria's office in Moscow was circuitous. By April 1940, he had been moved from Khabarovsk to the transit point for the north-east labour camps in Vladivostok, from which he was sent by boat to Magadan. At the end of April, the NKVD at the camp transit point forwarded Abram's appeal, together with a personal particulars note to Beria's office in Moscow. It arrived there a month later. It certainly caught their attention, though the response was probably not quite the one for which Abram had hoped.

No summons was issued for his despatch to Moscow under armed escort to convey his issues of national importance. In early July 1940, the NKVD secretariat simply sent the appeal all the way back to NKVD regional headquarters in Vladivostok, asking that they summon Abram and find out what it was he wanted to convey to Comrade Beria.

In mid-August 1940, Vladivostok sent the request on to Magadan asking them to respond to Moscow directly. Two months later, Magadan sent back to the NKVD secretariat a record of Abram's interrogation. This is the information I have been looking for ever since Abram first tossed the bait about 'matters of national importance' and political consequences of cross-border operations. Was there any substance to his claims or was it simply a try-on?

Question: What in detail were the issues of national importance which you wanted to convey to the NKVD chief of the USSR?

Answer: . . . while working in the 58th Border detachment at Grodekovo as a Chinese interpreter and *assistant to the chief of the Special Section, I personally developed an operational plan to bring from across the border the assistant Japanese station-chief from Sanchakou [a Manchukuo border post 40 kilometres south of Grodekovo] and a Russian White Guard agent ... The purpose was to get information on the Japanese network on this side of the border. My plan was approved, but deliberately thwarted by enemies of the people—by Osinin, the former deputy of the Far Eastern NKVD, and Malkevich of the International Department. Not long before my arrest, I had also received information about the escape to Manchuria of four prisoners from the Far Eastern Labour Camp. I told Malkevich about this, but he took no action ...*

The interrogator did not believe Abram. First he suggests that Abram had probably been planning to name other co-conspirators who had not yet been caught, but had changed his mind. Abram denies this. The interrogator then argues that Abram had written his appeal simply to get a summons to Moscow. Abram rejects the proposition and says his sole purpose had been to discuss his work in the border detachment—'that it was not taken seriously'—and in passing, to talk about his case as set out in his appeal.

Abram's appeal and record continued on its round. In December 1940, the NKVD secretariat sent the papers to the Special Section of the NKVD in Moscow for review. In late January 1941, they were forwarded to the Special Section of the Far Eastern Front in Khabarovsk for review and advice. On 18 February 1941 the papers were passed on to the Investigations Branch in Khabarovsk. Three months later, on 23 May 1941, the investigating officer reported his conclusions.

He found that the evidence of Morov, Markin and Novoselov—on the basis of which Abram had been convicted as a member of an espionage group—was 'dubious' since Malkevich, the former NKVD officer who initiated their cases, was subsequently convicted for 'falsifying investigations'. Given the terms of Abram's conviction, this should have been enough to turn his case around.

It wasn't. Instead, in a shrill tone redolent of xenophobia, the investigator created some new 'facts' from Abram's file. These include allegations that had been solicited by the same dubious investigators, which the earlier military tribunal had not seen fit to use, as well as some clear inaccuracies:

> While living in Hailar, Onikul had been linked with a number of people who aroused serious mistrust . . . While working in one of the border detachments, Onikul . . . used his cross-border network for personal aims, embezzling foreign currency intended for cross-border work. Moreover, while living in Vladivostok, Onikul had suspicious links with Chinese and lived beyond his means. Onikul's father still lives in Hailar and a number of his

relatives have been arrested and sentenced for counter-revolutionary activities.

On the basis of the above 'facts', and offering no concrete evidence, the investigator concludes that:

The appeal of the convicted Onikul A.G. be dismissed and the sentence of the military tribunal regarding Onikul, as a socially dangerous element, remain in force.

It was immaterial. Abram had already been dead for over three months. His diseased and tortured body lay buried in an anonymous pit in the ice of Kolyma.

————◆————

It is November 2000 and I am back in Khabarovsk with my friend Sasha Lavrentsov.

The light is fading fast as we walk across the snow to the entrance of the cemetery. At six o'clock on a winter evening, it is long closed. But the gate is unlocked. The naked birches stand silent witness as we slip through the loosely chained gate and make our way past the small chapel. In our dark hooded parkas with woollen scarves wrapped round our faces against the biting cold, we resemble grave robbers.

It is eerie. Looking up at the dome I can just make out the words mounted on the wall in black letters:

To the eternal memory of the murdered innocents.

Beyond it stretch rows of snow-covered gravestones, sheltered by tall pines. And underneath them, once mass graves with no stones.

At the remembrance wall, Sasha unzips his sports bag, hands me a large torch and pulls out a cordless drill. 'Do you have the plaque?' he asks, his voice muffled. I pull the bundle which I have wrapped in striped Cambodian silk from my rucksack and unwrap it, handing Sasha the white oval disk. 'Now climb up here and shine the torch so I can see where I'm drilling.'

I stand on the ledge above Anna Akhmatova's poignant words:

I would have liked to name each one in turn . . .

We work quickly and silently. I shine the torch, while Sasha drills two holes into the granite wall. My hands and feet are frozen. It must be even worse for Sasha. He has taken off his gloves to position the drill through the holes in the metal plaque. One hole. Two holes. The sound of the drill pierces the frozen silence. At last it is done.

Onikul
Abram Grigorievich

20	.	11
19 VIII 07		*19 II 41*

died in labour camp

reads the small white plaque Sasha has fixed to the remembrance wall. Another victim of Stalin's purges named.

I had called Sasha a few months earlier to say that I would be 'in the neighbourhood' and was thinking of flying over for a few days. He immediately told me that the remembrance wall had now been extended and the plaque I had ordered for Abram was ready. He would hold off mounting it until I arrived.

We had never intended that the deed be done covertly by night on my last evening in Khabarovsk. The plan had been to come out here in the early afternoon. But Sasha had been caught at work and time had slipped away.

Now it is too cold to stand around and too dark to take photographs, which causes me considerable distress. But Sasha assures me that we will come back the following day on the way to the airport.

'Great!' I shudder, 'Right now it must be minus thirty!'

'No more than minus twenty,' Sasha responds. 'And just remember, your great-uncle Abram stood much worse. Without your down-filled parka, mink hat and Orenburg scarf.'

On the way back to Sasha's apartment, where I am staying, I ask if we can pick up a bottle of the best local vodka in which to toast Abram's memory. Sasha chooses a small bottle called Doublet, explaining that it is a hunting term meaning 'double shot'. Later I find out why—it is fifty-six percent alcohol instead of the normal forty.

Sasha raises the first toast to Abram's memory. It is

strangely appropriate—a double shot from one former *chekist* to another.

There is no time for a long wake. Straight after dinner, Sasha and I get back to the business of reviewing Abram's file, which I have brought back with me from Sydney. Having laboured to make sense of it myself in all its tragedy and horror, I have grabbed the opportunity to check my interpretation with an expert. Sasha has spent years reviewing thousands of such files as part of his previous work with the KGB, old and new, right here in Khabarovsk. If he cannot explain some of its intricacies, there is no-one who can.

Staying for a few days with the Lavrentsovs in the very heart of what was NKVD territory in the 1930s, has given me a new perspective on Khabarovsk. The landmarks of Abram's most tragic days are now part of my everyday surroundings. When I walk to the centre of town, I pass the former Commune House where he had stayed in October 1937 while waiting to meet his superiors. Standing on the corner of Dzerzhinsky Street, its tall yellow walls open onto the main street like the folds of a piano accordion. My route back to the apartment follows the same path Abram took to the former NKVD headquarters. If I turn right a street early, I can walk straight to the gates of the present Ministry of Security, into which the van drove Abram after his arrest. Behind the windows on the second floor is the room where the military tribunal tried him.

Backing onto a derelict block directly across the road from Sasha's apartment block is the rear end of the prison where Abram was held for two years. Walking past it each day, I stare at the damp grey wall and see Abram. But it is not the carefree young man with film star looks whom I saw in his mother's photograph albums. Instead I see the tortured face and haunting eyes of his prison mug shot. He is crawling back to his clammy basement cell after a round of beating and interrogation, so luridly described in his appeals.

On the way to Khabarovsk airport, Sasha and I stop at the cemetery to see the results of the previous evening's clandestine labour. With the gates wide open and the sun shining, it is a very different place. The names leap off the white enamel plates on the remembrance wall—one after the other 'shot', 'shot', 'shot', mostly in 1937 or 1938, many of them in their thirties. In the six months since my first visit, the wall has been extended to three times its original length. I count the plaques. Abram's is the four hundred and ninety-first.

CHAPTER 13

REDEMPTION

IN MAY 1945, the Great Patriotic War against Hitler and fascism was over. The Soviet Union had emerged triumphant with its empire significantly expanded. But the cost was enormous: thirty million people dead, the country devastated, the economy in ruins. Scarred and exhausted, the Russian people exalted in their victory. Their bond to the Soviet regime had never been stronger. They had struggled together and won, proving their loyalty and devotion against unspeakable odds.

Few looked back to reflect that the disastrous situation they had faced had been exacerbated by Stalin's own miscalculations. They sang the Great Leader's praises and looked forward to a brighter future. Now that the war was over, their lives would surely become easier and more secure. Perhaps they could stop living in constant fear and learn to trust their neighbours? Perhaps the regime would treat them with a little kindness and even release the prisoners.

It was not to be. Stalin drove a relentless campaign of national reconstruction in preparation for the ultimate victory of the Socialist Camp against the West. Vigilance against enemies had to be maintained. Writers, poets, actors and musicians were publicly vilified for departing from ideological purity and repression continued.

It was in this climate that my great-grandmother Chesna finally emerged from her extended exile in Kazakhstan. The trouble was, she had nowhere to go. Though she had relatives in Moscow and Gorky, she could not get a residence permit to live there. Like all *zeks* (prisoners) who had served time for 'counter-revolutionary activities', Chesna was barred from all major cities, towns and a 101-kilometre zone around them. Even where she was not barred, she was not welcome for much longer than a month. So at the age of sixty-four, she drifted from town to town, alone.

Relating what Chesna told her in Harbin in 1957 about her life in those years, my mother conjures graphic images of a tall, old white-haired woman wandering from one place to the next, clutching a small bundle of belongings. Selling fried fish at railway stations to eke out a meagre existence, she bunks down in any corner she can find for a few hours of restless sleep.

From Uncle Lyova Rayak in Moscow, I learn that Chesna finally found sanctuary in the small town of Strunino, north-east of Moscow, thirty kilometres beyond the ancient church town of Zagorsk. Sometimes she would come to Moscow surreptitiously. Uncle Lyova would meet her at the station and spirit her away to the home of one relative or another. It was a dangerous business and Chesna never stayed more than a day or two. Being caught in Moscow without a permit, she ran the risk of being sent straight to prison camp. Her visits also put her relatives at risk for harbouring a 'socially dangerous element'. But there was some contact at least and the relatives could help her a little with food and money.

Chesna was desperate to know what had happened to her husband and her children whom she had not seen for ten years. No-one had heard a word about Girsh and Manya since their arrests in Gorky, nor of Abram in the Far East. At least Chesna could breathe a sigh of relief about her youngest son, Yasha. Even while she was still in Kazakhstan, she had heard from her niece, Fanya Klebanova in Gorky, that Yasha was still alive. Fanya, it appears, corresponded with them both. In Moscow, her relatives may have told Chesna of Yasha's whereabouts in a military construction area in Buy in the far north of the Moscow military district. But a meeting was out of the question. Someone might ask questions and dig into the past. It was safer that no connections be drawn.

I search Yasha's chronology to work out when Chesna's first reunion with her son may have taken place. One possibility is sometime in June 1946, before Yasha went to Riga to take up his new assignment. Another is early the following year when Yasha spent two months in Moscow on specialist training for sanatorium doctors.

The meeting may have taken place at the home of one of the relatives. Either way, in the prevailing climate of fear, it would have been quick and clandestine.

In 1948, a new wave of terror began in earnest. As in the 1930s, key targets were potential rivals among Stalin's own henchmen. Conspiracies were uncovered, leading to large-scale arrests at all levels of their power bases. Such was the fate of Stalin's deputy in the Council of Ministers, Voznesensky, and thousands of his men in the Leningrad Party. A massive campaign was also launched to root out 'homeless cosmopolitans' and those who 'kowtowed to foreigners'. Thousands of people, mostly Jews, lost their jobs or were arrested. All the prominent Jews whom Stalin had appointed to the Jewish Anti-Fascist Committee during the war were arrested, including the wife of foreign minister and Stalin's deputy, Vyacheslav Molotov.

Finally, in January 1953, the Soviet media exposed an alleged conspiracy by Kremlin Jewish doctors to curtail the lives of Soviet leaders by sabotaging their medical treatment. These 'monsters' were revealed to be agents of British and American intelligence operating through a 'bourgeois nationalist' Jewish organisation. Apparently, Stalin later intended to show that Zionists had penetrated to the highest levels by linking Molotov to the conspiracy through his wife. As the media whipped up an anti-Semitic frenzy, rumours swept Moscow that Jews would soon be deported to Siberia. People braced themselves for a new round of show trials and purges.

Where would it end?

———

But in early March 1953, Stalin died. Millions wept, uncertain of the future without the Great Leader. Even some of those who had suffered through his rule grieved. With Stalin they had won the war and turned the Soviet Union into a world power. Now what? But fears that the country would fall apart without Stalin's steely grip and that the West would exploit the trauma did not eventuate. Instead, a new reality emerged.

Within a month of Stalin's death, a general amnesty was declared, the doctors' plot was denounced as a fabrication and those arrested released. Security chief Beria, the one member of the new 'collective leadership' who might have asserted dictatorial rule, was arrested in July and shot by a firing squad in December 1953. In March 1954, the security police were downgraded from a Ministry (MGB) to become the Committee of State Security (KGB) under the political control of the Council of Ministers.

Strikes in several camps by political prisoners, excluded by the first amnesty, prompted the establishment of special commissions which visited camps and reviewed cases. More amnesties followed in 1954 and 1955. A cultural 'thaw', though interrupted by intermittent freezes, transformed Soviet intellectual life. Terror in the Soviet Union was not terminated entirely. But its tyranny was tamed.

Finally, in February 1956 the emerging new leader, Nikita Khrushchev, named the tyrant—Stalin. In a three-hour secret speech at the end of the twentieth Party Congress, he exposed Stalin's 'cult of personality' and the crimes of his dictatorship. These included 'mass arrests and deportations of many thousands, executions without trial and proper investigation'. Khrushchev told how innocent people had been murdered on trumped-up charges as 'enemies of the people', 'spies' and 'saboteurs'; among them the best and brightest of the Party. He revealed that their cases had been fabricated by the NKVD and confessions extracted through 'cruel and inhuman tortures'. All of these abuses of 'socialist legality' had been authorised by none other than Stalin.

The speech caused a sensation. Within days, the text was being read and discussed at Party meetings across the nation; later at open meetings where anyone could participate.

Khrushchev's efforts to distance himself from Stalin's excesses while implicating his key leadership opponents became clear in retrospect. But from the outset no-one believed that all the crimes could be attributed to Stalin alone. What had Khrushchev and the other leaders been doing? What were the guarantees it would not happen again?

To answer these questions in depth would require a fundamental analysis of the Soviet system itself, which no leadership would accept. But Khrushchev's new command did take measures to assuage popular concern.

Foremost among them: the release of hundreds of thousands of prisoners and rehabilitation.

Rehabilitation had, in fact, started much earlier. The conviction of security chief Beria as a traitor in 1953 had prompted a flood of letters from people seeking review of charges against their relatives. A special Rehabilitation Commission under the procurator general had been established sometime in 1954, and news was getting out of prominent figures being rehabilitated. By the time of Khrushchev's secret speech in 1956, some 8,000 people had been rehabilitated—most of them posthumously.

This was a minuscule percentage of the millions who had been arrested unlawfully. But 'rehabilitation' was a laborious process, conducted on a case-by-case basis and only when petitioned by the victim's family. The regime no doubt feared that a comprehensive and immediate rehabilitation of all the victims of the purges would totally undermine its credibility.

———

Chesna wasted no time in petitioning for a review of the cases of her family. I find the appeal she wrote to the procurator general on 10 April 1955 in her NKVD file. The letter is typed and contains a number of misspelt names and patronymics, which suggests it may have been prepared for Chesna by someone at the procurator's office. But the words and the signature are unmistakeably Chesna's own. The pathos is stronger for its simplicity:

From 1909 to 1936 my family lived in Harbin, where my husband worked as a representative of the Singer sewing machine company.

In 1936, after extensive petitioning, we were granted entry into the USSR and settled in Gorky, where my daughter, Maria Grigorievna Onikul, was working as a dentist at the outpatients clinic of the Gorky Avtozavod.

In 1937, my husband, daughter and son were all arrested. After a while, I was also arrested and exiled to a settlement in Kazakhstan for five years.

Having served my term in exile, on the basis of the amnesty decree, I returned to Moscow, where I was granted permission for permanent residence.

Since 1938, I have had no news about the fate of my husband and my children. During these long years, I have had to bear as wife and mother the painful and bitter burden of separation from my family. I myself was convicted without any charges being brought against me.

In the declining years of my life—I am 74 years old—I want to know the whereabouts of my family: my husband—Grigory Matveyevich Onikul, my daughter—Maria Grigorievna Onikul and my son—Abram Grigorievich Onikul, arrested in Gorky by the NKVD in 1937. I ask that the criminal cases against them be reviewed, and that you advise me of your decision and the fate of my family at the above address.

The address Chesna gives is that of her niece Tenya Tsirlin. This is apparently where she went to live after the amnesty of March 1953 put an end to her wanderings.

It is difficult to know whether Chesna deliberately named Abram among the family members arrested in Gorky or whether it was a typist's error. At the time, she had already established contact with Yasha but had no idea about Abram's whereabouts; whether he was free or had been arrested. Whatever the case, by naming one son and locating him in the place of the other, Chesna eventually got rulings on both.

It took nine months before any action was taken. But at the end of January 1956, the office of the chief military procurator sent Chesna's appeal, together with Manya and Girsh's files, to the KGB in Gorky requesting that their cases be reviewed. In separate covering letters, which I find in Girsh's and Manya's files, he questions the validity of their convictions as Japanese spies and the justice of their executions. The procurator also instructs Gorky KGB to review Yasha's case and notes that a request for the review of Abram's case had been sent to the military procurator in Khabarovsk.

The reviews of Yasha's and Chesna's cases were concluded in April 1956. In each instance, the military procurator of the Moscow Military District objected to their convictions on the grounds that the cases had been fabricated, and requested that the NKVD's verdicts from 1938 be quashed. In Chesna's case, the official 'Objection' reads:

... In the review of her case, no evidence was found that, while living in Hailar or in the USSR, she was involved in any activities hostile to the USSR or had any links with Japanese intelligence agents.

In view of the circumstances set out above, I believe that Onikul was illegally arrested and exiled. Therefore, pursuant to the Decree of the Presidium of the Supreme Soviet of the USSR of 19 August 1955,

I REQUEST:

That the decision of the NKVD Troika of the Gorky Region of 20 October 1938 in regard to Onikul, Chesna Abramovna be revoked and her case be dropped ...

In Yasha's case, the procurator found:

... no evidence that Onikul had been recruited by Japanese intelligence and conducted espionage activities in the USSR.

The accusation that Onikul was linked with Japanese agents ... is also unfounded.

The Military Tribunal of the Moscow Military District upheld the procurator's requests in each case. I find a copy of their handwritten 'Decision' dated 26 April 1956 in each file. Two days later, rehabilitation certificates were prepared for Chesna and Yasha—two of the little half-page *spravkas* among Chesna's papers that Galya had given me back in 1992.

According to another *spravka* dated the same day, Chesna was requested to come to the military tribunal's headquarters in Moscow's famous Arbat Street to collect the certificates of rehabilitation. I imagine that Chesna would have wasted no time in responding to this summons. Yet two months later, she had still not shown up at the tribunal offices. Correspondence in her file between the military tribunal, the KGB and the Central Address Bureau of the Moscow Military District indicates that Chesna had moved from her previous address in Moscow in 1955 but left no new one. Finally, four months later in August 1956, the KGB tracked her down in Riga.

In Galya's letter of 2001 in which she attempts to answer some of my questions, she says that after she and Yasha returned from Uzbekistan in mid 1955, they bought a room in a communal apartment in Riga 'so we would have somewhere to return to'. My own guess is that Yasha wanted to settle his mother there. Galya's letter continues:

> I think that was when Yasha brought Chesna Abramovna [from Moscow] and she lived in this room while Yasha and I were still touring, working in Estonia . . .

Then Chesna suffered another misfortune—breast cancer, which resulted in surgery. Under such circumstances, it is understandable that her earlier correspondence with the military procuracy may have slipped her mind.

In the meantime, the reviews Chesna instigated into the cases of Girsh and Manya had been completed. The review process was identical to that followed in Yasha and Chesna's cases. But as Girsh and Manya had incurred capital punishment, their reviews were conducted at the highest judicial level—the chief procurator of the USSR and the Military Collegium of the Supreme Court of the USSR.

In each case, an 'Objection' from the chief procurator dated 28 May 1956 summarises the results, including cross-checks against the cases of the alleged 'Japanese agents', whose 'evidence' had been used to convict Girsh and Manya. All had been baseless. The documents also identify by name the NKVD officials who took part in the investigations of their cases in Gorky—Lavrushin, Primilsky, Driven—and notes that they were themselves 'convicted for violation of socialist legality'. Each Objection concludes:

I request that:

> the decision of the NKVD and the Procurator of the USSR of 7 January 1938 in relation to Onikul . . . be revoked and the criminal case dismissed . . .

On 6 October 1956, nineteen years after their unwarranted arrests, the Military Collegium of the Supreme Court of the USSR did just that.

The certificates of rehabilitation on Girsh and Manya were finalised on 22 October. Each *spravka* contains three sentences:

> The case against Onikul . . . was reviewed by the Military Collegium of the Supreme Court of the USSR on 6 October 1956.

> *The decision of the NKVD of the USSR of 7 January 1938 regarding Onikul . . . is revoked and the case is dropped in the absence of criminal evidence.*
>
> *Onikul . . . is posthumously rehabilitated.*

After nineteen years, Chesna finally received advice about the fate of her husband and daughter. They were dead.

------◆------

From what my mother and other relatives tell me, Chesna was sceptical about the rehabilitation process. She believed in life and death and nothing in between. Her husband and daughter were dead. Abram's fate was still a question mark. She and Yasha had survived.

Still, she understood that in the eyes of the regime under which they were living, the rehabilitation certificates she and Yasha received restored their rights as citizens and were their tickets to a future. Most importantly, the Onikuls could stop hiding.

Were Chesna and Yasha compensated for the years they were unlawfully detained? No-one can recall. But my mother distinctly remembers Chesna telling her she had refused to take 'blood money' offered for her dead family. This is the first of many questions I address to the Memorial group in Moscow in early 2002. The advice I receive is that those who were rehabilitated received compensation of two months of their previous salary. In the event of posthumous rehabilitation, the compensation was paid to relatives. This clearly is the 'blood money' Chesna had refused.

But it is evident from Chesna's file that she did seek compensation for the family's personal property that had been illegally confiscated by the NKVD in Gorky at the time of their arrest. The letter she sent to the KGB in November 1956 bears her signature, but the handwriting is recognisably Yasha's, as is the politically skilful turn of phrase:

> ... *Our family were honest and loyal Soviet people. All our strength and thoughts were directed at serving the Soviet Union. Our innocence has at last been proven, truth has triumphed and we have been fully rehabilitated.*
>
> *I am now a very old and sick woman (I recently had cancer surgery). I am totally unable to work and very poor. This is why I ask you somehow to compensate me for the furniture and property taken from us in Gorky. A list of the main items illegally confiscated is attached.*
>
> *I seek your help.*

Two months later, the Gorky KGB reached the conclusion that property valued at about 24,695 roubles had indeed been taken illegally from the Onikuls. It recommended that Chesna be compensated and referred the matter to the Gorky regional finance department for assessment. This is contained in a formal document headed 'Findings' which I copied from Chesna's file in Nizhny in 1996. There is also a receipt for another 1,404 roubles for a Woodstock typewriter.

Thinking back to my time in the archive, I recall skipping over quite a few pages of tedious correspondence about property valuation. I did not appreciate its significance at the time.

***

I find it curious that nowhere in Chesna's correspondence does she mention her nephew Sanya Onikul, also arrested in Gorky in 1938. I cannot believe that she would not have been anxious to know his fate. I later learn from relatives that she did make approaches about Sanya, but got nowhere. The officials told her: 'It is not your business. He is not your son.'

With no direct relatives in the Soviet Union to petition on his behalf, Sanya's file lay buried in the KGB archives for fifty years, while his family in China could only guess at his fate. Only in 1989, when President Gorbachev initiated a comprehensive review of all cases from Stalin's purges, did Sanya's case get reopened. This explains the last page I find in his Gorky NKVD file. It is a *pro-forma* confirmation by the regional procurator in September 1989 that Sanya's case fell within the scope of the Supreme Soviet's decree on measures to restore justice to the victims of the repression. This is acknowledgment fifty years later that Sanya's sentence by the NKVD troika in 1938 and execution as a Japanese spy was illegal.

Chesna heard nothing about Abram for a long, long time. My mother says that in 1957, Chesna even made discreet enquiries as to whether her son may have somehow ended up in Australia with the displaced persons who were resettled there after the war.

In fact, the review of his case was completed in November 1956. At the back of Abram's NKVD file, I read the 'Findings' which the chief military procurator sent to the Military Collegium of the USSR Supreme Court on 12 November 1956. It notes in passing that Abram 'died in the ITL (corrective labour camp)' and confirms that there was no evidence to substantiate charges that he was an agent of foreign intelligence.

As in the cases of Manya and Girsh, it names the former NKVD officials who investigated Abram's case, including Osinin and Malkevich, noting that the two were 'subsequently convicted for illegal arrests of citizens and falsification of evidence against them'.

It recommends that:

> *The sentence of the military tribunal of the Khabarovsk NKVD of 4 October 1939 and the decision of the Military Collegium of the Supreme Court of 17 November 1939 . . . be revoked in the light of newly revealed circumstances and that his case be dismissed.*

The decision of the Military Collegium of the USSR Supreme Court of 6 February 1957 upheld the recommendation. The fact that this ruling countermanded its own 1939 decision to reject Abram's appeal is clearly a matter of some sensitivity. It specifically mentions that its decision took into account 'new circumstances of which the court was not previously aware'.

According to papers at the very end of Abram's file, the military collegium made three attempts to summon Chesna to their headquarters to convey the decision about Abram. These were sent to the same address in Moscow from which she had sent her original appeal. At the end of February 1957, Chesna had still failed to appear. Again, correspondence flew between various agencies. Responsibility to take the matter to completion fell on the military tribunal in Khabarovsk.

In mid-March, they sent the information about Abram's case to the Moscow militia, instructing them to advise Chesna about his posthumous rehabilitation and to return the documents together with her sign off. A month later, the papers were returned to Khabarovsk, still with no sign-off—just a barely legible handwritten note which mentions something about the register of tenants at Chesna's address in Moscow indicating she had left for Riga.

Yet at the end of April 1957, the military tribunal in Khabarovsk advised the military collegium in Moscow as follows:

> *I report that the decision . . . of the Military Collegium of the USSR Supreme Court of 6 February 1957 regarding the case of Onikul Abram Grigorievich has not been implemented since he died in the ITL. Efforts made to locate his relatives have not produced positive results.*
>
> *According to advice from the 9th district of the Militia of the City of Moscow, his mother, Onikul Chesna Abramovna, who lived in Moscow . . . has gone to live*

permanently with her daughter in the People's Republic of China.

This is astounding. As most people would be aware, emigration from the Soviet Union was banned at the time.

Still, the Moscow militia was partly right. In December 1956, Chesna had gone to Harbin—not for permanent residence but for a three-month visit. This in itself was a miracle.

In the post-Stalin period, restrictions on contact with the outside world had been slightly relaxed and Soviet people had begun to travel abroad. But these travellers were mostly officials or professionals. Carefully hand-picked, they travelled in delegations for purposes of scientific or cultural exchange or tourism—mainly to the fraternal satellites of east Europe and with minders.

How was it that Chesna, a recently rehabilitated 'enemy of the people', was allowed to travel alone for strictly personal reasons: to visit her family in China?

The exit visa application process was laborious, involving detailed documentation. It included obtaining a formal invitation from the Zaretskys in Harbin, with an undertaking of material support for Chesna while she was abroad. In her application form, Chesna would have had to fill in all the sorry details of her needlessly depleted family.

Perhaps the apparatchik who processed it took pity on Chesna. Perhaps he thought this harmless seventy-five-year-old woman had suffered enough.

CHAPTER 14

BACK TO HARBIN

DESPITE THE SUB-ZERO December weather, a crowd of relatives and friends turned up at Harbin Station to witness Chesna's homecoming in December 1956. All our family was there except me. They probably figured it was too cold and there would be excitement enough at the station without having to keep an eye on a precocious two-year-old child.

Years later my mother describes how, after a ten-day railway journey from Riga, Chesna emerged from the train, a stoic figure. She had brought with her a small suitcase full of gifts and a canvas bag with four enormous jars of blackberry jam she had made with berries from the Latvian forests.

It had been twenty years since Chesna had left Harbin. When she first arrived in Gorky in 1936, Chesna had exchanged intermittent lettercards with my grandmother Gita and some close relatives. But in the prevailing climate of xenophobia, this was a dangerous practice and there was little she could say about what was really happening. From the time of her arrest and through the war years, there was total silence. Only during the thaw years of the mid-1950s did she and Yasha re-establish correspondence with the Zaretskys. Still, their letters were circumspect and were sent under Galya's name.

Now Chesna was able to reacquaint herself with her Harbin family and other friends in person. There was a lot to catch up on. Her daughter Gita, a twenty-six-year-old brunette when Chesna last saw her, was now a silver-haired matron; her son-in-law Motya, an established Harbin figure. Her granddaughter Inna, who had been just seven years old, was now married to Alec, a young man of mixed Tatar-Russian extraction and had a two-and-a-half-year-old daughter—me—named after Chesna's daughter, Manya.

Whether from my own memory or from photographs and the stories of others, my impression of Chesna's visit is of endless conversations around the dining-room table surrounded by a changing cast of characters. Lunch, afternoon tea, dinner—the table was always laden with plates of *zakuski*, fruit, cakes, cups and goblets. A stream of visitors came to pay homage to Chesna. Most were from Harbin, but some travelled from Hailar; young people she had known as children. Their parents had passed on, some tragically. Each round of guests was punctuated by a pause for photographs with Chesna. Someone would pick me up, put me on their knee and tell me to 'smile at the birdie'.

All these photographs are in our family album together with the formal shots taken in the studio: Chesna and the family; Chesna, granny, my mother and me. Four generations of women. Though Chesna has aged, she looks much as she did in the photograph taken with Girsh and the Zaretskys before their departure for Gorky in 1936. With her white hair cut short, she sits erect and well groomed, wearing a dark-coloured dress. But the light in her eyes is gone.

Forty years later, I find the same photographs in Chesna's album in Riga, as well as one of the two of us in the Harbin city park. Chesna is sitting on a bench, a kerchief tied around her head—the archetypal Russian *babushka*. I stand on the bench beside her with my arm resting lightly on her shoulder, looking unusually serious. Perhaps even as a very young child I sensed that my great-grandmother was a living treasure, to be revered and treated gently.

———

So what did Chesna and the family talk about in those interminable conversations? According to my mother and other friends and relatives, Chesna wanted to know everything that had happened in Harbin and Hailar since her departure in 1936. How did they fare under the Japanese occupation? What happened when the Red Army came? Who married whom? Who died? What from?

Those who had stayed in Manchuria had survived their own tragedies: arrests, tortures, executions at the hands of the Japanese, deportations to the Soviet Union. At first, nobody dared tell Chesna about them. Hadn't she had enough grief? But she demanded to know. And the truth eventually came out. Years later they told me.

Chesna had not forgotten how Russian life in Manchuria had been turned upside down after the Japanese occupation. Suddenly people who for years had lived side by side, united by their Russian origins, became identified by the characteristics that divided them: 'White émigré' or 'Soviet', 'Orthodox Christian' or 'Jew'.

In garnering the support of Russian émigrés for their rule in Manchukuo, the Japanese rekindled old dreams and prejudices. Former White Guards and old Cossack warlords such as Ataman Semenov were spurred on by the promise of Japan helping to defeat the Bolsheviks and establish White rule in a breakaway Far Eastern republic. The 'blackshirts' of Konstantin Rodzaevsky's Russian Fascist Party (RFP) were enticed by the whiff of power.

By appointing RFP leaders to a number of key positions in the Bureau of Russian Émigré Affairs (BREM), established in 1934 to bring the discordant White factions under one umbrella, the Japanese gave implicit sanction to the RFP's fiercely anti-Bolshevik and anti-Semitic ideology. Some of the blackshirts also became involved in the Japanese Gendarmerie's seedy businesses and protection rackets, as well as other unsavoury operations.

Soviets, Jews and their shops and synagogues became the targets of RFP attacks. In the early 1930s, there was a spate of kidnappings of wealthy businessmen for ransom. Some of the victims were brutally murdered, most of them Jews. Though the perpetrators were Russian thugs linked to the RFP, the masterminds were the Japanese Gendarmerie. The climate of fear created by these incidents and the consequent departure of many entrepreneurs from Harbin advanced the Japanese goal of gaining control over major businesses in Manchuria.

When the Soviet Union sold out of the Chinese Eastern Railway (CER) in 1935, it lost influence in Manchuria altogether. The majority of Soviet citizens, many of whom were employees of the CER, left with their families for the Soviet Union. Others made for the international settlements of Shanghai and Tientsin. Those who remained were left at the mercy of the Japanese Gendarmerie and its White Russian cohorts. By the mid-1930s, the Onikuls were tired of living under such duress and pessimistic about future prospects for Russians in Manchuria. Thus, they left Hailar for the bright promise of the Soviet Union.

My mother was surprised to hear that despite Chesna's own troubles in the Soviet Union, she had still found the mental space to worry about her family in Harbin. Chesna's great fear was that her son-in-law Motya, being both a Soviet citizen and a Jew with a large and successful meat business, would be vulnerable to fascist banditry. She was relieved to discover that her fears had been unfounded. The Japanese did eventually arrest

Motya's brother Ruvim and closed down the Brothers Zaretsky & Co. meat business. But this incident occurred much later, in the 1940s.

The first in the Zaretsky family to feel the impact of being a 'Soviet' in Manchukuo was, in fact, my mother Inna—at the ripe age of eight. Inna tells me how on the morning of 7 November 1937—the anniversary of the Great October Revolution—she and her classmates had arrived at the Soviet school bubbling with excitement. To mark the occasion, her class was to perform a gymnastics routine in front of all the parents. Inna remembers being very pleased with the cute, white satin sailor suits and red berets they would be wearing but slightly nervous about the balance in the final pyramid. But there was no pyramid and no performance. Earlier that morning, the police had raided the premises and declared the Soviet school closed.

Though Soviet children already enrolled in émigré schools were able to continue their studies until around 1940, new Soviet pupils were not admitted. A number of teachers organised informal group classes for Soviet children, where they continued teaching them the Soviet syllabus with books provided by the Soviet consulate. But my grandparents decided that Inna should study at home with tutors, which she did for the next seven years. One was a young Cambridge graduate who taught her English and humanities according to the English grammar school syllabus. Though the end result was an excellent education, it was a lonely existence—especially since Inna was an only child.

Inna's social isolation was compounded when contact between émigrés and Soviets was forbidden after Japan's Axis partner, Germany, declared war on the Soviet Union in June 1941. This meant Inna could no longer study with her émigré music teacher or participate in concerts at the music school. Nor could she belong to either of Harbin's two Jewish youth organisations—Betar and Maccabi. She remembers walking her friends to meetings and sporting events to share a little of the excitement, then having to turn around and go home. But soon, even this was stopped as émigré parents were warned there might be 'consequences' if their children associated with Soviet friends.

Harbin's Association of Soviet Citizens, which coordinated the small community of Soviets and was their interface with the Manchukuo authorities, did what they could to create activities for their children. They built an ice-rink in the grounds of the closed Soviet school and hired a *dacha* (holiday house) with a summer playground on the other side of the Sungari. Activities were organised to amuse them. But it was difficult to overcome the sense of segregation.

While life under the Japanese occupation may have seemed tough for Soviet children, it was even harder for most of their parents. Those who had previously worked for the CER administration as teachers, clerks, engineers and railway workers had lost their jobs and housing. The compensation they received when the railway was sold enabled some to buy small properties. But finding employment was practically impossible. Soviets were barred from working in émigré firms. Many who were self-employed had their businesses closed. As the years went by, life became even harder.

The intention of the authorities was to pressure Soviets to surrender their Soviet citizenship and apply to BREM for émigré status. For many Soviets, the disruption of their children's education was the last straw finally driving them to become émigrés. By 1936, almost 2,000 former Soviets had undergone conversion.

From the family files I discover in the BREM archive in Khabarovsk in May 2000, I learn that some of my grandfather's relatives converted. The first step in this process was to sign a declaration giving reasons for the change of loyalties: 'I don't want to go to the USSR' or 'I am opposed to Communism'. A temporary émigré identity card was then issued, pending further approvals. Apparently, a contribution to BREM's coffers above the normal passport fee usually helped expedite the process.

Headed by a succession of White Russian generals and nominally under Russian control, BREM was the mechanism used by the Japanese Military Mission to control all aspects of émigré life—from education and welfare to legal affairs and provisioning. All émigrés over the age of eighteen had to register in order to receive identity papers, residence permits, employment cards or travel documents. This involved answering a biographical questionnaire of over seventy questions, including details of political affiliations and a year by year account of their lives since 1910. The BREM questionnaires I find in the files of my father's family provide me with a goldmine of information about a history I would otherwise never know; but how vulnerable they must have felt filling them in sixty years earlier.

By 1940, BREM held files on over 50,000 Russians. Ominously, the chief of its registration department, Mikhail Matkovsky, was a senior leader of the RFP, as were a number of BREM's other department chiefs. It is little wonder that Soviet counter-intelligence operatives were so keen to capture the BREM archive intact when they entered Harbin in 1945. To the detriment of many émigrés, they succeeded. It was handed over to them by none other than Matkovsky—who, it later emerged, had probably been a Soviet agent for some time.

By the early 1940s, BREM started issuing émigrés with identity badges which were to be worn at all times. At first these badges were striped white, blue and red, like the Tsarist flag. Later, at the *diktat* of the Japanese Military Mission, they were replaced by white disks with numbers. Poles and other citizens of the former Tsarist empire got yellow ones. Soviets were instantly conspicuous because they had none. Many émigrés resented having to wear these badges and irreverently called them 'dog tags'. Others compared them to the yellow stars forced onto Jews by the Nazis, noting that in Manchukuo, the badges were only worn by Europeans.

By the 1940s, through departures and 'conversions', the number of Soviet *Harbintsy* had dwindled to just over a thousand. Frustrated that she could not live like 'normal' children, Inna says she suggested to her parents more than once that they should give up their Soviet citizenship and become émigrés so they would have white badges like everyone else. Other friends and relatives had done it. Even her Uncle Ruvim had managed to swap his Soviet citizenship for Lithuanian. But my grandfather would not hear of it. He was convinced that being a stateless émigré was too risky since 'citizens of nowhere' had no diplomatic protection. In hindsight, he was right. But as a child, my mother could not comprehend this, and neither could Uncle Ruvim's wife. According to my grandmother Gita, her sister-in-law was most concerned that Motya's Soviet citizenship would put Ruvim at risk given they had the same surname.

In 1940 the Japanese struck. They arrested Ruvim and took over his meat retail business at the Harbin market. Ironically, however, they kept Motya on because of his experience in the wholesale business. What I later discover from Motya's BREM file is that the Japanese made him an adviser in their meat monopoly association, a role from which he was removed only in 1943—at BREM's behest.

Like many other Soviets who found themselves without work, Motya then resorted to a small home business. He bought a cow and a milk separator and made dairy products in the Zaretsky kitchen. Though the Zaretskys were also able to draw rental income from three apartments, these products gave them something to barter for food and other necessities. Compared to many other Soviets, the Zaretskys fared reasonably well.

———

In the early years of the occupation at least, life for Russian émigrés in Manchukuo went on much as before, or so it seemed. But as the years passed, the yoke of Japanese occupation began to weigh more heavily. Compulsory study of Japanese language in schools was one thing; few objected. But Japanese efforts to impose their belief system, including *wang dao* (the Imperial way) and the divine descent of the Japanese emperor, caused deep resentment.

My father, Alec, who attended the BREM public school, remembers how on some special occasions, like the birthdays of the emperors of Japan and Manchukuo, students would have to bow in the direction of each one's palace. To celebrate victories in Japan's Pacific war, they would bow east. On other special days, all schoolchildren would be taken to bow to the Japanese sun goddess *Ameterasu* at the Japanese shrine erected in the park opposite St Nicholas Russian Orthodox Cathedral. '*Rei!*' would come the call and all would bow to the divine progenitor of the Japanese race. Needless to say, the ritual was the subject of considerable private mockery.

By 1944, the Japanese were even considering placing effigies of the goddess in all Russian Orthodox churches, but this was cleverly thwarted. When Harbin's Orthodox archbishop got a whiff of the plan, he issued a public statement reminding believers that their religion forbade idol worship.

Adult émigrés were also required to attend certain celebrations and witness time and again the ceremonial reading of the scroll containing Emperor Pu Yi's

Manifesto on the occasion of his visit to Japan in 1935. This expressed the undying gratitude of the people of Manchukuo to the land of the Rising Sun for its hospitality and enlightened leadership. Russian émigré newspapers and magazines were full of similar tributes, hailing the new order Japan was creating in east Asia. All news adverse to Japan was, of course, censored.

But words were not enough for the new masters. Their émigré subjects were also expected to help build Japan's New Order in East Asia. As a primary schoolboy in the early 1940s, Alec and his classmates spent several weeks of their summer vacation at a 'voluntary' work camp, digging potatoes to feed Japanese soldiers. University students had to help on the construction of the Sungari River Dam.

An even worse fate awaited young men over eighteen. They could be drafted into the special White Russian military detachment set up as part of the Manchukuo Army in 1938. Named in honour of its Japanese adviser, the 'Asano Unit' was secretly trained for cross-border espionage and sabotage operations into the Soviet Union. Though service in Asano was 'voluntary', once the call came, it was not one that could be rejected without consequences.

Most oppressive for all *Harbintsy*, émigré and Soviet alike, was the climate of fear and distrust the Japanese created in their efforts to keep tabs on the Russian population. With the help of Russian collaborators with the Japanese Military Mission and the Gendarmerie, as well as BREM informers, an all-pervasive network of surveillance was established. Neighbours were asked to inform on each other, as I am shocked to discover from reading my grandfather's BREM file. A family friend tells me how, as a teenager, she and her émigré friends were asked by BREM to report on anything they heard of an anti-Japanese or pro-Soviet nature. Such an environment put people constantly on guard about what they said and to whom.

For those who transgressed against the authorities—be they BREM, the Gendarmerie or the Military Mission itself—there were heavy penalties. It would start with arrest and interrogation by the Gendarmerie or other police organs, and no-one really knew where it might end. The lucky ones got off with a written apology. Others spent time in jail. Arrests on trumped-up charges of anti-government behaviour were often ploys used to extract ransom money or to confiscate property. But the consequences were sometimes more sinister. Relatives might simply be presented with a sealed coffin. In other instances, people suddenly disappeared without trace. In all of this, stateless émigrés were the most vulnerable. Without consular protection, there was not much their relatives could do.

Years later, when the truth emerged about the bacteriological experimentation centres established by the Japanese in various secret locations in Manchuria, people realised the fate that may have befallen these missing persons. They were probably among the thousands of so-called 'logs'—live victims on whom the Japanese conducted hideous experiments in preparation for war.

At Unit 731 in Ping Fan on the outskirts of Harbin, most of the 'logs' were local. While the majority were Chinese, Koreans, stateless Russian émigrés and Soviets captured in border skirmishes were also among the victims.

Harbintsy were certainly aware that the Japanese were conducting experiments with bacteria. This was how they explained water wells around the city being contaminated with typhoid germs and prisoners receiving 'vaccinations' from which they later died. Even my grandmother attributed two bouts of typhoid which my grandfather survived in the early 1940s to Japanese skulduggery. But at the time, nobody knew the full scale of the horror.

Travel outside the main perimeter of Harbin was restricted and required police permission, which often took a long time to come through. In the later years of the occupation, Soviets were refused permission to travel out of their towns of residence altogether. This constraint was felt most acutely by Chesna's relatives in Hailar, who were barred from travelling to Harbin. In 1939, Chesna's great-niece, Ira Kogan, who was attending school in Harbin and living with the Zaretskys, was forced to abandon her education when permission to return was refused after she visited her parents in Hailar.

My mother still remembers the last vacation her family was able to take at the nearby mountain resort of Ertzendzandze during the summer of 1940. As always, she and Gita went away for the whole month, together with other female friends, both émigré and Soviet. Some men would catch the train from Harbin to join them at weekends, but my grandfather was always too busy working. I look at the photographs in my mother's album of tanned long-legged girls in wide-brimmed hats. It was their last carefree summer. By mid-summer of 1941, the Soviet Union and Germany were at war.

———•••———

News of Hitler's invasion of the Soviet Union on 22 June 1941 struck Russians in Harbin like a thunderbolt, both Soviets and émigrés alike. Even among White Guard stalwarts and fascist supporters, few relished the thought of Hitler's forces trampling on their Motherland. Besides, many Russians—like the Zaretskys—had family in the Soviet Union. Most had heard nothing from them since the late 1930s. Now fears for their safety were further compounded.

Heavy media censorship made it difficult to get a picture of what was going on in the war. Those who had access to shortwave radios disregarded official bans and strained to hear crackly Soviet broadcasts. On one occasion after the Zaretskys had been doing just that, a Russian policeman from the Gendarmerie turned up to interrogate them. Clearly their walls had ears.

Throughout the thirteen years of Japanese occupation, Russians in Manchuria were cut off from developments in the world outside. For information on Hitler's war in Europe, most *Harbintsy* relied on the newsreels shown before feature films in Harbin's movie houses, which screened mainly German footage. Images of the Nazi flag flying from the Arc de Triomphe in Paris as Hitler's soldiers goose-stepped down the Champs-Elysées did nothing to warm the hearts of Russian *Harbintsy*. Though publicly they could say nothing, many seethed inside. On the war between the Soviet Union and Germany, there was almost a complete news blackout.

In this respect, Soviets like the Zaretskys had a distinct advantage. At least they were invited to occasional screenings of Soviet newsreels at the Soviet consulate. My mother remembers her shock when she saw the carnage perpetrated by the Nazis in Russia—burned-out villages, buildings razed to the ground, young partisans strung up on gallows. For Soviet citizens, there was no ban on patriotic feeling. The Association of Soviet Citizens actively raised funds to support the war against fascism, to which my grandfather Motya contributed. My grandmother Gita was active in its Women's Committee, making up parcels to send to Soviet soldiers fighting in the 'Great Patriotic War'.

By the time Japan bombed Pearl Harbor in December 1941 and the Pacific war started, most Russian émigrés in Manchukuo were already profoundly alienated. Viewing footage of Japan's Pacific advances, with one Asian colony capitulating after another, did not make things any better. Most were aghast when the leadership of BREM pledged the community's full support for Japan's 'Great Asiatic War' against the 'Anglo-Saxons' and its commitment to building the New Order in east Asia. The price of subservience was getting too high.

It was becoming clear to all that Manchukuo was simply a supply base for Japan's war in Asia, and the emerging New Order for which they were being asked to make sacrifices served exclusively Japanese interests. By then, the Russians knew full well that in spite of their substantial number, the Japanese did not count them among the five races for whom they were building 'harmony' in Manchukuo. Even the ageing White generals in BREM and the leaders of the decaying Fascist Party began to see that a Japanese strike against the Soviet Union was not on the cards. It had begun to dawn on them that the promised puppet state of 'Siberi-kuo' with White Russian rule restored 'from Lake Baikal to the Urals' may have always been an illusion.

From the start of the Pacific war, Manchuria was placed on a total war footing. Almost all grain, meat, fuel and other necessities were requisitioned for the Japanese army. While Japanese civilians were not subjected to restrictions, Harbin's Russian population received small rations of poor quality bread, occasional sugar and salt, and dress fabrics only twice yearly. The Chinese population were given nothing but sorghum.

As the Zaretsky apartment was quite spacious for a family of three, my mother remembers that they rented out the second bedroom—first to friends who were preparing to leave for Shanghai, then to a German–Jewish refugee. To conserve fuel, in summer they cooked on a *hibachi* on the back landing. While my grandfather was still working in the meat business, he occasionally managed to bring home an ox tail from the abattoir or some goat meat from Hailar. Not realising what a luxury this was, my mother turned up her nose: 'Not tail again!'

The Japanese insisted that the Russian population of Harbin take civil defence as seriously as did their own people in Tokyo where 'every home was now a battle-ground'. The city was broken down into traditional Japanese *tonarigumi*—neighbourhood units of ten houses under a single coordinator, who supervised the digging of bomb shelters and blackout patrols. My mother remembers the heavy blackout curtains which had to be drawn at nightfall—black on the outside, red on the inside. God help any resident who let a sliver of light shine through! She describes the silly civil defence drills requiring everyone in the neighbourhood to line up outside the apartment block and pass pails of water down the line while dressed in dark blue shirts, hoods and cumbersome lace-up trousers.

For my father, as a teenage student at the BREM school, military preparations were more serious. They included marching and target practice with instructors from the Asano unit and Japanese advisers. Fortunately, he was still too young to be conscripted for military service in Asano or one of the other Russian military units that comprised the Russian Military Detachment of the Manchukuo Army. By 1942, this had become compulsory for all émigré men between seventeen and forty-five. Jews, Poles and the Baltic minorities were excluded, as well as the first son in a family.

Though there was little enthusiasm for participation

in 'Japan's army', the consequences of refusal at the hands of the Gendarmerie were far worse. Those who could afford to pay tuition fees could arrange a deferral by undertaking higher education. The only other way out was to move to one of the agricultural settlements whose development was being encouraged by the Japanese.

Russian patriotism in Manchuria, among both émigré and Soviets, grew stronger as Soviet victories over the Nazis mounted. In view of their diminished credibility, BREM and the Japanese found it more difficult to maintain control over a restive Russian population. By late 1944, many *Harbintsy* were crowding around the radio to listen to the crackly voice of the new underground radio station *Otchizna* (Fatherland). Broadcasting daily from somewhere inside Manchuria, it not only reported news from the Soviet war front, but even gave a running commentary on political developments inside Harbin. Who was behind the station? To this day, no-one seems to know for sure. Some *Harbintsy* speculate it was Matkovsky, head of BREM's administrative department. Others claim it was Colonel Nagolen, one-time commander of the Asano unit. Both appear to have been Soviet agents.

Chesna was saddened by all she had heard about the rigours of life under the Japanese in Harbin. But for her relatives and friends in Hailar, the intervening years had been considerably tougher.

By the time of Chesna's visit to Harbin, quite a number of them had moved there, among them Chesna's niece, Dora Kogan, and her daughter, Ira, as well as Ronia Onikul, daughter of Girsh's brother Nohum. Others came to see Chesna from Hailar, including Ronia's brother Jacob Onikul and Tima Litvin, whose family had been friends with the Onikuls and Zaretskys over many years. In 1957, they told Chesna what had transpired in Hailar after the Onikuls' departure in 1936. I hear the story many years later.

Chesna and Girsh had been right. Life under Japanese occupation in Hailar had gone from bad to worse, particularly for the hundred or so Soviet families, many of whom were Jewish. Living in the midst of an émigré community which included many former White Guards and Cossacks, they were highly visible targets for harassment by BREM and the Japanese Gendarmerie. As in Harbin, they were excluded from schooling and employment and, in later years, restricted from travelling beyond the town. Soviet houses in Hailar were conspicuous by the small wooden boards hanging from their front gates with 'USSR' painted on them in red letters.

By the late 1930s, opportunities in the lucrative livestock businesses in which many of the younger Russian Jews in Hailar were involved had dwindled. Japanese traders had established their own offices and did their own bidding, cutting out other players. In any case, various restrictions, including on travel and leaseholds, had made it impossible for the Russians to function. For a while, Tima Litvin operated a profitable camel transport business. But in 1942, first Russians then Mongols and Chinese were forbidden to work for him and he was forced to sell his business to a Japanese at half its value.

In 1943, as the Red Army routed the Nazis in Stalingrad and Japan came under pressure in the Pacific, life for Soviets in Hailar became more unpleasant. Some of the incidents Tima describes were simply annoying, like being ordered to bring in their radios to the Gendarmerie to have the shortwave cut. The Japanese were obviously anxious about news escaping of their military setbacks. More nerve-racking were the frequent summonses for interrogation, since it was uncertain where the process might end. Soviets also found themselves under fairly constant surveillance, though some of the 'shadows' with turned-up collars were so obvious in a small town that daring young men like Tima took delight in taking them on a wild goose chase.

But other incidents were tragic in their bloody-mindedness. When the wife of Ira Kogan's uncle, who was an émigré, dared to apply for a Soviet passport, the whole family was suddenly expelled from Manchukuo. In the dead of winter, Zalman Kogan, his wife who was still bleeding after an operation, and their two young children were taken by the Japanese to the Soviet border and sent on foot in the snow to find their way to their 'Motherland'. Somehow, they managed to survive.

In early 1944, first Tima Litvin, then a number of his associates, including Ronia's brother Jacob Onikul, were arrested by the Japanese Gendarmerie. All were Soviet citizens. All were tortured to extract a confession that they had been working for the Soviet Union. Tima's description of the tortures he endured at the hands of the Japanese over a period of eleven months remind me of those Abram Onikul had been subjected to by the KKVD in Khabarovsk. Who learned from whom?

Tima was beaten mercilessly, usually with metre-long cane rods with knots and spikes which cracked his head, tore his skin and ripped out his hair by the roots. Sometimes the interrogator used a rope soaked in water to make it as hard as steel. Water was poured into Tima's nostrils while he lay on his back, his hands and feet bound. When he began to choke and splutter, the interrogator would press hard on his stomach till he vomited and fainted. Cigarettes were stubbed out on Tima's face and hands and hot tea thrown at him. Most of the time his legs were shackled with heavy leg-irons. Despite this brutality, Tima did not capitulate.

In December 1944, both Tima and Jacob were sentenced to thirteen and ten years imprisonment respectively and sent to Harbin Prison. There they were set to work in the wood-filing factory where the sound of electric saws almost deafened them. Conditions in the prison were brutal. 'Political' prisoners like Jacob and Tima were not permitted to receive food parcels. But my grandmother found a way around these restrictions. She regularly packed a food box for a gypsy who shared her cousin

Jacob's cell and gave it to his wife to deliver. The gypsy then shared it with Jacob. Tima's aunt in Harbin did the same for him through another prisoner.

Partisans from Mao Zedong's People's Army were held in the same prison. When the commanders were led to their gallows in the prison yard, Tima remembers them shouting at the Japanese wardens: 'We are not afraid of death! Your turn will come!'

———

In time, it did.

In April 1945, the Soviet Union denounced its neutrality pact with Japan a month before Germany's unconditional surrender and Victory Day in Europe. Russians in Manchukuo secretly rejoiced but wondered what would happen next. They were particularly curious whether the Soviets would take on the Japanese in Manchuria.

This had, in fact, already been decided. In a secret agreement struck in Yalta in February that year, Stalin promised Churchill and Roosevelt that the Soviet Union would attack the Japanese in the Far East three months after the German surrender. In return, the Soviet Union would acquire territory in the Far East, including a restoration of its rights over the CER in Manchuria.

Late on 8 August, the Soviet Union advised Japan that the two countries would be in a state of war as of the following day. Shortly after midnight, in a finely orchestrated blitzkrieg operation, the Red Army invaded Manchuria with 1.5 million men. They attacked Japanese positions by air, land and sea along the full length of its 5,000-kilometre border. The Japanese Kwantung Army was taken totally by surprise.

In Harbin, the Japanese Military Mission wasted no time in arresting Soviet citizens. On the morning of 9 August 1945, men with Soviet passports were rounded up and taken away in cars by Russian and Japanese policemen. About two hundred ended up at the former Soviet school not far from the Zaretsky house. There they were held under guard by the Japanese Gendarmerie. My mother's beloved 'pink school' had now become a concentration camp.

News of the arrests spread fast. My grandparents were prepared for their turn, each with a small bag packed. Meanwhile, they sat on their balcony in Diagonalnaya Street with my teenage mother Inna, who was to go and stay with an émigré aunt. Inna remembers watching the black Gendarmerie car, with a Russian policeman hanging on its side, drive to and from the police station on the corner. By some miracle and much to my grand-father's surprise, he escaped arrest.

By 15 August, rumours were rife that the prisoners being held at the 'pink school' would soon be executed. But that afternoon, the Japanese guards simply disap-peared and the prisoners were able to disperse. Earlier that day, Japan's emperor, as Commander in Chief of the Armed forces, had announced an unconditional surrender.

Within a day, the 'pink school' was transformed into the headquarters of the Unit for the Defence of Harbin or SHOH, as it was known for short in Russian. SHOH's purpose was to secure the strategic sites around the city from saboteurs, snipers and looters during the power vacuum left by the Japanese surrender and pending the arrival of the Soviet army. This was the initiative of Vasily Panov, a youth organiser in Harbin's Soviet Citizens' Association. Panov, who effectively became the commandant of Harbin, was a family friend of the Zaretskys, having grown up in Hailar and attended school with Gita, Manya and Abram.

News of the establishment of SHOH spread quickly through the community. Soon hundreds of young Russians, both Soviet and émigré, descended on the school to offer support. SHOH's executive committee was comprised of younger members of the Soviet Citizens' Association, with older members assisting. But the vast majority of its 'fighters' were Russian students of all cultures and persuasions, including former employees of BREM and conscripts from the disbanded Russian military detachment. In all, between 1,000 and 2,500 people were involved.

With trucks and weapons confiscated from the Japanese and Manchurian police and military, SHOH teams took up guard at strategic locations—including the two railway bridges across the Sungari River, communication points, key utilities, transport and businesses, hospitals, the headquarters of the Japanese Military Mission and Japanese army stores. Other teams were sent out to disarm Japanese soldiers and deal with incidents of banditry. Doctors set up emergency first aid points. The Soviet Citizens Women's Committee, my grandmother Gita among them, prepared food for the SHOH teams around the clock. My grandfather Motya helped organise provisions. Even my mother helped carry supplies to the school, conscious that Japanese snipers were hiding on the roofs of major buildings.

Gita's connection with Vasily Panov proved to be a life-saver. On the evening of the Japanese capitulation, a gypsy stranger turned up at the Zaretskys', breathless. It was Jacob Onikul's cellmate from Harbin Prison, the one through whom Gita had been sending food packages. The gypsy told Gita he had come at Jacob's request. He told her he had just been released by the Japanese with other ordinary prisoners, but Jacob, Tima and other politicals had been sent into the yard to dig their own graves and would soon be shot.

Gita managed to track down Panov, who sent SHOH representatives to the prison. As Tima recounts it, late that night, he and Jacob were summoned to the prison administration building where the Chinese prison commandant and his Japanese adviser were meeting with two Russians. They were subsequently released. Earlier, SHOH teams had freed political prisoners held in cells at the Japanese Military Mission and the Gendarmerie. Jacob turned up at the Zaretskys' at dawn looking so beaten and ragged that they barely recognised him.

By the time the Soviet army's advance party of 120

landed at Harbin aerodrome on 18 August, SHOH, with some 1,200 volunteers had secured over five hundred of Harbin's key strategic establishments. They had also managed to capture the Japanese chief of general staff in Manchukuo, General Hata, his key aides and the Japanese consul general. These prisoners were handed over to the Soviets. SHOH led the Soviets to the barracks and command posts of the Japanese military. By the end of the month, the Soviet presence had been reinforced by the arrival of the head battalion of the First Far Eastern Front and the Amur flotilla of the Second Far Eastern Front.

These were heady days. Most *Harbintsy* greeted the Soviet army with flowers and euphoria. Hundreds lined the streets to get a glimpse of these wondrous creatures in their Soviet uniforms. They were Russians—their own—and they carried with them a sense of victory which the *Harbintsy* longed to share. On 4 September, the day the Japanese signed the act of surrender on board the *USS Missouri,* thousands gathered in the square in front of St. Nicholas Cathedral to celebrate the liberation of Manchuria. Two weeks later came the victory parade through streets festooned with Soviet and Chinese flags. For my sixteen-year-old mother, most memorable was the concert by the Red Army Ensemble that followed at the stadium. Never had she and her girlfriends heard such voices or been so moved by patriotic lyrics. The good looks of the singers no doubt consolidated this lasting impression.

Many *Harbintsy* showered the occupying army with kindness. Emigrés who had been apprehensive about their arrival began to feel more at ease. Even my father's mother Tonya, a dyed-in-the-wool anti-Soviet, allowed Alec to take a daily pail of fresh milk to some young soldiers billeted nearby. Many invited officers to their homes for meals. Friendships were struck up. Romances flourished. Young Soviet soldiers in uniform who had never before set foot inside a church married Harbin girls in Orthodox ceremonies. Few of these couples saw each other again after the Soviets left Manchuria in May 1946. In some instances, the officers were already married with families back in the USSR. The progeny of these unions were nicknamed 'trophy children'.

But many of these friendships were genuine and some Soviet officers talked more openly with the relative strangers they met in Harbin than among themselves. As my grandfather was involved in meat procurement for the army, the officers he worked with were frequent guests at the Zaretsky home. My mother recalls one of them, a major from Khabarovsk, describing how, at the height of Stalin's purges, the men in his work group had all disappeared, one after the other. As the only survivor of the original group, he had felt sure that people around him assumed he had informed on the others, which he claimed was not the case. Another of Motya's colleagues, a young captain, advised the Zaretskys against going to live in the Soviet Union—hardly patriotic behaviour on the part of a Red Army stalwart.

As with any occupying force, the Soviet army had its less refined elements. Some of the troops who entered Manchuria at the start of the war had come straight from the German front. War-weary and brutalised by the horrors they had experienced, they were more accustomed to meeting the enemy head on than relating to peaceful civilians. Among them too were hardened criminals, released to fill out the ranks of the army. Their behaviour towards the Chinese was particularly thuggish. Drunken soldiers accosted people in the street, demanding watches and sometimes, women. But soon they were replaced by fresh young conscripts whose role was to maintain order.

More sinister was the arrival of the slick operatives of the military counter-intelligence organisation, Smersh (Death to Spies!). Naturally, their first targets were Russians who had collaborated with the Japanese. Top of the list were old Cossack generals, like Ataman Semyonov and General Baksheev; leaders of BREM and the Russian Fascist Party, including its leader Rodzaevsky; employees of the Japanese Military Mission and the Gendarmerie; and officers of the Russian Military Detachment. The more prominent were sent to Moscow for highly publicised trials and executions. Lesser beings were sent to the Gulag. Smersh's hunt for 'enemies' was made considerably easier by the fact that Matkovsky, BREM's deputy and keeper of the archive of émigré files, and Colonel Nagolen of the Russian Military Detachment were both apparently Soviet agents.

Thousands of innocents were rounded up in the process. This included young men who, without choice, had been conscripted into Asano or another of the Russian military detachments. Even fifteen-year-old youths who had spent two weeks as part of their school training camps were taken in the process. Russians who had illegally crossed the Soviet border to escape collectivisation after 1930 were also hunted down.

Hundreds of representatives of Harbin's various communities and social organisations also found themselves under arrest, among them Jewish community leader Dr Abraham Kaufman. All had been tricked into attending what they thought was an introductory meeting with the Soviet High Command at the Yamato Hotel. Their crime? Representing the interests of their communities to the Japanese authorities.

Smersh had no qualms about the methods they used to catch their prey. One relative who had crossed illegally from Vladivostok in 1930 was caught after a senior operative cajoled information about his whereabouts out of his five-year-old daughter. All were deported to the Gulag.

Chesna would have been only too familiar with what these people had experienced. Many of them were convicted on trumped-up charges under various clauses of the infamous Article 58, just as she and her family had been seven years earlier. The lucky ones survived long enough to be rehabilitated and reunited with their families.

———◆———

The fiercest battle of the brief August 1945 war between the Soviet Union and Japan in Manchuria took place in Chesna's old hometown of Hailar. It was also one of the war's most needless tragedies. These were the horrors about which no-one wanted to tell Chesna. But their impact on the lives of those closest to her was so profound that they could not be kept hidden.

Chesna had been bracing herself for the meeting with the family of her nephew Sanya, especially his father Nohum. She dreaded having to break the news that Nohum's brother Girsh had been executed by the NKVD and that a similar fate may have befallen his son Sanya. But Sanya's sister Ronia, who had moved to Harbin, told Chesna that both her parents had died, her mother from cancer. What about Nohum? Ronia changed the subject and told Chesna that her brother Jacob would soon be coming to visit from Hailar. What about her younger brother Zalman? He had been a teenager when the Onikuls had left in 1936. 'He's dead too.' 'What from?' Another silence. Chesna's question about her niece Dora Kogan's husband, Yacov, was met with the same response. What about Tima Litvin's father? Also dead. Silence. It went on and on.

Chesna demanded the truth and the story eventually unfolded.

Chesna had been vaguely aware that the Japanese had been building a large military base near Hailar. Construction had started before the Onikul departure, but Chesna had no idea of the scale. In fact, the Japanese were building a huge fortified underground city. Built on the backs of tens of thousands of Chinese 'coolie' labourers brought from the south and worked to death or killed, the base was a key target for Soviet attack. The

Soviet onslaught started very early on 9 August, with heavy aerial bombardment which went on for several days until the five thousand-strong Japanese garrison capitulated.

Waking to the sound of shelling, the people of Hailar found leaflets dropped by the Soviet bombers warning citizens to leave town. As people scrambled to get out, the Japanese Gendarmerie drove around town arresting male Soviet citizens, many of them Jews. Ronia Onikul was stunned when she saw the young Russian from the Gendarmerie arrive at their house. With him was her older brother Zalman, who had been next door helping their neighbour. He was under arrest. Now they had come for her father.

'Where are you taking them?' Ronia cried.

'That is not your business.'

Distraught, Ronia and her mother joined the other people fleeing to the hills from the burning town. The Kogans, the Litvins and others had similar stories.

Days later, when the fighting had subsided and Red Army units had taken control of the town, people started returning. Some, like the Kogans, found themselves homeless. Their houses had been completely burned out in the bombing. Other houses that were still standing had been ransacked by looters. But there was no sign of the men who had been arrested—not in the prison nor the cells of the Gendarmerie. While most of the missing people were Soviets, a couple of émigré Jews had also been taken away. As the weeks dragged on, hopes that the men would return home faded.

Then one day in September, on a block behind the Soviet commandant's office on the edge of town, someone stumbled on a piece of cloth protruding from a sandy mound. Brushing away the sand, a hand was revealed, then a body.

As the surrounding area was dug up, the full horror of the carnage was revealed. Forty-two bodies were unearthed. Almost all of them had been beheaded. Young and old. Russians and Jews. In deep shock, the families of the missing men came to identify the mangled bodies. Some had to search for heads which lay far from the bodies. Ronia found her brother Zalman's head had not been completely severed from his body. In agony, he had torn his shirt to shreds. Among the corpses of local Russians, there were bodies of Russians who nobody knew. The locals guessed they were probably Soviet prisoners the Japanese had captured in cross-border operations.

But Japanese bloody-mindedness in Hailar in the final days of the war was not restricted to Soviet citizens. Over twenty disarmed men from the Hailar unit of the Russian Military Detachment were machine-gunned and stabbed to death by the Japanese cavalry on 10 August.

There was retribution. When trials of Japanese military started in Hailar, many were sentenced to death for the atrocities they had committed. When the chief of the Japanese Military Mission was brought to the scene of the massacre from his prison cell, he admitted that he had personally given the order for the beheadings. On their return to Hailar, Jacob Onikul and Tima Litvin were called to give evidence in the trial of their torturer, who was sentenced to execution. As with the posthumous rehabilitations of the Onikuls in the Soviet Union, it was cold comfort.

———•———

After all the years apart from her family, Chesna's time in Harbin passed too quickly. But the Chinese Public Security Bureau treated her kindly. First they extended her initial three-month visa to six months. All it took was a letter saying that, in view of her old age and ill-health, she wanted to stay with her daughter for a longer time. Then with the help of a letter from the Zaretskys' dentist, she extended her stay for another month, until June 1957.

By that time, like other *Harbintsy,* my family was looking at leaving China and considering where we might go. Chesna strongly encouraged us to come to the Soviet Union. She was sure that Yasha would find a way to get us to Riga and help find good employment and accommodation. Chesna left Harbin confident that this was still an option. Even if it had been, the experience with our next visitor from the USSR would have closed it.

———•———

Yasha arrived in Harbin on the Moscow-Peking Express several months after Chesna returned to Riga in late 1957.

A photo I find in Chesna's album shows my mother, my aunts Ronia Onikul, Ira Kogan, her mother Dora, the Litvins from Hailar and me, rugged up in warm coats at Harbin Station. On the back of the photo, the inscription reads:

On the platform before meeting Yasha

My mother explains that the photograph, taken by my father, had been sent to Chesna in Riga. She points out that I am wearing the cherry red and white knitted scarf, hat and mittens which Chesna had brought me from Riga earlier that year. From our warm clothing, we figure it must have been in October or November 1957.

I am amazed that not just Chesna, but Yasha too had been allowed to visit relatives in Harbin in the late 1950s. It suggests a far more liberal travel regime in Khrushchev's Soviet Union than I had ever realised. My mother laughs and explains that Yasha did not come to stay with us but was travelling with a delegation on a familiarisation tour of the People's Republic of China.

'The train stopped in Harbin for about an hour on its way to Peking,' she says, 'so we went to see him at the station.'

From a stack of tourist photographs Galya gave me in Riga, I can see that Yasha's tour included Peking, Tientsin, Shanghai, as well as model villages in the countryside. Such visits to cement ties with workers in fraternal socialist countries became popular during the Khrushchev years. But as I learn from my mother, cementing ties with family living abroad was definitely not on the agenda.

In spite of Khrushchev's thaw, having 'foreign' relatives was still something that raised question marks about a Soviet citizen's 'biography' and many tried to keep it hidden. Until the time when he died in the mid-1980s, Yasha still sent us mail under Galya's surname.

Looking carefully at the photograph, I notice something curious.

'How come granny and grandpa aren't there?' I ask my mother. 'I would have thought Gita more than anybody else would have been desperate to see her brother after twenty years?'

'She did,' my mother says, 'but that came later.' Inna then goes on to explain how 'chance' meetings with relatives during Yasha's trip in China had been orchestrated with tradecraft worthy of a clandestine intelligence operation.

As Yasha's Moscow-Peking Express pulled into Hailar, Yasha's cousin Jacob Onikul and his wife Lika got on the train. Later, Lika tells me how they had reserved a private sleeper for the journey to Harbin. When they went to dine in the restaurant car, they saw Yasha sitting at one of the tables with his colleagues. They observed each other for a long time but made no sign of recognition.

As they were leaving the restaurant car, Jacob and Lika walked close to Yasha's table. In a loud voice she dropped into the conversation with her husband the number of their cabin. Later that night, after everyone had settled in their sleepers, Yasha coughed outside their door and they let him in. He stayed with them till the morning, catching up on all that had happened over the years.

When the train got to Harbin Station and the greeting party was milling around with Yasha at one end of the platform, my grandfather was bidding farewell to Gita as she boarded the same train further along the platform en route for Peking. My mother told Yasha the number of Gita's carriage and sleeper so Yasha could pay his sister a visit that night.

After Gita returned to Harbin, it was my mother's turn. Inna went to stay with an aunt in Tientsin at the time when Yasha's delegation was there for a couple of days. As arranged during their brief encounter on the platform in Harbin, Yasha called for Inna at her aunt's apartment and the two of them went shopping. He had managed to get out of a factory tour by feigning illness. Just as they were paying the bill for a pile of Chinese down-filled silk jackets, disaster struck. Through the shop window they caught the nonchalant gaze of a tall figure with a pale European face. It was the delegation's KGB minder.

All my mother remembers is Yasha grabbing the two bags of jackets and making for the door. Stunned at how fast it had all happened, Inna saw him walk up to the stranger. Then the two walked away together. Inna ran all the way to her aunt's house, shaking. What was going to happen to her uncle?

That night Yasha turned up fleetingly at her aunt's house to put Inna's mind at rest. He told her everything had been 'sorted', which she took to mean the booty had been shared. Next day, Inna went to the lobby of the Hotel Astor to see Yasha's delegation leaving for the station. Yasha passed her without acknowledgment. My hunch is that the penalty for getting caught shopping was much less than fraternising with 'foreign' relatives, whom he had probably omitted to mention in his 'biography'.

This was the last time my mother saw her Uncle Yasha. But I saw him one more time.

Another photograph in our family album shows Yasha at Harbin Station with my grandparents and me. It was taken by my father the day Yasha transited Harbin on his way back to the Soviet Union. The absence of my mother suggests that she was still in Tientsin.

The photograph captures a grim, grey scene on a bitterly cold day. Standing against a granite wall, my grandfather and I are both in fur hats and collars. My grandmother has wrapped her head in a warm Orenburg shawl, while Yasha shivers in a scarf and fedora. Behind us is the big black hole of the train tunnel. The adults are gloomy. I am grimacing. Was it simply the weather or the knowledge that we would soon go in different directions and might never see each other again?

CHAPTER 15

KHRUSHCHEV'S 'VIRGIN LANDS' OR SYDNEY?

In April 1954 Harbin was abuzz with excitement. The Soviet government had just given permission for Russians with Soviet citizenship living in China to take part in Khrushchev's 'virgin lands' campaign. As almost all Russian *Harbintsy* were now Soviet citizens, this meant they could join the hundreds of thousands of young people from all over the Soviet Union to develop the wilds of Siberia and Kazakhstan.

Hundreds flocked to the Soviet consulate to sign up and arrange departure. As in the mid-1930s, Harbin Station became the backdrop for countless farewells. Again tears were mixed with hurrahs, as train after train left for the Soviet Union laden with people, their hopes, fears and belongings. Everything was packed—brooms and buckets, crates of books, even the odd grand piano. People had no idea where they might end up so they took whatever they owned. Baggage was not restricted.

Patriotism had triumphed over ideology. Since the end of the war in 1945, many *Harbintsy* had been clamouring to return to the Soviet Union to help rebuild their homeland after the ravages of war. Now their chance had come. This was the first mass migration to the USSR since Chinese Eastern Railway (CER) employees and their families returned after its sale in the mid-1930s.

Did these *Harbintsy* know what they were doing? Surely they were aware that 'repatriation' to the USSR from Harbin had a distinctly tarnished history? Had they forgotten how their CER compatriots had disappeared without trace? Not to mention those deported by Smersh in 1945.

The *Harbintsy* remembered these tragedies only too well. But times had changed. Stalin was dead and the most evil of his lieutenants had been eliminated. The new Soviet leadership under Khrushchev seemed to be genuinely trying to build a more humane society. Many *Harbintsy* whose relatives had been deported to the USSR in 1945 signed up for the virgin lands program in the hope of reuniting with their loved ones. Some had received messages. Others were going without having heard a word.

Besides, life in Harbin had long lost its former Russian charm. Now that the Chinese were at last masters of their country's destiny, many Russian *Harbintsy* were finding it hard to adapt to life with an increasingly Maoist flavour.

Harbin was the first major city where Mao Zedong's Communist forces established tenuous control—well before the People's Republic of China (PRC) was proclaimed in October 1949. But few Russian *Harbintsy* noticed. It happened at the end of April 1946, as Soviet occupation forces pulled out of Manchuria while the rival forces of Mao and Chiang Kai-shek's Kuomintang continued their long battle for control of China.

But any notion that the Chinese Communist advance in Harbin was assisted by the Soviets would be misplaced. While the Soviets abandoned the Manchurian countryside to Mao's Communists, they dutifully handed back the cities to the Kuomintang, as agreed in the treaty signed with Chiang Kai-shek after the war. This secured for the Soviet Union the spoils agreed by the Allied Powers in Yalta, including joint administration of Manchurian ports and railways. The Soviets also stripped the Manchurian industrial plant of its equipment and rolling stock as 'reparations'. This retarded Manchuria's industrial development and ensured the PRC's dependence on its Soviet 'brother'.

At the time, most Russian *Harbintsy* knew little about these Sino-Soviet machinations. Busy rebuilding their lives after thirteen years of Japanese occupation, it mattered little to them which of the Chinese factions, Communist or Kuomintang, controlled their city. Times were tough, with wartime currency rendered useless and shortages of basic necessities, electricity and heating fuel. Their hardship was exacerbated by the Soviets sending home from China huge quantities of coal, grain and foodstuffs as more 'reparations'.

Harbintsy also had to adjust to the new institutions and practices which the Soviet occupation had established. All *Harbintsy* with Soviet citizenship now had to register with the Society of Soviet Citizens (SSC), created to administer the affairs of Russians in Manchuria, much as BREM did during the Japanese years. The SSC operated in close collaboration with the Soviet consulate, as BREM had with the Japanese Military Mission. Young people were encouraged to join the Union of Soviet Youth (SSM), a politico-cultural organisation modelled on the Soviet Komsomol.

For students like my parents, whose main preoccupation at the time was education, there was much anxiety and excitement as educational institutions reopened and Soviet curricula were introduced. With the re-opening of my mother's old Soviet school, she was able to complete her final two years of high school with other students in a classroom instead of studying at home alone.

Even more exciting was the reopening of the Harbin Polytechnical Institute (HPI), Harbin's premier institution of higher learning, which the Japanese had closed to Russians in 1937. It now trained a generation of Russian engineers who later spread from Novosibirsk and Tel Aviv to Sydney and Sao Paulo. Though the HPI's director was Chinese, as in most other government enterprises and institutions, the management was effectively Soviet. With the exception of several hundred Chinese graduates brought from Shanghai to study Russian, in the early days there were still few Chinese students.

When the Chinese Communists came to power in October 1949, Stalin had little choice but to welcome their victory and to offer aid. For his part, China's new leader, Chairman Mao, had no option but to accept it, complete with thousands of Soviet advisers who helped steer China's industrialisation in a Soviet direction. But Mao significantly improved the terms of the alliance signed earlier by Chiang Kai-shek in China's favour. The timetable for handover of the Manchurian railways was brought forward by twenty-three years to 1952, with no compensation to the Soviets.

That left just enough time for my father to graduate as a Chinese linguist from HPI and spend a year as interpreter to the Soviet inspector of sport for the railway administration. This involved travelling around China with the inspector, monitoring the establishment of fitness programs and presiding at sporting competitions. Not bad for a first job.

By 1951, my parents were both working as technical interpreters at the Sugar Refinery Construction Bureau, which developed plans for local plant construction, based on foreign designs. Unusual among Russian *Harbintsy,* both of them were fluent in Chinese, having graduated from HPI's newly established Faculty of Oriental and Economic Studies. Their work involved interpreting at meetings between Russian engineers and Chinese officials, as well as translating design documents. Speaking Chinese almost like a native, my father worked directly for the chief engineer and was often called on to interpret for various eastern European experts at board meetings.

By this time, Chairman Mao had launched the first of his many political campaigns—the crackdown on counter-revolutionaries. Aimed at weeding out anyone with past connections to the Kuomintang, the initiative had strong shades of the Soviet campaign against people of dubious social origin in the 1920s and 1930s. Suspects were subjected to long interrogations and constant sur-veillance, while investigation committees delved into every last detail of their background. Some confessed to crimes they had not committed simply to avoid being sent to prison. Quite a number committed suicide. This was the path chosen by one Chinese couple from Shanghai who worked as engineers in the same office as my mother. She had often been struck by how elegant the woman always managed to look, even in the drab and shapeless navy blue Mao suit she was obliged to wear. Well born and Western-educated, they were easy targets.

The next campaign, launched in late 1951, targeted the 'three evils'—corruption, waste and bureaucracy—among workers in government departments and state enterprises. My parents witnessed their Chinese col-leagues sit through endless 'self-criticism' and 'criticism' sessions, confessing their guilt to misdemeanours such as stealing two pencils. Those who had nothing to confess would be made to 'think harder'. Sometimes they would make things up just to get out of the room. Russian employees were also expected to participate, but most refused.

The next year, the campaign against the 'five evils' hit harder. This time, the goal was to uncover bribery, tax evasion, theft of state property, cheating on government contracts and stealing economic information among capitalists, factory owners and merchants. The campaign was used by the authorities to raise badly needed revenue for the state's coffers. Suspects were detained by the Public Security Bureau (the Chinese equivalent of the KGB, whose Russian acronym was DOB). Most were fined heavily for their alleged misdemeanours. As DOB relied on the evidence of informants, the process also opened the way for score-settling and personal vendettas. As well as thousands of Chinese, some Russian business-men in Harbin also got caught in the process

In a number of instances, the consequences were tragic, as a family friend in California tells me fifty years later. While trade in foreign currency was illegal, this did not stop the Chinese authorities buying foreign exchange from Harbin's Russian 'Gold King' well into the early 1950s. Then they called in their chips, demanding that he name all the other people who traded with him. Rather than divulge, he threw himself under a train at Harbin Station. Another merchant, arrested for possession of US $10,000, much of which was acquired before 1949, had the full amount confiscated and such a heavy fine imposed that he could not raise it even after selling all his property. He too chose suicide.

Realising that nationalisation of private business enterprises was imminent, at the end of 1952 my grand-father and his partners liquidated the meat and livestock business in Hailar which they had set up in the late 1940s. Motya still kept several hundred head of livestock in

Mongolia, where he travelled a couple of times a year for the colourful Mongol Ganjur livestock fair. But from 1951, his main occupation was as a director and manager of cash transactions at the Jewish Bank in Harbin. From his personal papers, I also discover that in his last years in Harbin, Motya was the *shochet*, performing the kosher slaughter of animals for the dwindling Jewish community, as well as being a member of its audit committee.

—•••—

In a multicultural Russian city like Harbin, cross-cultural marriages were not uncommon—especially between Russians and Jews or Russians and Tatars. My parents did one better. When my Jewish mother married my father, who was half-Russian Orthodox, half-Muslim Tatar, they brought all three cultures together in one family.

While my two wise grandfathers, both Jew and Tatar, were philosophical about the whole business, both grandmothers were unhappy. Curiously, the one who objected the most was my father's mother Tonya, who had herself married outside her Russian Orthodox faith. My Jewish grandmother Gita came around fairly quickly. After the wedding, my father came to live with the Zaretskys and was readily accepted by the whole extended family.

In mid-1954, my mother stopped work long enough to give birth to me and establish a bond that would ensure neither of us took the other for granted. In fact, I saw quite a lot of my parents, even on working days. We lived with the Zaretskys in Diagonalnaya Street, just around the corner from my parents' workplace. Most days the whole family would eat lunch, the main meal of the day, at home. The rest of the time, I was looked after by my Russian nanny under the watchful eye of my grandmother Gita.

My grandmother Tonya mellowed with my arrival. She started coming to our house for family occasions and became firm friends with my grandfather Motya. When her husband died two years later, she accepted Motya's offer to come and live in the apartment downstairs with Ira Kogan's mother, Dora. Growing up with two doting grandmothers in such close proximity was, for me, the best of all possible worlds. For them, it was a constant source of tension. Years later, an aunt describes how, as a three-year-old, I returned from a walk with Tonya. Asked where I had been, I made a perfect sign of the cross in the Russian Orthodox way and announced that I had been to the house where people did 'that'. 'She'll have her baptised soon,' Gita muttered.

Thinking about it after I hear this story, I realise that this was probably not the only time Tonya had taken me to church on our walks around Harbin. It may explain why I have always been drawn to the ceremony and ritual of Orthodox churches, wherever in the world I come across them. And why I always light a candle for Tonya.

For years, I wonder what it was that Tonya had found so confronting in my parents' marriage. Was it just because my mother was Jewish? I sense there was more to it than that. The files of Tonya's family which I find in the archives in Khabarovsk and Harbin give me an insight into her background and the complex emotions my parents' union may have aroused.

In Tonya's eyes, the life of my mother's family in Harbin was as far removed from her own as she could have imagined. The Zaretskys had come to live in Manchuria by choice, long before the 1917 revolution. They were established, wealthy and lived in the heart of Pristan, the city's commercial district. My grandfather Motya owned hundreds of head of sheep and cattle. My grandmother Gita had a fairytale marriage and appeared to Tonya to live a charmed and pampered life.

Tonya's own life stood in stark distinction. Arriving as refugees from the Bolshevik Revolution, her family had to scrape together an existence. Her own marriage had been a matter of practicality rather than romance. Her house was not even on the right side of the river, let alone the top end of town. By the 1950s, she and her husband lived by selling milk from their six cows. The contrast in the life of the two families underlined for her the bitterness of exile.

Tonya had once been destined for a good life. This is clear from the uncompromising gaze with which she regarded the world as a small child in a fragment torn from what had probably been a family photograph. There she stands—Antonina Shelamanova, aged around six, posing on a chair in the classic white drop-waisted dress little girls wore in pre-revolutionary Russia. At the time, her family lived in Novouzensk near Saratov on the Volga. Her father was a prosperous farmer who had been elected as a deputy to the provincial Peasant Congress in Samara. Her future looked assured.

But what might have been, did not eventuate. Dispossessed by the Bolsheviks, Tonya's family fled to the Far East with the White Army. They spent the Civil War in Nikolsk-Ussuriisk, near Vladivostok. After the White defeat in 1922, they sought refuge in Harbin. Life in exile was a struggle. Tonya's parents split. Her father died. Her mother remarried. Her brother disappeared.

Dark-haired and attractive, at seventeen Tonya married my grandfather, a Tatar fifteen years her elder. Born in a village near Kazan, the ancient Tatar capital on the Volga, Muhamedjian Mustafin had arrived in Harbin in 1920. Having fought on both sides of the Civil War without real allegiance to either, he was glad to get away from the turmoil. In Harbin, he worked as an electrician and maintenance man for wealthy property owners or large companies. The work was hard and did not pay all that well, but it had the benefit of on-site accommodation. He supported Tonya and my father, while Tonya studied to be a nurse. When she qualified in the mid-1930s, Tonya went to work at the Kasem Bek Hospital, a job to which she returned in 1956, after her husband died.

Tonya and Muhamedjian lived together well enough, respecting each other's differences. Tonya gave up neither her name nor her religion. All the main Orthodox festivals were celebrated in their home. Each Sunday she would go to the Russian Orthodox church in whatever neighbourhood they were living. For many years, when they lived in the Novy Gorod district, Tonya went to St Nicholas Cathedral across the square from their house. Built entirely of wood without a single nail and full of precious icons, this was the centre of Russian Orthodox life in Harbin.

On Fridays, my grandfather Muhamedjian went to the grand old Tatar mosque, which stood a block from the main synagogue in Artilleriiskaya Street on the Pristan side of town. He was active in the Tatar community and served for several years on the board of the community association. My father, known to Russians as Alec and Alimjan among Tatars, would go to church at Christmas and Easter, and attended Orthodox scripture at school to please his mother. His father would take him to the mosque on major festivals like *Kurban-bairam* (the feast of the sacrifice) and to the traditional Tatar *Sabantui* horseraces held at the Harbin racecourse. But the focus of his life was secular—school and sport.

◆·····◆

Though my family paid no attention to the 'virgin lands' campaign when it was first launched, they could not ignore it for long. With people leaving all around them, herd mentality became a powerful magnet: 'Everyone is going to the virgin lands. Maybe we should too?' Even my grandfather Motya raised the possibility once or twice. But my parents dissuaded him on the grounds that I was too young to be taken into such uncertainty.

Leaving Harbin, the 'virgin lands' volunteers had absolutely no idea of their final destination. Only when they arrived on the Soviet side of the border were heads of families summoned before a special commission which decided where they would be sent—Kazakhstan or Siberia, wheat farm, hydroelectric plant or tractor factory. By then, there was no option of going back. Once the destination was agreed, people were transferred with all their belongings from the passenger train to a goods wagon or cattle car for the onward journey.

By 1956, the truth about the joys of building the 'socialist paradise' had begun to filter back to Harbin. As Soviet mail was censored, it came in code, in the subtext of letters, which interspersed glowing reports of life in the virgin lands with glaring non sequiturs. One family friend wrote praising his new life, then added:

> It is so good here that you should all come—just as soon as Marochka finishes university.

How were the censors to know that I was barely two at the time?

Comparing the letters they all received, my parents and their friends formed a composite picture of the sort of future that lay before them: a family still dressed in elegant Harbin clothes standing in a field surrounded by all their possessions—suitcases, furniture and a grand piano. Before them in the grasslands, they see a sign that reads, 'Future Virgin Lands *Sovhoz* (State Farm)'. The sun is setting fast, as the truck which brought them from the train disappears into the dusty distance. The image was not so far-fetched.

Was this really Soviet revenge against those who had escaped from the Bolsheviks or some sort of penance for abandoning their homeland? This is certainly how some *Harbintsy* later described it in some anti-Soviet émigré publications. But it is far from the truth. Khrushchev's virgin lands program was aimed primarily at the 200,000 young Soviet Komsomol patriots who came from all ends of the Soviet Union. The extension of the campaign to include Russians from China was well intentioned but ill-conceived.

Soviet farms needed workers and practical people. Many of the ballerinas, violinists, doctors, teachers and highly qualified engineers arriving from Harbin were more a hindrance than a help. Once they acquired proper Soviet passports, no-one held them back on the farms. Many were able to find jobs and accommodation in towns and cities. Eventually some even got through to Moscow and Leningrad. Only people without other qualifications stayed on the farms.

But back in Harbin, pressure on Russians to return 'home' to the USSR was getting stronger, especially from the Soviet consulate and its comrades in the SSC and SSM. The approach was a combination of stick and carrot. It was widely publicised that those who signed up for the 'virgin lands' program would be able to sell their property to the Chinese authorities and liquidate their businesses for good returns. They could take all their property with them and transfer their funds to the Soviet Union. Those who intended to emigrate elsewhere were warned they would get next to nothing for their property and would not be allowed to export their capital. The quantity of gold, silver and foreign currency they could take out would also be severely restricted.

Not long after the 'virgin lands' campaign was first announced in 1954, processing of exit permits for those who wanted to emigrate to countries other than the USSR almost ground to a standstill. Then in October 1954, all who had made such applications were summoned to public meetings where representatives of the consulate told them permission had been refused. There was 'only one way for Soviet citizens' to go from China: back to the Soviet Union.

Soon members of the SSM who had not registered for the virgin lands program were being reviled at special meetings and expelled from the organisation as 'traitors to their Motherland'—just as Komsomol members had been vilified as 'enemies of the people' in the Soviet Union in the 1930s. While this was punishment of sorts, most of those expelled were strong enough to grin and bear it. My parents were not affected at all. My mother had managed to get herself expelled from the SSM much earlier for refusing to wait on tables at a union workers' function. My father had never joined.

In 1956, the Soviets struck where it hurt. At the instigation of the SSC, Chinese government institutions were ordered to dismiss all Russian employees who had not registered for the virgin lands program. Left without means to live even while they tried to organise visas elsewhere, thousands were forced to go to the Soviet Union.

My parents were more fortunate. Language teachers were in high demand and both were able to find employment teaching Russian to the Chinese at the Institute of Foreign Languages after they were sacked from the construction office.

From photographs of my Harbin childhood, I can see that despite these tensions, we still enjoyed plenty of lighter moments. In summer there were outings to Sun Island and boating on the Sungari River. Until travel was severely restricted in 1958, we continued to spend a month each summer at a *dacha* we rented on the other side of the Sungari or in the mountains at Maoershan. My father still sailed regularly on the Sungari and went duck-shooting and skiing with his friends. My parents went to tea dances and parties at the Soviet Club. And to countless farewells.

But our days in China were numbered. Apart from Soviet pressure, life in the new People's Republic was becoming increasingly difficult, even for *Harbintsy* who spoke fluent Chinese. By the late 1950s, the Chinese authorities were open about wanting to rid the country of foreigners. Chinese were discouraged from working in Russian houses, while young people were indoctrinated against 'foreign devils'. On the streets, a new hostility became palpable. Chinese children would harass Russian passers-by without reprimand—spitting at them; throwing stones, ink or slander.

DOB's intrusions into the life of *Harbintsy* had also

become more frequent and increasingly more annoying. On the pretext of checking the resident books, DOB policemen regularly came to people's houses to conduct inquisitions in broken Russian. The same questions would be asked time and time again: 'What's your name? Who lives here? Are you going to the USSR? Why not? Last year you said . . .' Even people who were usually polite were driven to despair. Sometimes they ventured into the kitchen to see what was cooking in the pots and harass the residents as to where they might have acquired a chicken.

My mother's confrontation with a DOB policeman over a domestic of mixed Chinese-Korean extraction was more serious. By this time, it was risky for Chinese to work for foreigners, let alone live in their houses. But the Zaretskys took pity on this woman and gave her work and a place to stay. She had been warned never to admit this to the DOB policeman. But one afternoon the domestic got flustered by his questions. 'Yes,' she blurted out when he asked, 'Do you live here?' This directly contradicted what my mother had told him just five minutes earlier. 'I am arresting you,' he told my mother and insisted she accompany him immediately to the police station. Only the excuse that I was ill and could not be left alone enabled her to stall until my father came home from work. The reprieve he negotiated was a written apology to DOB. More than forty years later, I find it in my mother's file in the DOB archive in Harbin.

Other friends tell of being summoned for interrogation for four days running after being caught playing a social game of *mah jong*. Each time they are accused of gambling for money and ordered to write confessions, naming names.

The Chinese authorities insisted that foreigners remaining in China had to live under the same conditions as the Chinese, with no special privileges. As part of Chairman Mao's Great Leap Forward in 1958, my family were expected to 'make steel' like everyone else in China. This meant feeding scrap metal into the neighbourhood furnace set up on the street near our house. They also had to participate in his neighbourhood campaign to kill sparrows by clattering saucepans on the roof till the birds fell out of the sky. The logic was that because they ate crops, the sparrows were partly to blame for the famine sweeping China. When the local policeman called a neighbourhood meeting to explain this, the invidious task of interpreting for the Russian residents fell to my mother. Again, she almost got herself arrested for bursting into laughter from disbelief at what she was translating. Soon domestic pets were also being killed as superfluous creatures who ate food required by humans.

It was time to leave.

———◆◆◆———

Contrary to statements by the Soviet consulate in 1954 that there was only 'one way' for Soviet citizens to go

from China—to their homeland in the Soviet Union—
my family discovered several other alternatives.

As Jews, we were automatically eligible for emigration
to Israel. Since the establishment of the Jewish state in
1948, many friends and relatives had already taken this
route. The Soviet consulate made loud noises about refusing to allow Soviet citizens to go there and belittled a
homeland of 'sand and stones'. Exit permits were,
nevertheless, given. Letters from relatives living in tents
on the outskirts of Haifa and Tel Aviv left us with no illu-
sions about the challenges of the life we would face there.
But somehow my family sensed that helping to make the
deserts bloom among the sand and stones in Israel would
ultimately be more rewarding than tilling the virgin soils
in the Soviet Union. In 1957, we got Israeli visas.

At the same time, we explored the possibility of
emigrating to Australia, one of the few countries taking
Russian refugees from China at the time. However
remote and unknown Australia was, however foreign its
Anglo-Celtic culture, it was peaceful and held the
promise of a stable future. Friends from Sydney wrote
that there were plenty of job opportunities, especially
since my parents and my grandfather already spoke
English. We found sponsors and applied—my grandparents first, my parents several months later.

At the time, Australian consular affairs in China were
handled by the British embassy in Peking. In my grandfather's DOB file in the archive in Harbin, I find the
embassy's confirmation of permission for my grandparents to enter Australia in July 1957. This was based on

advice from the Department of Immigration in Canberra of 23 May 1957 and was valid for two years. Ours took much longer. Although Canberra's advice to the embassy is dated 27 July 1957, it was only confirmed in November 1958. Perhaps my parents' linguistic abilities and work with Chinese and Soviet officials complicated their security profile?

Conscious that the term of their Australian entry permit was beginning to run out, my grandparents nevertheless waited for our permits to come through so we could leave Harbin together.

Meanwhile, my parents prepared for Australia. Having heard that engineers were in high demand, they went to night school to study draughtsmanship to build up their technical qualifications. As Soviet books in Harbin were very cheap, they bought up books on everything from *kolkhoz* chicken farming to plumbing, metallurgy and embroidery. One just never knew when they might come in handy! Not knowing what Australia would have in the way of tailors and dress-makers, on whom *Harbintsy* relied for clothing, my mother sat through a dressmaking course, which she loathed.

By the late 1950s, the Russian community in Harbin had dwindled to a couple of thousand and a couple of hundred Jews. As with all minorities, they had become very close knit. Almost everyone was 'sitting on suit-cases'—waiting for visas, fighting with DOB about exit permits and packing up their lives. The bush telegraph worked overtime, reporting the latest obstacles DOB might throw up or where to get packing crates and suitcases. News received in letters from abroad spread like wildfire.

What was this Australia really like? What should we take with us? The picture *Harbintsy* got from friends already in Australia was very confusing. Some heard the country was very warm and there was no need for winter clothes; others, that it was cold and they should bring everything. Some letters said household items were hard to find and expensive; others advised there was no point bringing anything but 'greenbacks' (US dollars).

Harbintsy had little idea about the vastness and geographical diversity of the continent to which they were headed, though they all knew that Australia's national animal was the kangaroo. They did not distinguish between the cities from which letters came or comprehend that Brisbane was as far from Melbourne, both geographically and socially, as Harbin was from Shanghai. In their minds, whatever particular city they were bound for was simply 'Australia'.

When the time came for us to prepare for departure, my family bought items to cover all contingencies. We were fortunate enough to have money to spend and knew we could not take it with us. Everything was packed—from supplies of soap and toothpaste to brooms, buckets, washboards, mattresses and a metal baby bath. As taking out bolts of cloth was illegal, suit lengths of wool and brocade were sewn into large bags. Nobody told us that it would be much cheaper to buy clothes off the rack than to find a tailor in Australia. A Chinese tailor worked for days making camel-hair quilts and jackets to protect us against the Sydney cold!

Securing entry to Australia was the first victory. The next challenge was getting approval to exit China. This tortuous process involved three agencies—the Soviet consulate, on whose passports we would be travelling; the SSC, who administered the affairs of the Soviet community; and finally, the Foreign Department of DOB, which would ensure that we met our obligations to the People's Republic. Between them they ran people ragged. First one would hold out on permission, then another. Sometimes, they would change their mind. Meanwhile the applicants' visas would expire.

Essentially, the game was about money. The consulate and the SSC wanted 'voluntary contributions'; DOB wanted as much as it could extract through nefarious taxes, fines and sheer blackmail. Working at the Jewish Bank, my grandfather saw what happened to others. He knew that only once his business affairs were in order was there any point in sending our passports to the British embassy to have our Hong Kong and Australian visas issued.

As soon as our permits for Australia came through, Motya went to Hailar to sell up his remaining sheep and cattle. My parents did not know exactly what transpired in Hailar. But they remember that Motya came back tired, angry from arguing with the authorities over evaluations and taxes and fed up with their excessive bureaucracy. He wanted to get out as soon as possible.

Before embarking on the battle with DOB in Harbin, Motya sent all our passports to the British embassy to get visas. According to copies of the correspondence from the British embassy in Motya's DOB file, this was at the end of January 1959. By this time, my grandparents' two-year permission to enter Australia had barely four months to run. In the first week of February, our passports were returned with visas stamped. The Hong Kong transit visa was valid for twelve weeks, the entry visa for Australia for four months. We were on a countdown and DOB knew it.

The price of four exit visas (as a child, I did not count) from China and tickets to the border at Canton was my grandfather's two-storey apartment block at 155 Diagonalnaya Street. This deal with DOB was brokered by a senior Party official, who lived across the street and wanted to move into our apartment, complete with all our furniture. Even permission to give our old grandfather clock as a gift to our long-time family doctor was declined. Whatever 'voluntary contributions' the Soviet consulate and SSC demanded, we paid. We were lucky we could afford it. Others were less fortunate. With contributions set above their means, some were left bargaining to the last minute, others even after their intended date of departure. Soviet consular officials did not stop reminding us that it might all have been otherwise—if only we had chosen the right way.

By the time our permission for Australia came through, my grandmother Tonya had decided she was not coming with us. She had applied for an Australian visa, but this had been half-hearted. What was there for her to do in Australia? Having to abandon her Russian culture and way of life would be bad enough. But she would also lose her profession as a nurse, which she had worked so hard to acquire. Without English, she had no hope of requalifying or doing anything but menial labour. This she was not prepared to do. Nor was Tonya ready to become a dependent at the age of forty-seven. She could probably think of nothing worse than staying at home and arguing over my upbringing and household chores with my grandmother Gita.

Tonya decided to return to her homeland. She had a niece in Saratov, a town on the Volga River, not far from the village where she was born. This was where she went shortly after we left Harbin. She did find work as a nurse and lived in a Russian culture of sorts. But her life was hard and heart disease killed her four years later. When my aunt Ira Kogan saw Tonya in Saratov in 1962, she was already ill and despaired that she had not come with us to Australia. My father blamed himself for not being more insistent. Every couple of months until she died, Tonya sent me parcels of Russian books to make sure I did not forget my heritage.

———•┈•———

Our last day in Harbin was 16 April 1959. That evening, it was our turn to wave farewell to relatives and friends at Harbin Station. With piles of crates, trunks and suitcases, we left Harbin on the Moscow-Peking Express. Three generations of *Harbintsy* were leaving their homeland.

Early that morning, in a final act of bloody-mindedness, DOB had made us move all our belongings into one small room and denied us access to the rest of the house. But unbeknown to DOB or to my grandfather, my father had got in first. Several days earlier, in partial revenge for our confiscated property, he had stripped and sold the metal sheets from the apartment block roof to Chinese traders—to help China's steel industry.

In our last week in Harbin, many of our farewells had been spiritual. The Zaretskys visited the Jewish cemetery where my grandfather Motya said *kaddish* at the graves of his parents and other relatives. My father went to his father's grave at the old Tatar cemetery to say goodbye. We had all been for a walk down to the Sungari.

There had, of course, been a farewell dinner with friends at the restaurant at the Soviet Club, practically the only Russian restaurant still operating at our end of town. It was a small affair as most friends had already left. Some had gone to the Soviet Union; others to Israel, Brazil and Australia. In all, there were just over a thousand Russians left in Harbin, one-tenth of them Jews.

My mother laughs when I ask her if they went to say goodbye to their old haunts in their last days in Harbin. 'What for? By that time, we had been saying goodbye for years.'

When the train finally moved off, sadness was mixed with relief. The long goodbye was over.

———

From Harbin we went to Peking—without passes or permission.

Having visited the ancient palaces and peaceful gardens of the capital in earlier days, my parents decided to go there one more time. After the stresses of packing up their lives in Harbin, they relished the thought of wandering around the Temple of Heaven and the Forbidden City to absorb the grandeur of China's history and civilisation before leaving.

But applying for permission from the DOB apparatchiks would further complicate our exit process and neither of them had the stomach for any more applications or interrogations. Everyone had had enough of bureaucracy.

So they decided to take the risk and just do it. Instead of changing trains for Canton at the station before Peking, we simply stayed on board. Knowing what a stickler for the rules my grandfather was, my parents led him to believe we had the necessary passes. By the time the railway officials came to check our permits, we were miles beyond the transit station.

While my unsuspecting grandfather insisted that we had permits, my father explained in excellent Chinese that I had fallen ill and they urgently had to take me to the hospital in Peking. As was the case so often in China, the excuse of a sick child worked. Meanwhile our enterprising friend Tima Litvin from Hailar had booked us rooms in an excellent little hotel where he usually stayed.

The interlude in Peking fulfilled my parents' expectations and offered us a brief respite before our four-day train journey to Canton and the next battle—clearing customs. It took almost a day, as all our crates and trunks were turned inside out in the search for contraband. The limit on hard currency was about ten US dollars per person and gold and silver were severely restricted. Taking out more than allowed was a risky business as it could lead not only to confiscation but also arrest.

From Canton, it was a short train ride to the British colony of Hong Kong. There, everything had to be repacked again and other immigration formalities completed. With the help of the Hebrew Immigrant Aid Society (HIAS), we got berths on the SS *Eastern Queen* and set sail for Australia on 5 May, with sixty other 'White Russian migrants from the Far East', as we were described by Australian authorities in official documentation. With my grandparents' entry permits for Australia due to expire on 23 May, we were forced to take the first available option.

I don't remember much about the journey other than the fact that we crossed the equator a couple of days after my fifth birthday and I was given a birthday cake. From the Australian Immigration travel control document I find in the Australian archives forty years later, I see that I was the only child under ten, and the only girl on board.

When I ask my mother about the journey, she tells me that I am lucky I don't remember too much. For us this was no luxury cruise on a Jardine Matheson liner, as it was for the passengers on the upper deck. We were the migrants travelling steerage—below deck, men and women split in dormitories. As a special privilege, my mother and I were allocated bunks in a small cabin for four, with my grandmother and another woman. The trouble was, the room was directly opposite the kitchen so it was noisy, hot and smelly.

After rocking on the Pacific Ocean for some two and a half weeks, we finally reached Australian shores. We docked in Melbourne and that night flew to Sydney, which was to be our new home. It was 22 May 1959, the day my grandparents' permits to enter Australia were due to expire.

CHAPTER 16

CONTINUITY

IN MAY 2000, I return to Harbin with my parents for the first time after forty-one years. It is a journey we have long talked of taking. But as always, it is an opportunity seized on the spur of the moment. They join me at the end of one of my visits to Shanghai and we fly north together.

I know that this visit is for my benefit as my parents have always made clear that if not for me, they wouldn't be going back. They would much prefer to leave intact their memory of Harbin as they knew it in their youth. But they want to show me the city where I was born and where four generations of my family lived to help me put places to all the stories—or at least as many places as are still standing. To re-establish roots.

Walking through the streets of Daoli (the former Pristan district) in the bright spring weather, Inna and Alec are like two pied pipers. They point out familiar buildings, explaining in a mixture of three languages what the places used to be, recounting incidents. Behind them walks a small entourage taking notes and snapping photographs —two Harbin scholars interested in the history of the Jewish community; my friend Sasha Wang Zhicheng, the Russian expert from Shanghai; a couple of friends from Sydney whom we met up with in Harbin; and me.

For me, the 'homecoming' has all the excitement of a new adventure. I remember little of the city of my birth and have no real expectation of finding the old 'Russian' Harbin. My heart leaps each time I glimpse something Russian—a baroque facade, art nouveau touches in a gateway, a cupola in the distance. Having spent most of the 1990s in the newly modernising cities of the former Indochina, I am accustomed to spotting remnants of colonial splendour beneath the squalor of poverty and the sterility of progress. I carry with me some old photographs of myself as a child in front of key Harbin landmarks and am delighted each time I find one still standing.

For my parents, their return provokes much more complex emotions. Rationally, they know that forty turbulent years have passed since they were last in Harbin. The city has withstood the ravages of the Cultural Revolution and a huge influx in population. There are now three million people living in the city proper. But in their mind they still see the beautiful city of their youth—wide boulevards, elegant buildings and shady gardens. The reality that confronts them as they walk around the former Pristan area where we once lived is at once familiar, yet unrecognisable.

The main street is now a showpiece pedestrian mall and many of its old buildings, like the former Hotel Moderne where we are staying, have been renovated. Some are marked with preservation plaques, though sadly few of these identify the building's history. But most of the side streets are shabby and dilapidated. A few grand old houses still stand, crumbling amidst built-on wooden shopfronts, but many have disappeared or are disfigured by poorly executed extensions.

Our different perceptions prompt argument and harsh words between me and my parents. They are stressed. I am excited. After forty years, I rejoice in what remains. They mourn what has been lost. My eye searches out familiar details—a sculptured head on the remains of an art nouveau frieze, the witch's hat of a Gothic roof. Why can't they see it? They say their vision is clouded by the strangeness of the new perspective and tears of relived pain. Why can't I see that?

Like all returnees, we seek out the key landmarks of our former lives, starting with the house where we once lived. Though none of us says so, each silently hopes that the apartment block my grandfather built on the old Diagonalnaya Street in 1933 will still be standing. That would be a real sign of continuity. It is a blow to find that an ugly commercial building was constructed in its place only a few years ago.

Happily, the two schools my parents attended are still functioning and have changed little in appearance. A fine Romanesque construction set in leafy grounds, my mother's Soviet school is still a high school. With its distinctive rose colour, I can see for myself why everyone simply called it the 'pink school'.

My father's school is even more of a surprise. Even before I know what the Moorish-style building is, I am struck by the Stars of David in its arched windows. Located next door to the main synagogue, it was a Jewish school until the mid-1920s, when it was sold to the Harbin municipality and became a Russian public school. During the Japanese occupation, it was run by BREM. Today it is a Korean school. With many of its original features well preserved, for me the building encapsulates Harbin's multicultural past—and present.

Former religious shrines have not fared so well. The old Tatar mosque with its faded maroon and beige stripes and tall minaret, is in a pitiful state. In spite of the brass 'preserved building' plate fixed on its front wall, it is crumbling and dilapidated and inhabited by thirteen squatter families.

The Main Synagogue in Pao Dui (formerly Artilleriiskaya) Street has been transformed into a guest house for railway wagon factory workers. The New Synagogue further up the road in Jin Wei (formerly Diagonalnaya) Street is a club of the Public Security Bureau (known as DOB in Russian), though no longer in use. At least these buildings are still standing.

The former Blagoveshchenskaya Church near the Sungari River has disappeared altogether and been replaced by a modern hotel. On the other side of town, St Nicholas Cathedral, the most important shrine for Harbin's Orthodox Russians, was torn down by the Red

Guards in August 1966 during the Cultural Revolution.

In search of the graves of the Zaretsky relatives and my grandfather Mustafin, we hire a minibus to take us to the Huangshan Cemetery, almost twenty kilometres from the city. It is a surreal place. Beyond ceremonial gates at the end of a drive guarded by Chinese sacred animals, stands a Disney-like castle in which we find the genial young director, Liu Jun. He and his assistants chat in Mandarin with my parents and lead us to the Jewish cemetery.

Set in its own walled area, there is row upon row of old gravestones with familiar names. We spread out in different directions to hunt for the Zaretskys. Suddenly my mother cries out, 'I've found them.' The graves of her great-grandparents, uncles and aunts lie in one row and are in good condition. From this point, everyone's mood lightens.

We congratulate Liu Jun on the excellent restoration work his team has recently completed. It has been a long time coming and is a happy ending to a saga that spans forty years. Most of the 800 Jewish graves at Huangshan today were transferred from the old cemetery in central Harbin after the Chinese declared its 'liquidation' in 1958. This massive task was completed by the leaders of the minuscule Jewish community with financial support from former Harbin Jews scattered around the world.

For almost thirty years the graves lay neglected. With the establishment of diplomatic relations between China and Israel in 1992, efforts commenced through the Israel-China Friendship Association to have the cemetery restored. They were led by Teddy Kaufman, the son of Dr Abraham Kaufman who led the Harbin Jewish community through most of its turbulent years.

Sadly, our efforts to find the grave of my Tatar grandfather at the Muslim cemetery in Huangshan are unsuccessful. Apart from the Jews, none of the other Harbin communities moved their graves en masse. My father remembers burying his father under a tree near the wall of the Tatar section of the old cemetery in the city. But it is long gone.

Approaching the Russian cemetery, we see many people of mixed Russian-Chinese extraction milling outside the small blue chapel, visiting grave sites. It turns out to be *Radonitsa,* the festival commemorating the dead in the Russian Orthodox Easter calendar. Suddenly my parents recognise Valya Han, an old acquaintance from their days at the Harbin Polytechnical Institute in the 1950s. An attractive Russified Korean in her mid seventies, she is one of the last remaining 'old *Harbintsy*' who stayed on in China. We had been given her contact details by friends in Sydney and were intending to get in touch with her.

In the following days, we meet Valya several times. To my parents' delight, Valya shows us a Chinese restaurant which still cooks the style of Harbin food they remember and we dine there together several times, exchanging stories. Having survived ten years incarceration during the Cultural Revolution, Valya now divides her time between teaching English and Russian to Chinese children and looking after the dwindling number of old Russians who, for one reason or another, never left Harbin.

They are old and ailing and live in very poor conditions, supported by money and medicines sent by former *Harbintsy* from Australia and the United States. Valya has become their lifeline, selflessly tending to both their spiritual and practical needs and maintaining constant contact. She takes us to visit one of them, Mikhail Myatov, a frail old man in his eighties whom my father remembers from old times.

———

Six months later in the November chill, I visit Harbin again, this time with two friends from Sydney interested in the former Jews of China. Thanks to my earlier visit with my parents, I now have my bearings and am able to show my friends around the key landmarks of Jewish and Russian Harbin. I also have the chance to spend more time with people I met briefly the first time and to see the city in a perspective beyond my own roots.

Harbin in November 2000 is a city full of aspirations and contradictions, aptly summed up by a couple of signs I see along the four-lane freeway from the airport into the city. The first is a traffic sign prohibiting horse-drawn carts and tractors between the hours of 0630 and 2100. The other is a road sign pointing the way to the 'high technology development zone'.

Despite being one of China's key industrial centres, Harbin's northern isolation and conservatism kept its doors closed to reform and renewed foreign contact long after they had swung open in cities like Shanghai and Beijing. Now its leadership is striving to make up for lost time with energy and enthusiasm, embracing free-market imperatives, making efforts to attract tourists and prospective foreign investors. In this brave new world, Harbin's unique multicultural and architectural heritage is recognised as an asset.

But history is never without its complications. For the Chinese, Harbin's Russian past has long been caught up in the intricacy of historical, political and ideological rivalry between the two states. The demise of the Soviet Union eliminated the ideological dimension and the relationship with Russia is now developing along more pragmatic lines. But Tsarist Russia's exploits in Manchuria, including the establishment of Harbin as headquarters of the Chinese Eastern Railway, are still portrayed as an act of colonial aggression.

Nevertheless, the role Russians played in Harbin's development is increasingly acknowledged. Renewed efforts are being made to preserve old Russian buildings and Harbin's daily newspaper, the *Heilongjiang Daily*, runs regular features about former *Harbintsy*. Whether through architecture or people's stories, Harbin's Russian history is being preserved.

Not surprisingly, the centenary of Harbin's establishment in 1998 presented the authorities with a political dilemma. Plans for a joint Chinese-Russian academic conference in Harbin and Khabarovsk were scuttled by Beijing and the centenary went unmarked. Or did it? Given the Chinese propensity for indirectness and symbolism, the timing of two events in the heart of the old Russian area of Pristan (Daoli) was most significant.

First, the former Church of St Sophia was refurbished, complete with Orthodox crosses on its domes and the large bell from the desecrated St Nicholas Cathedral mounted in its bell tower. St Sophia was opened in the second half of 1997 as the Harbin Architectural Museum, just in time for Harbin's centenary. The motive was, of course, to attract tourists. But the building has now become the symbol of Harbin and the museum inside it is a testament to its Russian history.

The second notable event was a celebration organised by the Harbin authorities in mid-1998 in Zhongyang Street, the main street of Daoli (formerly Kitayskaya Street in Pristan) so dear to Russian hearts. Ostensibly, it was to celebrate the anniversary of its conversion into a pedestrian mall a year earlier. But it just happened to coincide with the hundredth anniversary of both the street and Harbin.

Compared with the complexities that confront Chinese authorities in grappling with Harbin's Russian past, the issue of the former Jewish community is relatively straightforward. The Jews who came to live in Harbin are regarded simply as subjects of the Tsarist empire who sought refuge from hardship and persecution. In November 2000, preserving vestiges of their former life in Harbin has become a priority, endorsed by the provincial and municipal governments. As well as the intrinsic historic and cultural value of the work, the aim is clearly to attract Jewish tourists and investors.

Qu Wei, the enterprising new president of the Heilongjiang Academy of Social Sciences who is spearheading activities through the newly established Jewish Studies Centre, talks of imminent government approval to transform one of the former synagogues into a permanent Jewish museum and shows me publications in progress.

But the prize for innovation has to go to the director of the Huangshan Cemetery, Liu Jun. He announces that he is putting the Harbin Jewish Cemetery online in the hope that descendants who see images of their relatives' graves will be moved to visit the cemetery in person. Two months later it happens: photographed and identified, the Jewish graves, which eight years ago were still overgrown with nettles, are now accessible on the World Wide Web!

———•◦•———

The situation with dusty old files and papers is a different story. On each visit to Harbin I have sought access to material on my family from the Public Security Bureau's files of former Harbin residents. I know that thousands of such files are held in the Heilongjiang Provincial Archive, along with the records of the former Russian and Jewish communities. But getting access as a foreigner appears to be impossible. My Harbin friends shrug and mumble about the complex clearance process involved which cuts across both state and provincial levels.

But midway through my second visit, Qu Wei has good news for me: I have been granted permission to visit the archive. Zhang Tiejang from the Jewish Studies Centre and Sasha Wang Zhicheng, my friend from Shanghai who is a visiting fellow at the Heilongjiang Academy, are to accompany me.

The archive has recently moved to a fancy new building quite a distance from the city centre. Driving through the snow-covered streets, we pass block after block of new buildings. The predominant architectural style is a strange concoction of modern glass and concrete with classic columns and cupolas—the new Harbin imitating the old. I think back on the various archives I have visited over the past four years and wonder what gems I will find in this one.

My arrival at the archive creates consternation. The staff are clearly unaccustomed to foreign visitors, especially one like me with big demands and little time. Who is this *waiguoren* (foreigner)? Why does she want old files of people with unpronounceable Russian names from the Public Security Bureau archive? Zhang and Sasha explain that, though I don't speak Chinese, I was born in Harbin and that my family lived here for fifty years. It is their history I am now researching. The archive officials shake their heads. They have not had one of my kind in the archive before.

I write the names of the files I am seeking in Russian and English and Sasha adds the Chinese. While waiting for the files to arrive, I look at some of the old Russian books lying on the table. One is a jubilee album of the Chinese Eastern Railway, with photographs of its construction and its stations. When I take out my digital camera to photograph a picture of Hailar Station, all hell breaks loose and the book is whisked away. I offer to pay. It makes no difference.

Just then, a pile of large envelopes arrives, bearing the names of some of the people I have requested. My own is the least interesting: two small cards and one page that sets out my name and the barest biographical details. The others each contain foreigner registration forms with photographs from various periods—Manchukuo, the Chinese Republic, the People's Republic, biographies, permits for travel and other official documents in Chinese and Russian. My lack of Chinese means I can only make sense of half the material. But it is Friday and time is too short to have Sasha translate the material for me. It becomes even shorter when we are told the archive will close for a two-hour lunch break. I mark up the Russian pages for photocopying as fast as I can.

In the afternoon, the officials are more friendly towards me. The climate of suspicion and need to assert authority through denial have abated. Sasha tells me later that I have won respect for my persistence. 'How can she stand up for three hours straight, looking through all those old papers without even a pause for a cup of tea?' one of the women asked him. They look in awe at the number of pages I want photocopied. They warn me there are fees for copying, conservation and retrieval. Sasha assures them not to worry, I will pay.

I return several days later on my way to the airport. It is my last chance to follow up on a couple of files that were not found on my first visit. To speed up the retrieval process, the archivist lets me look through the card index myself. Sensibly, it has been left in Russian alphabetical order.

<hr>

On my last Saturday afternoon in Harbin, Sasha and I visit Valya Han, the remarkable Korean Russian whom I met with my parents on our first visit. Since that time Valya has become my Harbin reference point whom I consult for advice on Harbin matters. In spite of recent illness, Valya is as always well groomed and radiates positive energy. With her is a Chinese journalist from the *Heilongjiang Daily*, Zeng Yizhi, who calls herself 'Isabella'. I later discover that one of Isabella's briefs is to write stories about Russian life in the former Harbin and to interview returning visitors. Thus her interest in meeting me.

As we sit drinking hot tea from old Russian tea glasses and eating mandarins, I look around the room, crammed with books and memorabilia. A large photo-portrait of Valya's parents has pride of place on the piano. On the bureau and the bookshelves are photographs of family in Russia, friends around the world and a beautiful young Valya in her twenties. Among the utilitarian Chinese household items are a few vestiges of another life—the Russian tea glasses from which we drink, the white lace draped across the top of the bureau and a crystal vase of the style I have seen in the houses of *Harbintsy* the world over.

When I ask about her family, Valya explains that her parents were Russified Koreans who were themselves born in Siberia and fled to Harbin from Vladivostok in 1923 after the Bolshevik victory. She and her brothers were brought up in the Russian culture and the Orthodox church. I notice several beautiful old icons set against traditional pussy willow on a small table in the corner of the room.

How is it that Valya ended up staying in Harbin all these years? It was by accident, rather than intention. A talented pianist who was working at the Harbin Polytechnical Institute, she and her parents had fully intended to follow her two brothers who left for the Soviet Union during the 'virgin lands' campaign. But they did not manage to get visas in time before the Sino-Soviet split and the Cultural Revolution. In 1964 Valya was arrested.

It is difficult to believe that this tiny woman survived ten years incarceration during the Cultural Revolution. For what? Being a Soviet spy, of course! In order to answer her interrogator's questions in prison, Valya says she taught herself Chinese by translating *The Thoughts of Chairman Mao* with the help of a Chinese-Russian dictionary. By the time she was released, her father was dead and her mother was old and frail. She herself contracted a deadly liver disease and was sent home with only two months to live. By some miracle, she recovered. Contact was re-established with her brothers and Valya travelled several times to the Soviet Union as an interpreter with various Harbin delegations.

I have brought Valya a couple of parcels from the

Harbintsy in Sydney containing winter provisions for the old Russians she looks after. Valya tells me that Mikhail Myatov, whom I had visited with my parents six months earlier, recently died. This leaves less than a handful of old Russians remaining in Harbin.

'If Sasha and I come with you to church tomorrow, perhaps we can meet some of the old Russians afterwards,' I suggest. Of the sixteen Orthodox churches still standing in Harbin, only the Pokrovsky Church in Nangan (the former Novy Gorod) is still functioning.

'Too late,' Valya laughs. 'The priest died two months ago, after a long illness. Father Grigori—he was Chinese. At least while Myatov was alive, we were all right. He knew the service backwards and I know a little. Between us, we could lead the others. Now only I am left. As for the old Russians, they are too frail and too ill to come to church anyway.'

Valya explains that between ten and twenty people attend church on Sundays, mostly middle-aged women of mixed Chinese-Russian extraction. The younger people sometimes come at Christmas and Easter. So far, the authorities have not assigned a new priest to replace Father Grigory and it is unclear whether they will.

I ask if there are some old Russians we could visit.

'Sure,' says Valya 'They would be delighted to see you. But as you only have tomorrow, there's probably only time for me to take you to one.' Valya reels off several names, all unfamiliar to me. 'Which one would you like to see?'

'I don't mind. You choose.'

Valya decides on an old woman by the name of Nikiforova. 'Efrosinya Andreyevna is almost ninety years old, a former pharmacist. But she still has her wits about her and a good memory. I think she'll like you.'

Efrosinya Nikiforova's tiny one-room flat lies at the end of a narrow dingy passageway on the second floor of an old communal apartment in Nangan. From her tone of voice as we squeeze one by one into the room, I can tell this is a no-nonsense woman.

'This is Mara Mustafina,' Valya introduces me as a former *Harbinka* visiting from Australia. 'And this is Efrosinya Andreyevna. Many young people call her *Tyotya* (Aunt) Frosya.'

'Mustafina? Don't know the name,' says the old lady, coming into view. She is a solidly built grandmother figure in a dark grey woollen cardigan, her silver hair brushed back from her strong-featured face. It is hard to believe she is almost ninety. My own grandmother Gita had been so frail when she died at that age just a year earlier.

'My mother's name was Zaretsky,' I say, 'Perhaps you knew them?'

'Zaretsky,' she muses. 'Was she a dancer?'

Not as such.

'No, no, that one was Zarutsky,' the old woman corrects herself and invites us to sit down.

416

We crowd round the square table covered in patterned plastic that occupies most of the room. On it are a few Russian books and papers, a large magnifying glass, and a plate of fruit. Sitting face to face with her, I can hear that Frosya is breathing heavily and cannot see very well, in spite of her thick glasses. An exchange about respective ailments prompts Frosya to give Valya a quick diagnosis and recommend treatment.

'I was a pharmacist at the Kasem Bek Hospital for twenty-six years,' she explains.

'Really? That's where I was born!' I exclaim, seizing on a point of common ground.

'I didn't work in obstetrics,' Frosya laughs politely.

Frosya talks about her life. As she speaks, her gnarled hand shuffles constantly along the table as if gathering imaginary crumbs. She talks of coming to Harbin as a teenager in the early 1920s from Siberia; being Soviet, then émigré; wearing the dreaded badges with numbers during Japanese times. There were rations and restrictions, first under the Japanese then in Chinese Communist times—even restrictions on going to the cemetery.

Seeing an opening, I ask about the closure of the cemetery in 1958. Frosya says the Harbin authorities hoped all 80,000 Russian Orthodox graves would be moved. But it did not happen. I ask her if she knows what happened to the Tatar cemetery, explaining that my grandfather was buried there. Frosya says she visited it once with a friend and describes where it used to be. As in the Russian Orthodox part, she says all the graves were levelled when the area was turned into a recreational park in the 1960s.

As I listen to Frosya, it dawns on me that my grand-mother Tonya once worked at the Kasem Bek Hospital.

'I wonder if you might have known my grand-mother?' I say quietly. 'Her name was Shelamanova.'

'Tonya?'

'Yes.'

'Oh my God!' Frosya slaps the table and her eyes brim with tears. 'That's why the name Zaretsky sounded so familiar.' Her thoughts tumble out in unfinished bursts. 'Tonya died . . . I pleaded with her not to go . . . When her family went to Australia, she was heartbroken . . . She loved her son . . . Most of all, she adored her granddaughter.'

'I am her granddaughter,' I say.

Silence.

'Who would have imagined. What a surprise . . . Oh Tonya, Tonya . . . I was thinking about her just the other day . . . What upset her most was that she would never see her granddaughter again . . .'

At risk of being overwhelmed by all the emotion, I concentrate on capturing the moment in multimedia. It is moments like this that convince me that lugging around my mini-disk recorder, digital video and two stills cameras in my rucksack is worthwhile, whatever their weight. In the long and rambling conversation that follows, I get answers to questions that have puzzled me for years and confirmations of facts I already know. Frosya has an incredible memory and an incisive wit. What is even more exciting is that I am getting a picture of my grandmother Tonya from an independent source, without the filter of family sensitivities.

Frosya first met Tonya in 1936 when she joined the pharmacy at the Kasem Bek Hospital where Tonya was working as a nurse. She describes Tonya as highly competent, with a responsive and generous spirit. The two became close friends. In summer, they would go swimming near Tonya's house on the other side of the Sungari. Later, after Tonya's husband died, Frosya visited her in the apartment downstairs from us. That was where she first saw me. 'What a house!' Frosya says. 'It could have stood for another hundred years. They don't build houses like that these days. But they tore it down just a year and a half ago.' Why? 'Because they think anything old is an eyesore.'

Frosya remembers going with Tonya to visit my grandfather's grave. This was the visit to the Tatar cemetery she had told me about earlier. She says his grave was right next to the wall that divided the Jewish and Tatar cemeteries. It is probably still there, except the gravestone has been removed, like all the others.

A couple of themes recur in Frosya's conversation. The first is Tonya's distress at parting from her granddaughter. It is interesting that Frosya continues to talk about me in the third person. I guess I don't quite fit the image of the four-year-old Tonya talked about. Frosya's second theme is her own failure to persuade Tonya not to go to the Soviet Union. It is clear that her untimely death still preys on Frosya's mind.

'She was so upset when the family went to Australia. I kept telling her to wait—but she would not listen. She had a sister in Saratov, so she went there. I tried to persuade her not to go. "Wait till they get jobs," I told her,

419

"then you'll go too." But she was in a hurry. She even tried to persuade me to go with her. I told her to wait. What upset her most was that she would never see her granddaughter again . . .'

'So why did she go to Saratov. Why didn't she come with us?' I ask.

'She probably had her reasons. She was torn between the two. Saratov was her homeland . . . and Australia . . . well . . . Anyway, she made a mistake. She went to Saratov and worked in a hospital—too hard. She had a bad heart. If she'd gone to Australia, she would not have died so early . . .'

Whether by accident or by design, Isabella, the journalist from the *Heilongjiang Daily*, arrives while we are talking, armed with provisions for *Tyotya* Frosya. Frosya accepts them under protest, saying Isabella is constantly showering her with kindness. The two are obviously very close. While Sasha and Valya update Isabella on the afternoon's developments in Chinese, I seize the opportunity to ask Frosya a few sticky questions. What have I to lose? From what I have gathered Frosya is fairly forthright. She'll either answer or she won't.

I ask her what Tonya said about my mother's family, the Zaretskys. How did she cope with her son marrying a Jew? Did she reconcile herself to my mother in the end? Frosya's responses are diplomatic.

'What could she say about the Zaretskys? She never complained about anyone. She only worried about her granddaughter. Her greatest distress was that she could not take her granddaughter to church! She cried about it.'

'She didn't take my father to church all that much either,' I observe.

'She didn't talk much about him. Mostly about her granddaughter. She was always knitting things for her. Whenever she had a spare moment, she would go and play with her.'

'I remember.'

What about my parents' marriage? Frosya says Tonya was 'powerless'. 'She would not stand in the way of her son's happiness.'

'It was a great love story,' Valya interjects. 'At the Institute, Inna and Alec were inseparable.'

'If my grandmother was such a strong Orthodox believer, how was it that she married a Tatar Muslim?' Frosya talks about the difficulties Russian refugees faced in the 1920s as they started to put their lives together in Harbin. Finding work was hard. People had to live somehow. Tonya was introduced to my grandfather by one of her relatives.

'Did she love him?' I ask.

'I don't know, I didn't ask,' she scoffs. 'But they lived well together.'

Frosya remembers that she has some group photographs taken at the Kasem Bek Hospital that include my grandmother. She taps the table impatiently as she thinks where they might be, but cannot remember. I suggest that when she finds them, she give them to Isabella to copy and email to me. Isabella, who has been writing furiously, stops and pulls out her portfolio of newspaper features on Russians. She flicks through them till she finds the one on Frosya. Among the photographs is one of a group of medical sisters and doctors outside a hospital.

'Is my grandmother here?' I ask, passing it to Frosya, together with her magnifying glass.

'Here is Tonya right next to me,' she answers and begins to list the names of others in the photo.

As we are about to leave, disconnected fragments come flooding to Frosya's mind. Frosya says Tonya told her about hiding from the Soviets in 1946 when they were rounding up 'enemies' after the war. But what reason did Tonya have to hide? I ask. She had been strongly anti-Communist. Tonya managed to avoid arrest by never being in the place where Smersh came to find her. Next Frosya remembers the frenzy at Harbin Station when Tonya was leaving for Saratov. Fifteen minutes before the train was to leave, Tonya remembered that she had left something very important back at the apartment. What it was, Frosya could not remember. Only that my Aunt Ira Kogan's husband had to race back on his motorbike to fetch it. The recollection jogs Frosya's memory about a gift Tonya had left her. It was a book of old Russian songs. If she found it, she would let me know.

Emerging into the snowy Sunday afternoon, I thank Valya for her prescience in deciding to bring me to visit *Tyotya* Frosya. She insists it was my grandmother's spirit that had brought me here. She is serious.

'Remember you told me you lit the candle in her memory in the church in Khabarovsk? Now your grandmother has brought you to her friend.'

'No,' Sasha points to the white jade pendant hanging

on a red string around my neck, with a wink in his eye. 'I think it was the talisman of *Guanyin,* the goddess of Mercy, which you bought at the Temple of *Jilesi* (Bliss). She is the protector of women.'

———

Fate? Coincidence? Serendipity? It was not the first time amazing things had happened on this journey. A couple of weeks earlier in Shanghai, my friend Andrew Jakubowicz and I had managed to stumble across the building where his family had found refuge from the Nazi Holocaust in Europe. The building was in the process of being demolished to make way for a metro. When I return to take another look the day after I leave Harbin on my way back to Sydney, it has been reduced to a pile of rubble.

History does not stand around waiting for you to find it—but if you make the effort, it sometimes meets you halfway.

———

I return to Sydney just in time to attend the tombstone consecration of my grandmother Gita, who died a year earlier. At the centre of her grave we have put a simple tribute in memory of her father Girsh, sister Manya and brother Abram—'victims of the purges'.

Two weeks later, I receive an email from my new friend Isabella in Harbin. *Tyotya* Frosya has found the book my grandmother gave her and wants me to have it. Before sending such precious cargo, Isabella wants to test the waters and has sent me a couple of newspapers which arrive safely a few weeks later.

One day the package arrives by registered post. It is covered in stamps, including a large one of the goddess *Guanyin*. Inside is a small book with the title *Russian Songs of the XIXth Century* embossed in faded gold on a rust red cover. Frosya has tied it together with strands of yellow ribbon to protect its cracked spine. The book is a collection of old Russian songs and ballads written and sung in pre-revolutionary Russia and published in wartime Moscow in 1944. It had been sent for sale in Harbin sometime after its liberation from Japanese occupation. Its yellowed pages exude a strong musty smell, reminding me of the smell of the Onikul files in the archive in Nizhny Novgorod.

As I am closing the book, I notice something written on its front page. It is my mother's name in her handwriting. My mother had left the book with my grandmother Tonya when we departed Harbin in 1959. Now, forty-one years later, through a circuitous route, it has made its way to me in Australia. Another journey across continents and generations.

NOTES

General

The people described in this book were subject to a number of different and sometimes competing cultures, languages and political systems which governed such aspects of their lives as their personal names (eg. Yiddish, Tatar, Russian), calendars (Jewish used in *shtetls*; Julian used in Russian empire until 1918; Gregorian post 1918; Manchukuo imperial calendar) and place names (eg. in Russia—Tsarist, Soviet and post-Soviet; in Manchuria—Chinese, Russian or Manchukuo).

Formally, Russians are called by their name, patronymic (derived from their father's name) and surname. Informally, they are known by their first name, which may be shortened (eg. from Aleksandr to Sasha or from Marianna to Mara). A diminutive form may be used as an endearment (eg. Marochka).

Jews of the Tsarist empire, whose predominant

language was Yiddish, were given Yiddish or Hebrew names, but also adopted the Russian patronymic style. For example, my great-grandfather Girsh Onikul, whose father's name was Morduh, was known in Russian as Girsh Morduhovich. In Soviet times, this name was russified to Grigory Matveyevich and his children took on the patronymic from Grigory. Thus, Manya and Abram were known formally as Maria Grigorievna and Abram Grigorievich.

For the sake of simplicity, I have used the personal names by which the characters were most commonly known. Although politeness would dictate use of patronymics for elderly people like my great-grandparents, I have only used patronymics in instances where this was my usual form of address and retained them in quotations.

I have not adhered strictly to any particular system of transliterating Russian names but generally followed the most common usage. For the 'people of Harbin', I have deliberately used *Harbintsy* (rather than *Kharbintsy*) based on the accepted spelling of the city's name.

For Chinese placenames, I have used the form and spelling most commonly used by the people I am writing about at the time the events took place.

As identified in the text, the primary sources for most of the material in this book are the personal files of my family, obtained in various archives in Russia and China, photographs in my possession and the oral histories of family and friends, identified in the text or in the acknowledgments. In order to put this material in historical and political context, I have also drawn on a wide range of valuable secondary sources. These notes provide details of key publicly available material, as well as additional information on some points of interest.

Chapter 1: Riga Treasures

For a graphic portrayal of the final years of the Soviet Union and its collapse, see David Remnick, *Lenin's Tomb: The Last Days of the Soviet Empire*, Random House, New York, 1993; David Steele, *Eternal Russia: Yeltsin, Gorbachev and the Mirage of Democracy*; Faber & Faber, London, 1994. Monica Attard, *Russia: Which Way Paradise?*, Doubleday, Sydney, 1997 presents the Soviet demise and the emergence of the new Russia from the perspective of ordinary Russians.

For a history of Memorial, see Nanci Adler, *Victims of Soviet Terror: the Story of the Memorial Movement*, Praeger, London, 1993. Memorial's website at http://www.memo.ru provides background on the organisation, its research and activities, and valuable documentary information on the purges.

Adam Hochschild, *The Unquiet Ghost: Russians Remember Stalin*, Penguin, New York, 1995 explores how Russians, including both the perpetrators of the repression and its survivors, began confronting the Stalinist past in the early 1990s. In 1991, he was given access to the KGB files of several American victims of the purges.

Chapter 2: Gorky Tears

The files of Girsh, Chesna, Manya and Yasha Onikul were made available to me by the State Archive of the Nizhny Novgorod Oblast of the Russian Federation.

Chapter 3: On the Steppes of Manchuria

For background on the Chinese Eastern Railway (CER) and the early history of Russian Manchuria, I have drawn on R.K.I. Quested, *'Matey' Imperialists: The Tsarist Russians in Manchuria 1895–1917*, University of Hong Kong, 1982; David Wolff, *To The Harbin Station: The Liberal Alternative in Russian Manchuria, 1898–1914*, Stanford University Press, Stanford 1999; G.B. Melikhov, *Manchzhuriya Daliekaya i Blizkaya* [Manchuria Far and Near], Nauka, Moscow, 1991; Søren Clausen and Stig Thøgersen (eds), *The Making of a Chinese City: History and Historiography in Harbin*, M.E. Sharpe, New York, 1995.

In 1898, the Chinese awarded Russia a concession to construct a southern spur on the CER from Harbin to Port Arthur and a leasehold on the Kwantung Territory in the Liaodong Peninsula. These were ceded to the Japanese following Russia's defeat in the Russo–Japanese War in 1905. Under Japanese control the southern spur from Changchun to Port Arthur was renamed the South Manchuria Railway.

On early Russian life in Harbin, see Georgi Melikhov, 'Glimpses of Old Harbin', *Far Eastern Affairs*, No 4, 1990.

The internal debate in the Tsarist Government about settler policy for the CER, including on Jewish settlers, is detailed in Wolff (Chapter 3).

According to the 1913 census, there were twenty-two nationalities living in the commercial Pristan district of Harbin (half of them minorities of the Tsarist empire).

See excerpt from V.V. Levitsky, 'Pristan na Sungari' [Pristan on the Sungari], 1998 in the *Bulletin of Igud Yotzei Sin (Bulletin IYS)*, No 336, Nov–Dec 2000. Elena Chernolutskaya, 'Religious Communities in Harbin and Ethnic Identity of Russian Émigrés', in Thomas Lahusen (ed), *Harbin and Manchuria: Place, Space and Identity*, *South Atlantic Quarterly*, Winter 2000, Duke University Press, Durham, provides an overview of the various communities.

On the Jewish community in Harbin see Wolff (Chapter Three) and articles by Zvia Shickman-Bowman, 'The Construction of the Chinese Eastern Railway and the Origins of the Harbin Jewish Community, 1898–1931' and Boris Bresler, 'Harbin's Jewish Community 1898–1958: Politics, Prosperity and Adversity' in Jonathan Goldstein (ed), *The Jews Of China*, Vol 2, M.E. Sharpe, New York, 2000; Herman Dicker, *Wanderers and Settlers in the Far East: A Century of Jewish Life in China and Japan*, Twayne Publishers, New York, 1962; Joshua A. Fogel, 'The Japanese and the Jews: A Comparative Analysis of their Communities in Harbin 1898–1930', paper presented at Conference on *Paris of the Orient? The Worlds of Harbin 1898–1945*, USC-UCLA Joint East Asian Studies Center, 1999. Since 1988, the Russian language *Bulletin of Igud Yotzei Sin (Bulletin IYS)* has serialised 'Posyolok Harbin' [The settlement of Harbin], a history of the Harbin Jewish community (1900–1933) by its leader Dr Abraham Kaufman and regularly publishes memoirs of former Jews of China.

The first Jewish settlers in Manchuria came from Siberia—the descendents of former conscripts of Tsar Nicholas II's army, who by serving the full 25–year term were granted the privilege of living outside the Pale of Settlement. With a population of 500 in Harbin in 1903, the Jews were recognised as a 'community'. Its numbers were soon swelled by demobilised Jewish soldiers (25,000 of whom had been stationed in Manchuria during the 1904–05 Russo-Japanese war) bringing their families out to Manchuria.

Only those laws of the Tsarist empire which were specifically mandated by the CER Administration applied in the CER Zone. Although there is no evidence of Jews being employed by the CER before 1915, David Wolff points out that there was no legal basis for their exclusion and suggests it may have simply been in defer-ence to the hiring practice in Russian state enterprises. By 1909, Jews comprised twelve of the forty members of the Harbin municipal council, (something from which they were barred in the empire proper).

The Finance Ministry in St Petersburg made it a prac-tice to have issues concerning Jews and other minorities resolved locally, where efforts to impose restrictions were deflected. One such attempt by the Governor General of the Maritime Province Gondatti was successfully thwarted by the CER Administrator General Horvath himself. The incident is described by Kaufman in a lecture on 17 February 1962, reprinted in the *Bulletin IYS*, No 336, May–June 2001.

For background on Russian life and émigré politics in

Manchuria in the 1920s and 1930s covered in this and the next chapter, I have drawn on the following sources: John J. Stephan, *The Russian Fascists: Tragedy and Farce in Exile 1925–1945*, Hamish Hamilton, London, 1978; Elena Taskina, *Neizvestnyi Harbin* [Unknown Harbin], Moscow, 1992; Pyotr Balakshin, *Final v Kitae: vozniknoveniye, razvitiye I ischeznovaniye Beloy Emigratsii na Dalnem Vostoke* [Finale in China: formation, development and disintegration of the White Russian Emigration in the Far East] Vol 1, Sirius, Munich, 1958; Victor Sannikoff, *Pod Znakom Voskhodiashchego Solntsa v Manchzhurii: Vospominaniia* [Under the Sign of the Rising Sun in Manchuria: Reminiscences], Sydney, 1990; Olga Bakich, 'Émigré Identity: The Case of Harbin' in Thomas Lahusen (ed), *Harbin and Manchuria: Place, Space and Identity, South Atlantic Quarterly*, Winter 2000.

On the Zionist movement in Harbin and other cities in China, see Yaacov Liberman, *My China: Jewish Life in the Orient 1900–1950*, Gefen Publishing House, Jerusalem, 1998 and a jubilee volume *Betar v Kitae 1929–49*, [Betar in China], 1969.

Chapter 4: Coming Apart

The term 'cradle of conflict' in relation to Manchuria was coined by the American writer Owen Lattimore, *Manchuria: Cradle of Conflict*, New York, Macmillan, 1932.

Peter Hopkirk, *Setting the East Ablaze: On Secret Service in Bolshevik Asia*, Oxford University Press, 1984.

For background on the Russian Far East and Manchuria during the Russian Civil War, I have drawn on John J. Stephan, *The Russian Far East: A History*, Stanford University Press, Stanford, 1994; G.B. Melikhov, *Rossiiskaya Emigratsiya v Kitae (1917–1924)* [The Russian Emigration in China (1917–1924)], Institute of Russian History, Russian Academy of Sciences, Moscow, 1997 and Pyotr Balakshin, *Final v Kitae* [Finale in China] Vol 1, Sirius, Munich, 1958.

George Lensen, *The Damned Inheritance: The Soviet Union and the Manchurian Crisis 1924–35*, The Diplomatic Press, Tallahassee, 1974 provides a detailed account of developments during the period of Soviet-Chinese joint control of the CER, including the Sino–Soviet conflict and the sale of the CER to the Japanese in 1935, based on Soviet, Japanese and British foreign relations documents.

Anti-Soviet moves by Zhang Hsueh-liang in Manchuria in 1929 should be seen in the context of earlier moves by Nationalist leader Chiang Kai-shek against Chinese Communists and the closure of Soviet consulates in areas under his control. R.K.I. Quested, *Sino–Russian Relations: A Short History*, George Allen & Unwin, Sydney, 1984, provides a concise overview of Sino–Soviet Relations.

On the Mukden incident in 1931, which the Japanese Kwantung Army used as a pretext for its occupation of Manchuria, see David Bergamini, *Japan's Imperial Conspiracy*, Granada Publishing Ltd, London, 1971; Takehiko Yoshihashi, *Conspiracy at Mukden: The Rise of the Japanese Military*, Yale University Press, London, 1963; John K. Fairbanks, Edwin O. Reischauer, Albert

M. Craig, *East Asia: The Modern Transformation*, George Allen & Unwin, London, 1967.

On the life of Pu Yi see Pu Yi, *From Emperor to Citizen: The Autobiography of Aisin-Gioro Pu Yi*, Oxford University Press, Oxford, 1987 and Edward Behr, *The Last Emperor*, Futura, London, 1987.

On life in Manchuria under Japanese occupation, including the activities of the Japanese secret police, collaboration between the Japanese and militant White Russians, the establishment of the Bureau of Russian Émigrés in Manchuria (BREM) see John J. Stephan, *The Russian Fascists: Tragedy and Farce in Exile 1925–1945*, Hamish Hamilton, London, 1978; Raymond Lamont-Browne, *Kempeitai: Japan's Dreaded Military Police*, Stroud, London, 1998; Amleto Vespa, *Secret Agent of Japan*, Little Brown, Boston, 1938; Sabine Breuillard, 'General V.A. Kislitsin: From Russian Monarchism to the Spirit of Bushido', in Thomas Lahusen (ed), *Harbin and Manchuria: Place, Space and Identity, South Atlantic Quarterly*, Winter 2000, Duke University Press, Durham; Pyotr Balakshin, *Final v Kitae* [Finale in China] Vol 1, Sirius, Munich, 1958; Victor Sannikoff, *Pod Znakom Voskhodiashchego Ssolntsa v Manchzhurii: Vospominaniia* [Under the Sign of the Rising Sun in Manchuria: Reminiscences], Sydney, 1990.

The USSR sold the CER to Japan for 140 million paper yen, of which one third was to be paid in cash and two thirds in kind over three years. It was a far cry from their original asking price of 250 million gold rubles (equivalent to 625 million paper yen). By the basic agreement, the USSR ceded to Manchukuo all rights concerning the CER, its subsidiary enterprises and properties. The land and buildings occupied by the Soviet consulate general and its officials, and one school and one hospital together with their lands were to be leased rent-free and sine die to the USSR. (Lensen, *The Damned Inheritance*).

Chapter 5: From Manchukuo to the Radiant Future

The exact number of 'returnees' from Manchuria to the USSR after the Soviets sold the Chinese Eastern Railway to Japan in 1935 is not known. Estimates vary between 21,000 and 100,000. See discussion in Steven Merritt, 'Matushka Rosiia Primi Svoikh Detei! [Mother Russia, Receive Your Children] – Archival Materials on the Stalinist Repression of the Soviet Kharbintsy' in *Rossiiane v Azii* [Russians in Asia], No 5, Autumn 1998. I have chosen to use the ambiguous figure of 'over 30,000 families', as used by A. Suturin, *Delo Kraevovo Masshtaba: o zhertvakh Stalinskovo bezzakoniya na Dalnem Vostoke* [A Matter of Regional Scale: the victims of Stalinist illegality in the Far East], Khabarovsk Book Publisher, 1991.

By the late 1930s, Shanghai's 25,000 Russians comprised its largest European community. Among them were some 5,000 Russian Jews, who had also established their own community institutions.

On the life of Russians and Russian Jews in Shanghai, see Pyotr Balakshin, *Final v Kitae* [Finale in China] Vol 1, Sirius, Munich, 1958; Antonia Finnane, *Far From*

Where? Jewish Journeys from Shanghai to Australia, Melbourne University Press, Melbourne, 1999; Rena Krasno, *Strangers Always: A Jewish Family in Wartime Shanghai*, Pacific View Press, Berkeley, 1992; Nora Krouk, 'Nam ulybalas Kvan In' [Guanyin smiled on us], *Rossiiane v Azii* [Russians in Asia], No 7, 2000; Bernard Wasserstein, *Secret War in Shanghai*, Profile Books, London, 1999.

Wang Zhicheng, *Shang hai e qiao shi*, [A History of the Russian Émigré Community in Shanghai], Sanlian, Shanghai, 1993.

Among other publications, Pan Guang has edited two photographic histories, *The Jews in Shanghai*, Shanghai Pictorial Publishing House, Shanghai, 1995 and *The Jews in China*, China Intercontinental Press, Shanghai, 2001.

V.D. Jiganoff, *Russkie v Shanghae* [Russians in Shanghai] 1936.

The Hoover Institution Archive at Stanford University in Palo Alto California holds a valuable collection of Russian émigré materials, including on Russians from China. It has recently completed a project to put on microfilm the more significant materials from collections held in the Museum of Russian Culture in San Francisco.

On the Gorky Avtozavod (GAZ), sotzgorod and Gorky in the 1930s, see interview transcripts of Vladimir Posner, Russian journalist; Sergei Dyakonov (son of former GAZ director 1932–38); and Feodor Chinchenko (former GAZ worker) from the Abamedia documentary *Yanks for Stalin* about US aid in the industrial development of the Soviet Union during the 1920s and 1930s at http://www.pbs.org/redfiles/rao/catalogues/trans/index.html

Sir Walter Citrine, *I Search for Truth in Russia*, George Routledge & Sons, London, 1936; Victor Herman, *Coming Out of the Ice*, Freedom Press, Oklahoma City, 1979.

Building the 'radiant future' [*svetloe budushchee*] was a key theme of Stalinist propaganda in the 1930s, closely linked to the doctrine of 'socialist realism', which instructed artists and writers to present life as it would become, rather than as it was. As Sheila Fitzpatrick, *Everyday Stalinism: Ordinary Life in Extraordinary Times: Soviet Russia in the 1930s*, Oxford University Press, London, 2000, explains, people were encouraged to see that 'an empty ditch was a canal in the making; a vacant lot where old houses or a church had been torn down, littered with rubbish and weeds, was a future park'.

Chapter 6: Black Ravens in October

On the key political developments in the USSR in the 1930s and the purges which are covered in Chapters 7 to 11, I have drawn on the following sources: Sheila Fitzpatrick, *Everyday Stalinism: Ordinary Life in Extraordinary Times: Soviet Russia in the 1930s*, Oxford University Press, London, 2000; J. Arch Getty and Oleg. V. Naumov, *The Road to Terror: Stalin and the Self-destruction of the Bolsheviks 1932–39*, Yale University Press, New Haven, 1999; Veronique Garros, Natalia Korenevskaya and Thomas Lahusen (eds), *Intimacy and*

Terror: Soviet Diaries of the 1930s, The New Press, New York, 1995; Marc Jansen and Nikita Petrov, *Stalin's Loyal Executioner: People's Commissar Ezhov 1895–1940*, Hoover Institution Press, Stanford, 2002; Roy Medvedev, *Let History Judge*, Spokesman Books, London, 1976; Edvard Radzinsky, *Stalin*, Sceptre, London, 1997; Robert W. Thurston, *Life and Terror in Stalin's Russia 1934–1941*, Yale University Press, New Haven, 1996; Robert Conquest, *Stalin and the Kirov Murder*, Hutchinson, London, 1989; Robert Conquest, *The Great Terror: A Reassessment*, Oxford University Press, New York, 1990; Arkady Vaksberg, *The Prosecutor and the Prey: Vyshinsky and the 1930s Moscow Show Trials*, Weidenfeld & Nicolson, London,1990.

Some foreigners who came to help build socialism were also arrested during the purges—some shot, others sent to the Gulag. Adam Hochschild, *The Unquiet Ghost: Russians Remember Stalin*, Penguin, New York, 1995, was told that the KGB had files on several thousand American victims. He describes several cases to which he was given access. Victor Herman, *Coming Out of the Ice*, Freedom Press, Oklahoma City, 1979, survived to tell his own tale.

The article about the dangers of sexual entrapment by foreign spies in Gorkovskaya Kommuna was cited by Sheila Fitzpatrick, see above.

Chapter 7: Japanese Spies in Gorky
On the NKVD's practices and treatment of political prisoners in Gorky, I have drawn on L.P. Gordeeva,

V.A. Kazakov, V.V. Smirnov, *Zabveniyu Ne Podlezhit: Neizvestnye Stranitsy Nizhegorodskoy Istorii (1918–1984)*, [Not to Be Forgotten: Unknown Pages of Nizhny Novgorod's History (1918-1984] Vol 2, Nizhny Novgorod, 1994 and Victor Herman, *Coming Out of the Ice*, Freedom Press, Oklahoma City, 1979.

Chapter 8: The Ravens Return

Lazar Kaganovich's comment on accidents is cited in Steven Merritt, 'Matushka Rosiia Primi Svoikh Detei! [Mother Russia, Receive Your Children] – Archival Materials on the Stalinist Repression of the Soviet Kharbintsy' in *Rossiiane v Azii* [Russians in Asia], No 5, Autumn 1998.

The text of the joint resolution of the CPSU Central Committee and the Council of People's Commissars of 17 November 1938 is contained in J. Arch Getty and Oleg. V. Naumov, *The Road to Terror: Stalin and the Self-destruction of the Bolsheviks 1932–39*, Yale University Press, New Haven, 1999.

Chapter 9: 'All Harbintsy are Subject to Arrest'

Key books mentioned on the Great Terror are Aleksandr Solzhenitsyn, *The Gulag Archipelago*, Collins and Harvill, Sydney, 1974; Eugenia Ginsburg, *Journey into the Whirlwind*, Harcourt Brace, New York, 1975; Nadezhda Mandelstam, *Hope Against Hope*, translated by Max Hayward, Penguin Books, London, 1972.

Anna Akhmatova's *Requiem* (both Russian and English texts) is contained in *Poems of Anna Akhmatova*, selected and translated by Stanley Kunitz with Max Hayward, Collins Harville, London 1994. On her life, see Roberta Reeder, *Anna Akhmatova: Poet and Prophet*, Allison & Busby, London, 1994 and Amanda Haight, *Anna Akhmatova: A Poetic Pilgrimage*, Oxford University Press, Oxford, 1990.

NKVD Operational Order 00593 of 20 September 1937 was first published in Memorial's information bulletin, *Memorial-Aspekt*, July 1993. At the same time, Moscow Memorial announced the formation of a 'KVZhD [CER] section' to bring together former employees of the CER who suffered during the purges.

My translation of the full text of the Harbin Order is on p. 449.

For background on the NKVD's operation against *Harbintsy*, see Steven Merritt, 'Matushka Rosiia Primi Svoikh Detei! [Mother Russia, Receive Your Children] – Archival Materials on the Stalinist Repression of the Soviet Kharbintsy' in *Rossiiane v Azii* [Russians in Asia], No 5, Autumn 1998; Mark Jansen and Nikita Petrov, *Stalin's Loyal Executioner: People's Commissar Ezhov 1895–1940*, Hoover Institution Press, Stanford, 2002 (Chapter 4) put the operation against the *Harbintsy* in the context of other mass arrest 'national' operations.

Although the NKVD order refers to '25,000 so-called Harbintsy (former employees of the CER and returnees from Manchukuo) working in the Soviet transport and industry sectors', this number probably only includes post-1935 returnees without their families. From Merritt's survey of the literature, the number of

Harbintsy (in the widest sense of Russians from China) in the USSR after 1936 could have been in excess of 100,000.

On Japanese recruitment of Russians for intelligence operations against the USSR, see Pyotr Balakshin, *Final v Kitae* [Finale in China] Vol 1, Sirius, Munich, 1958.

Kaganovich's remark about *Harbintsy* at the February–March 1937 Plenum is quoted in Merritt.

Text of NKVD Operational Order No 00447 of 30 July 1937 regarding kulaks, criminals and other anti-Soviet elements is contained in J. Arch Getty and Oleg. V. Naumov, *The Road to Terror: Stalin and the Self-destruction of the Bolsheviks 1932–39*, Yale University Press, New Haven, 1999.

Chapter 10: The Survivor

The handbook on the Soviet Gulag prepared by Memorial's Research and Information Centre, N.G. Ohotin and A.B. Roginsky, *Sistema Izpravitelno-Trudovykh Lagerey v SSSR 1923–60* [The System of Corrective Labour Camps in the USSR 1923–60] Zvenya, Moscow, 1998 gives a comprehensive breakdown of labour camps and prisons. It is accessible on Memorial's website at http://www.memo.ru/history/NKVD/GULAG/index.htm

Yasha's wife, Galya Sviderskaya died in Riga in May 2002.

Chapter 11: Our Man in Khabarovsk

On Kolyma camps see Robert Conquest, *Kolyma: The Arctic Death Camps*, The Viking Press, New York ,1978; Eugenia Ginzburg, *Journey into the Whirlwind*, Harcourt

Brace, New York, 1975 and *Within the Whirlwind*, Harcourt Brace Jovanovich, New York, 1982; Stanislaw Kowalski's account of his imprisonment, *Kolyma: The Land of Gold and Death*, can be accessed online at http://www.personal.psu.edu/users/w/x/wxk116/sjk/kolyma.html

John J. Stephan, *The Russian Far East: A History*, Stanford University Press, Stanford, 1994 is a valuable source on the history and politics of the region, including the tensions between the centre and periphery, the purges and Kolyma. He describes a visit to Kolyma in 1944 by the US Vice-President Wallace and officials who were completely duped about what was really going on in the region.

The files of the Bureau of Russian Émigré Affairs in Manchukuo (BREM) were among materials brought out of Harbin by the NKVD and Red Army after the Soviet occupation of Manchuria in 1945. Classified 'secret', the BREM files were held by the KGB. In accordance with a Presidential Decree of 1991, 58,367 files were declassified and handed over to the State Archive of the Khabarovsk Krai between 1992–94. I was able to access family files held there in 2000.

By November 2000, the Khabarovsk Memorial group had published three volumes of its books of memory— A.P. Lavrentsov, T.G. Bespalova, O.V. Radchenko (eds), 'Hotelos by vsekh poimenno nazvat' ['I would have liked to name each one'], Khabarovsk. The books are 'dedicated to the memory of Far Easterners and citizens of neighbouring states, who were subjected to unwarranted political repressions during the years of Soviet rule'. Work is in progress on a fourth volume.

Abram Onikul's file was made available to me by the Federal Security Bureau (FSB) of the Khabarovsk Krai.

Chapter 12: Spies in the Far East

On Soviet foreign intelligence operations, see Christopher Andrew and Oleg Gordievsky, *KGB: The Inside Story of its Foreign Operations from Lenin to Gorbachev*, Hodder & Stoughton, London, 1990; Christopher Andrew and Vasili Mitrokhin, *The Mitrokhin Archives: The KGB in Europe and the West*, Allen Lane, 1999.

On the purges in the Far Eastern State University (DVGU), see *Dalnevostochnyi Gosudarstvennyi Universitet: Istoriya I Sovremennost 1899-1999* [Far Eastern State University: Past and Present 1899–1999], DVGU, 1999.

On the purges in the military and intelligence apparatus in the Russian Far East, as well as the defection to the Japanese of regional NKVD chief Lyushkov, see John J. Stephan, *The Russian Far East: A History*, Stanford University Press, Stanford, 1994; Marc Jansen and Nikita Petrov, *Stalin's Loyal Executioner: People's Commissar Nicholai Yezhov 1895–1940*, Hoover Institution, Hoover Institution Press, Stanford; Article by S. Nikolaev, 'A byla li taina [So was there a secret?], 1990, reprinted in A.P. Lavrentsov et al (eds) 'Hotelos by vsekh poimenno nazvat' [I would have liked to name each one], Vol 3, Khabarovsk, 2000.

Chapter 13: Redemption

On the post-war Stalin period see Edvard Radzinsky, Stalin, Sceptre, London, 1997; Roy Medvedev, *Let History Judge*, Spokesman Books, London, 1976.

On the Khrushchev period, see Giuseppe Boffa, *Inside the Khrushchev Era*, George Allen & Unwin, London, 1959; Edward Crankshaw, *Khrushchev's Russia*, Penguin, London 1959; Harrison Salisbury, *To Moscow and Beyond: A Reporter's Narrative*, Michael Joseph, London 1960; Strobe Talbot (ed) *Khrushchev Remembers*, Sphere, London 1971; Dimitri Volkogonov, *Autopsy for an Empire: The Seven Leaders Who Built the Soviet Regime*, The Free Press, New York, 1998.

The English text of Khrushchev's speech at the 20th CPSU Congress, with an introduction by Anatole Shubb and annotations by Boris Nicolaevsky is available at http://www.trussel.com/hf/stalin.htm.

An apocryphal story told about Khrushchev's speech is that as he was railing against Stalin's crimes, a voice at the back of the hall called out: 'Comrade Khrushchev, what were you, a high Party official, doing while Stalin was committing all these crimes?' Momentarily flustered, Khrushchev stared at the audience then asked 'Who said that?' Silence. He repeated the question. More silence. No voice was heard. No hand was raised. After prolonged silence Khrushchev responded: 'Now you know what I was doing.'

Chapter 14: Back to Harbin

For useful sources on life for Russians in Manchuria

under Japanese occupation see note on Chapter 4.

Amleto Vespa, *Secret Agent of Japan*, Little Brown, Boston, 1938 provides an insider's account of the campaign of kidnappings, which culminated in the brutal murder of Semyon Kaspe, the young pianist son of a wealthy Harbin Jewish businessman late in 1933. His funeral brought thousands of Harbintsy of all nationalities and religious denominations out onto the streets in protest. See also John J. Stephan, *The Russian Fascists* and Pyotr Balakshin, *Final v Kitae*. Boris Bresler, 'Harbin's Jewish Community 1898–1958: Politics, Prosperity and Adversity' in Jonathan Goldstein (ed), *The Jews Of China*, Vol 2, M.E. Sharpe, New York, 2000, notes that eight of the twelve people kidnapped between mid–1932 and the end of 1933 were Jews, four of whom were murdered.

Elena Taskina, *Neizvestnyi Harbin* [Unknown Harbin], Prometei, Moscow, 1992 and Victor Sannikoff, *Pod Znakom Voskhodiashchego Solntsa v Manchzhurii: Vospominaniia* [Under the Sign of the Rising Sun in Manchuria: Reminiscences], Sydney, 1990 provide firsthand accounts of life in Harbin and Manchuria during this period. Interesting memoirs of the period have also appeared in the Russian periodicals *Russkie v Kitae* [Russians in China] (Ekaterinburg) and *Na Sopkakh Manchzhurii* [In the Hills of Manchzhuriya] (Novosibirsk).

On Unit 731 and Japanese bacteriological experiments, see Williams, Peter and David Wallace, *Unit 731: Japan's Secret Biological Warfare in World War II*, The Free Press, New York, 1989; Sheldon H. Harris, *Factories of Death: Japanese Biological Warfare 1932–45, and the American Cover-Up*, Routledge, London, 1994. In Minoru Matsui's documentary, 'Japanese Devils' [Riben Guizi] 2001, fourteen Japanese soldiers give graphic accounts of atrocities they committed during the Sino–Japanese war, including in Manchuria.

My account of the activities of the Unit for the Defence of Harbin (SHOH) and of the Soviet entry into Harbin in August 1945 relies substantially on Elena Taskina, *Neizvestnyi Harbin* and the account of P.K. Fialkovsky, *Russkie v Kitae*, September 1997 and V. Shirokolobov in *Na Sopkakh Manchzhurii*, August 1998.

A. Kaufman, *Lagernyi Vrach* [Camp Doctor], Am Oved, Tel Aviv, 1973 and Grigory Pasternak and Eugene Raleigh, *To Reach This Season*, Judah L. Magnes Museum, Berkley, 1983 give first-hand accounts of what happened to them after they were arrested by Smersh.

Among the forty-two Soviet citizens beheaded by the Japanese in Hailar on the eve of the Japanese capitulation were: Nohum Onikul (Ronias and Jacob's father); Zalman Onikul (Ronia and Jacob's brother); Yakov Kogan (Ira's father); S. Litvin (Tima's father); A. Friedman; B. Freidman; M. Genkin; L. Levitan; A. Levitan; B. Borkovsky; F. Grigerman; L. Apatoff; Pulin (father); Pulin (son); Shmelev; Komarov; F. Zaharenko. (Names based on a list provided by relatives of the deceased and account of K.F. Tulakina in *Russkie v Kitae*, No 2, 1995.

After the bodies were identified, they were initially buried in coffins in a single grave in the Hailar city park and were subsequently reburied by their families and friends in the appropriate sections of the city cemetery.

Chapter 15: Khrushchev's 'Virgin Lands' or Sydney?

In the late 1990s memoirs of *Harbintsy* who joined the 'virgin lands' campaign appeared in Russian periodicals including *Russkii v Kitae* [Russians in China], published in Ekaterinburg since 1995 and *Na Sopkah Manchzhurii* [In the Hills of Manchuria] published in Novosibirsk since 1993.

On Sino–Soviet machinations and the manoeuvres between Mao Zedong's Communists and Chiang Kai-Shek's Nationalists to secure advantage in Manchuria in the wake of the Japanese defeat, see the introduction of Donald Gillin and Raymond Myers (eds), *Last Chance in Manchuria: The Diary of Chang Kia-Ngau*, Hoover Institution Press, Standford, 1989; section 4 of Søren Clausen and Stig Thøgersen (eds), *The Making of a Chinese City: History and Historiography in Harbin*, M.E. Sharpe, New York, 1995; C.P. Fitzgerald *Revolution in China*, Cresset Press, London, 1953; R.K.I. Quested, *Sino–Russian Relations: A Short History*, George Allen & Unwin, Sydney, 1984.

Elena Taskina, *Neizvestnyi Harbin* [Unknown Harbin], Prometei, Moscow, 1994, is a useful source on Russian life in Harbin during this period.

Chairman Mao's political campaigns are well covered in Jung Chang, *Wild Swans: Three Daughters of China*, Flamingo, London, 1992 and Harold C. Hinton, *An Introduction to Chinese Politics*, Wren Publishing, Melbourne, 1972.

The BREM files of my relatives were made available by the State Archive of the Khabarovsk Krai. Their

Public Security Bureau (referred to by the Russian acronym 'DOB' in the text) files were made accessible by the Heilongjiang Provincial Archive in Harbin.

Gary Nash, *The Tarasov Saga: From Russia through China to Australia*, Rosenberg, Sydney, 2002, describes the route taken by many White Russians fleeing the Bolshevik Revolution of 1917, including my paternal grandparents through the Far Eastern Republic, then to Manchuria.

There is a brief description of the Tatar community in Harbin in Elena Chernolutskaya, 'Religious Communities in Harbin and Ethnic Identity of Russian Émigrés', in Thomas Lahusen (ed), *Harbin and Manchuria: Place, Space and Identity*, South Atlantic Quarterly, Winter 2000, Duke University Press, Durham.

Chapter 16: Continuity

On the politics surrounding the centenary, see Peter Berton 'A Trip to Khabarovsk, Birobidzhan and a Nostalgic Return to Harbin after Fifty-seven Years', in the *Bulletin of Igud Yotzei Sin* (English language supplement), Nos 357–359, 1999; James Carter, 'A Tale of Two Temples: Nation, Region and Religious Architecture in Harbin, 1928–1998' in Thomas Lahusen (ed) *Harbin and Manchuria: Place, Space and Identity, South Atlantic Quarterly*, Winter 2000, Duke University Press, Durham.

My friends Igor and Alla Savitsky have created a scale model of St Nicholas Cathedral on the basis of drawings made from photographs by a Khabarovsk architect, which has been exhibited in various Australian cities.

On the efforts of the Israel–China Friendship Association for the restoration of the Harbin Jewish Cemetery, see articles by Teddy Kaufman in the *Bulletin of Igud Yotzei Sin* Sept 1992, May/June 1994 (including a list of the 515 graves identified at the time) and Oct/Nov 1994 (English supplement).

The Harbin Jewish Cemetery website can be accessed at www.hrbjewcemetery.com

The Public Security Bureau (referred to by the Russian acronym 'DOB' in the text) files of the former Russian community are held in the Heilongjiang Provincial Archives in Harbin.

In September 2002, Efrosinia Andreyevna Nikiforova, is the last remaining old Russian in Harbin.

Andrew Jakubowicz has produced a website about the Jews of Shanghai, 'The Menorah of Fang Bang Lu' which can be accessed at http://transforming.-cultures.uts.edu.au/ShanghaiSite

OPERATIONAL ORDER OF THE USSR PEOPLE'S COMMISSAR OF INTERNAL AFFAIRS NO 00593

20 September 1937
Moscow

The organs of the NKVD have registered up to 25,000 people, so-called 'Harbintsy' (former employees of the China Eastern Railway and returnees from Manchukuo), working in railway transport and industry sectors of the USSR.

Operational intelligence materials show that the overwhelming majority of *Harbintsy* who have arrived in the USSR are former White officers, police, military police, and members of various émigré fascist spy organisations etc. The overwhelming majority of them are agents of Japanese intelligence, which over a number of years has sent them to the USSR to conduct terrorist, diversionary and espionage activities.

Evidence from investigations also serve as proof of this. For example, over the last year, up to 4500 *Harbintsy* have been subjected to punitive measures / repressed for terrorist and diversionary-espionage activities in railroad transport and industries. Investigations of their cases have revealed a carefully planned and executed operation by Japanese intelligence to organise on Soviet territory a diversionary-espionage base from among the *Harbintsy*.

Enclosed with this order is a classified letter about the terrorist, diversionary and espionage activities of Japanese agents among the *Harbintsy*, with the purpose of crushing all spy cadres among them who have been planted in the transport and industry sectors in the USSR.

I therefore order that:

1. As of 1 October 1937, a comprehensive operation be commenced to liquidate diversionary-espionage and terrorist cadres among the *Harbintsy* in the transport and industry sectors.

2. All *Harbintsy* are subject to arrest who are:

a) exposed and suspected of terrorist, diversionary, espionage and destructive activities;

b) former Whites, returnees, those who emigrated during the civil war, as well as those who served in the forces of the various white formations;

c) former members of anti-Soviet political parties (Socialist Revolutionaries (SRs), Mensheviks and others);

d) members of Trotskyist and right formations, and all *Harbintsy* linked with the activities of these anti-Soviet formations;

e) members or various émigré fascist organisations (the 'Russian Armed Services Union', the 'Cossack Union', the 'Union of Musketeers', the 'Yellow Union', the 'Black Ring', the 'YMCA', the 'Russian Student Organisation', the 'Brotherhood of Russian Truth', the 'Peasant Workers Party' etc);

f) former employees of the Chinese police and armed forces, both before the occupation of Manchuria by the Japanese and after the establishment of Manchukuo;

g) former employees of foreign firms, primarily Japanese, but also White Guard firms (eg. Churin & Co and others);

h) Harbin graduates of well known courses 'International', 'Slavia', 'Praga';

i) owners and co-owners of various enterprises in Harbin (restaurants, hotels, garages, etc);

j) those arriving in the USSR illegally without proper Soviet documents;

k) those who held Chinese citizenship before transferring to Soviet citizenship;

l) former smugglers, criminals, traders in opium and morphine etc.

m) members of counterrevolutionary sectarian groups.

3. The arrests are to be conducted in two steps:

a) First to be arrested, all *Harbintsy* working in the NKVD, the Red Army, railway and water transport, civil aviation and air force, military plants and defence workshops of all other plants, electrical power facilities of all industrial enterprises, in gas and oil refineries, in the chemical industry;

b) second, all other *Harbintsy*, working in Soviet establishments, soviet farms, collective farms etc.

4. Harbıntsy, not falling under the categories set out in point 2, regardless of the presence of compromising information, are to be immediately removed from railway, water and air transport and from industrial enterprises, simultaneously taking measures to ensure their exclusion from these sites in the future.

5. The investigations of the cases of the arrested *Harbintsy* are to be rolled out in such a way that all participants in the diversionary-espionage and terrorist organisations and groups are exposed in the shortest period of time.

The new network of spies, saboteurs and diversionaries exposed in the course of the investigation of the *Harbintsy*—ARE TO BE ARRESTED IMMEDIATELY.

6. All arrested *Harbintsy* are to be divided into two categories:

a) in the first category—are all Harbintsy who have been exposed in diversionary-espionage, terrorist, sabotage and anti-Soviet activities. They are subject to execution.

b) in the second category—are all other, less active *Harbintsy*. They are subject to imprisonment in jails and camps for a period of 8–10 years.

7. On those *Harbintsy*, classified in the first and second categories as a result of the investigation process, an album is to be compiled every 10 days (with individual certificates on each prisoner), with a

concrete presentation of investigation and intelligence materials, identifying the degree of culpability of the prisoner.

The album is to be forwarded to the NKVD of the USSR for confirmation.

The classification of arrested *Harbintsy* into the 1st or 2nd category is derived on the basis of intelligence and investigative information—by the NKVD chief of the republics—the chief of the NKVD directorate of the region (oblast or krai), the chief of the NKVD's DTO of State Security, together with the corresponding procurator of the republic, region or railway.

8. After the confirmation of the lists by the NKVD chief of the USSR and the chief procurator, the sentence is to be carried out immediately.

9. The release from prisons and camps of *Harbintsy* convicted earlier upon completion of their sentences for espionage, diversion and sabotage—IS TO CEASE.

Materials on these people are to be presented for examination by a Special Board of the NKVD USSR.

10. The operation against the *Harbintsy* is to be used to acquire qualified intelligence agents, taking measures to ensure that double agents are excluded from the secret service.

11. The operation is to be concluded by 25 December 1937.

12. My Order No 00486 of 15 August 1937 will apply in relation to the families of repressed *Harbintsy*.

13. I am to be informed on the progress of the operation by telegraph every five days (on 5th ,10th, 15th , 20th , 25th , 30th of each month).

Signed People's Commissar of Internal Affairs—Chief Commissar of State Security

YEZHOV

ACKNOWLEDGEMENTS

This book is the result of curiosity, good fortune and the willingness of people across the globe to help uncover truth, restore memory, and piece together the fragments of broken lives.

Firstly, I would like to thank all those who helped in my journey of discovery long before this book was imagined—friends, relatives and total strangers with whom I formed many lasting bonds. Some helped me unearth information, others shared their own experiences and stories, which broadened my perspective.

Unfortunately, Galya Sviderskaya did not live to see this book published. I am eternally grateful to her for holding onto the papers and photographs of the Onikul family—most of whom she never knew—and passing them on to me.

In Australia, my sincere thanks go to Olga and Bradley Wynne; Igor and Alla Savitsky; Ronia Onikul; Ira Kogan/Levinsky; Lika Onikul; Ida Chernouss;

Isador and the late Ira Magid; Efim and Nora Krouk; Rachel Kofman and Jenny Poliak.

In Russia, Uncle Lyova Rayak; Anya, Borya and Sasha Tsaliuk; Leonid Zirlin (now in Germany); Alyosha Kalinin; Olga Andreyevna Kalinina; Vadim Sadovsky; Alexei P. Arefiev and staff of the Nizhny Novgorod State Archive; Boris Nemtsov's adviser, Aleksandr Kotiusov; Sasha Lavrentsov and his family; Nadezhda Fedorovna Evdokimova; Valentina Dmitrievna Rodintseva; Natalya Nikolaevna Bendik and Marina Gennadievna Smorchkova at the Khabarovsk State Archive; Dr Galina Ivanovna Kanevskaya at the Far East State University; and Elena Petrovna Taskina.

In China, Valia Han; Efrosinya Andreyevna Nikiforova (Tyotya Frosia); Zeng Yizhi (Isabella); Director of Harbin's Huangshan cemetery Liu Jun; Professors Qu Wei, Li Shu Xiao and Zhang Tiejiang at the Heilongjiang Academy of Social Sciences; Professors Pan Guang, Wang Zhicheng and Huang Renwei at the Shanghai Academy of Social Sciences.

In the USA, my thanks go to Rena Krasno; Professor Albert Dien of Stanford University; Elena Danielsen and Ron Bulatoff of the Hoover Institution Archive; Dmitry Brauns and Georgy Tarala of the Museum of Russian Culture in San Francisco; Elia Poliak; Lily Blake-Klebanoff; Lou and Mara Grossman; Leo Hanin; Cy and Olga Kaufman; Professors Peter Berton, Greg Grossman, Nicholas Riasanovsky and Joshua Fogel; Isia Goldin; Golda Lazarovich; Tania Kalugin. In Canada, Rita and Nikolai Vorontsov. In Israel, Tima (Chaim)

Litvin; David Friedman; Cecilia Lyubman; Valery Tsirlin.

Secondly, I wish to thank those who played a role during the writing of *Secrets and Spies*. It was the late John Iremonger of Allen and Unwin who kick-started the whole process by telling me to stop talking and put pen to paper. Barbara Mobbs and the Australian Society of Authors', Rob Pullen, gave me invaluable advice about dealing with publishers. I thank the team at Random House for making my first experience as a writer a challenging and rewarding one—in particular, my publisher (and fencing partner), Jeanne Ryckmans, who enthusiastically embraced my proposal and courageously backed an unknown horse and kept me on the track with encouragement and good humour; my editor Nadine Davidoff, who with sensitivity and insight, asked all the right questions and helped me shape the narrative; others whose skills assisted the finished product—James Mills-Hicks, Anna Warren, Justine O'Donnell, Frances Paterson.

I am grateful to all the friends, too numerous to mention, who gave me ideas, advice, encouragement and moral support through a very solitary process, including Colin Benjamin; Steve Waters; Richard Wu; Michael Keck; Professor Garth Nettheim and David McKnight.

I would particularly like to thank Geoffrey Jukes and Zhanna Dolgopolova, my former university teachers, who ensured that I observed academic integrity and got my historical facts right; Natasha Goosev, a friend from a prominent White Russian Harbin family, who provided me with wise counsel and a context against which to set the experiences of my own family; my friend Ann Reich, who meticulously read every draft and gave me valuable feedback from the perspective of an avid reader; and Andrew Jakubowicz, who shared parts of the journey and inspired me to change my life and find the voice with which to tell the tale.

Most of all I am indebted to my parents, Inna and Alec Moustafine. Initially uncomfortable at the prospect of public exposure of their lives and skeptical that anyone would be interested in reading about them, they sifted through often painful memories and answered my endless questions, coming to understand that by making real the life of one family I could tell the tale of many.

INDEX